WILLIE IRVINE

Together Again

WILLIE IRVINE

Together Again

with Dave Thomas

SPORTS
BOOKS

Published in Great Britain by
SportsBooks Limited
PO Box 422
Cheltenham
GL50 2YN
www.sportsbooks.ltd.uk

© Willie Irvine 2005
First Published October 2005

Front cover designed by Kath Northam.

Main photograph by Andy Ford.
A catalogue record for this book is available from
the British Library.

ISBN 1 899807 33 0

Printed and bound in England by Creative Print and
Design Ltd, Wales.

Contents

Acknowledgements

Rita, Darren, Jonathan and Stephen Irvine.

Jimmy McIlroy and Bobby Irvine.

The *Burnley Express*, Howard Talbot, Margaret Potts.

Randall Northam at SportsBooks for suggestions, editing and advice.

For help with Preston North End information: Chris Hudson, Ivor Holden, John and Dominic Thompson.

In Brighton, Tim Carder (Brighton and Hove Albion Collectors' and Historians' Society) and Mel Peatfield.

At Everton, George Orr.

In Northern Ireland, Roger Bell, Tommy Reid, Joan Irwin and Malcolm Brodie.

And Dave Thomas.
Dave spent a year working on this book with me, helping me get my thoughts and stories down on paper, nudging me to remember more and more and helping me to find out just a little bit more about my early family. It wouldn't have been written without him. Thanks, Dave.

Harriet Thomas for sorting out all computer problems.

Dedications

**To my wife Rita, and my sons Darren, Stephen
and Jonathan.**

Rita, you have stuck by me through thick and thin, through
the good and bad times. Being a footballer's wife is not easy
and you have been the rock on which the family has been
built and the strength that has held us together.

Darren, Stephen and Jonathan; a man could not have three
finer sons.

Willie Irvine

**To the memory of Alan Bailey who passed
away far too soon.**

1946 to 2005.

Alan was a dedicated Burnley fan whose work eventually
took him to Wakefield. It never stopped him from supporting
the Clarets and getting to Turf Moor as often as possible. I
first met him four years ago when he worked on a project to
set up a "sheltered home" for my daughter and two of her
friends. Then we lost touch. Out of the blue he telephoned me
in December 2004 to say that he had a collection of Burnley
scrapbooks for which he was looking for a good home, and
having read *No Nay Never* and tracked me down, asked would
I like them. He explained that he knew he was terminally ill
and wanted them to go to a good home before he died. I
visited him and instead of collecting "just a few" scrapbooks,
there were four huge tote boxes full of memorabilia, a suitcase
full of priceless Burnley books, three boxes full of Burnley
videos and matches he had taped himself, and a shopping
bag full of programmes going back to the sixties. God bless
you, Alan and thank you.

Dave Thomas

PROLOGUE

The face is kindly and the grey hair thinning. Maybe he looks just a little older than he really is but that's not surprising when you've heard his story. But the eyes smile. The voice is soft and gentle and there's still a clear Irish brogue even after all these years in Lancashire. He's back in the place today where he spent just six years of his working life but people still know and remember him well. On a plaque fixed to a wall of one of the towering stands is his name. It's the plaque of legends and he is one of them.

As usual a group of people is assembling, waiting to be shown round the scenes of his triumphs and playing days. This is matchday at Turf Moor, the home of Burnley FC. It was once a power in the land, a big club set in a small town whose fortunes had once been based on cotton and coal. Burnley FC, cotton, coal. The holy trilogy. The three slowly declined together.

There's a quietness and a modesty in his approach to the people who gather round him. He looks quite small. You could pass him by in the street outside, or in the local corner shop, and have no idea who he is or that he was once a household name. He played at Preston North End, too, where his goals are remembered when relegation was avoided, and at Brighton & Hove Albion when his goals that season took them to promotion. It is nearly 40 years since he played at Burnley and only a few of this group will have any idea of what he was like then; the athletic physique, the boyish looks, the huge mop of hair, the sharpness, the exuberance of his celebrations after a goal.

The group waits patiently for the few remaining stragglers. Only a few of them will have any notion that the ground he shows them round now bears no relation to the one in which he played. The only similarity is the patch of green grass in the middle, the playing field, which today is a lush glistening surface; marked out with its crisp white lines, the myriad drops of moisture caught by the sunlight so that the whole surface looks as if it is sprinkled with diamonds.

"Are we all here then?" he asks quietly. There is a polite nodding of heads. The group is almost complete. They wait patiently.

Not everybody in the group knows who this unpretentious, self-effacing man is. But I do. I saw him play. I saw the instinctive positioning, the lightning strikes, the flashing headers, the speed of foot, the bravery and the goals he scored followed by the exultant, arms-raised celebration. For others in the group, the stadium tour is just the necessary prelude to the matchday lunch and a glass of Sauvignon served by lines of well-drilled waiters. But for those with a mind for history, or who watched Burnley games in the sixties, the walk around the ground with their guide is a pilgrimage, and they hang on his every word, for this man truly was a prodigy. In only six short years he left his mark and a record that stands to this day. It was a tackle from an Everton player that did the damage and snapped his right leg when he was only 24. He has never forgiven the player who did it. He has never forgotten the searing pain and his teammates calling out for the game to be stopped. There are landmarks in all our lives. This was his.

"He was a gud 'un", an older member of the group remarks to nobody in particular. Our guide and host hears and smiles. It took him a long time to learn to understand Lancashire dialect when he first arrived in Burnley and there were times when he felt as if he was in a foreign land.

He was indeed a "gud 'un", but after that Everton match he was never the same. Once recovered, his career continued but that precious spark that separates the gifted from the merely good was gone. Like so many before and after, he was eventually sold to another club. A footballer then was a chattel, owned by the club, to be sold at his master's whim. Two reasons sufficed. The player had outlived his usefulness or the club needed the money; in his case, a mixture of both. A snapped leg, recovery, but a level of performance just that fraction diminished from what it once was. In football today there is no room for sentiment. Then, there was even less.

Prologue

Neither were there any great fortunes to be made from the game. Glamour had yet to arrive. A basic wage and bonuses and that was it, maybe a newspaper column. A footballer was still a working-class man and rubbed shoulders with supporters on the bus or train, in the town and even on the way to the ground on a matchday.

The group is assembled and he motions for them to follow. The route he takes them on is tried and tested as is his patter and the anecdotes he tells as they slowly make their way round the perimeter of the pitch, then indoors along corridors and stairways and up into the chairman's room with its oak panels and solid furniture. Pictures of great moments hang on the walls along with framed newspaper features and the international shirts of former players. The group at this moment are in the smaller of the three stands and from there they move to the oldest stand behind the goal. Deep below the rows of seats above their heads, they see the changing rooms and the old baths and then walk down the same tunnel that the players run down onto the pitch, although in his day the players' tunnel was down a different side of the ground. From this point it's back across into the colossal main stand, through the press room and then up the stairs and into the gigantic hospitality area that runs from end to end of this enormous structure. Great windows look out onto the pitch. The tables are set for lunch in partitioned corporate areas. The bar staff are in position. Nearly an hour has passed by.

"If there is anything you need or want, just let me know," he tells them all. "I'll be here during the game and while you're eating. There'll be coffee at half-time and after the game there's no hurry to leave."

He looks across at me and winks. His job is done, unless someone has a complaint, which is rare, or a question about his goalscoring, which is frequent. He has told them stories about a hat-trick at Tottenham, the legendary chairman Bob Lord, about manager Harry Potts, then his renowned scoring partner Andy Lochhead and finally the mercurial Irishman he knew so well, Jimmy McIlroy. He has shown them the exact places from where he scored this twenty yarder in a league game or that equalising header in a cup game. He can remember them all. It's funny how the great goalscorers – and with 97 goals from 144 games for Burnley he was clearly that – can do this. Somebody has asked him which was the best. "All of them, I loved them all," he replies, smiling.

The group disperses to different tables up and down the length of the dining area which itself is the complete length of the football pitch. Content, he leans against the bar and watches them settle down. It is a brief moment when he sometimes finds his mind drifting back to his playing days and sometimes the days before that in Carrickfergus. Just occasionally he thinks of the father he never knew.

For the last few months he's been telling me his story and jotting things down in his notebook for me to read. The notebook started as something simple and uncomplicated to hand down to his grandchildren and contained a few details of his life and family, his mother and brothers and sisters or at least what he thought he knew about them. But he could hardly have known of the things he would learn about himself and his past as he wrote it. The jottings in his notebook begin with just a few hazy ideas about his family background, just a few things that have been handed down but to which he has given little thought, or has ever questioned. But as the book has progressed he has found out so much that he didn't know before.

This is his story and the group who are now starting their meal don't know the half of it. They don't know that it starts in the Belfast Blitz of World War Two.

Northern Ireland was ill prepared for wartime and the Luftwaffe raids of 1941. Families sent their sons to fight but the war seemed far away from Stormont. Rationing and the blackout were the reluctant acknowledgement of its existence but the possibility of an attack on Belfast itself was almost unrecognised. The government resented the spending of money on defences. Firefighting equipment orders were cancelled and there was a near absence of air raid shelters. Belfast was one of the most undefended cities in Europe. There were in fact just four public shelters. This was the city where Alex Irvine worked as a full-time fireman at the

Harland and Wolff shipyard. Each day he caught the train from the tiny station at Eden Halt. He could never have imagined the destruction that was to come.

The three raids that came in April and May devastated the city. In total more than 1,200 people lost their lives and ten times that were made homeless. The docks were a specific target and Harland and Wolff was destroyed, with Alex Irvine and his colleagues in the thick of the attempts to control the fires and rescue the injured. The fires after the third raid could be seen from 45 miles away and the Luftwaffe had free rein to come and go as they pleased. At home Alex could barely bring himself to talk about it or describe the horror of blazing buildings and trapped people. In one raid he suffered injury himself when hit by falling rubble resulting from one of the enormous blasts that seemingly hammered all night at Harland and Wolff.

Recovering from the injury, he and Belfast, after the raids, somehow returned to a semblance of normality. What remained though was a devastated and disrupted city where the burial of the dead lasted for weeks. After May 1941 there were no more raids, but what did remain was the blackout. Designed to save lives it did anything but, doing just the opposite. Not one chink of light had to escape from a window or doorway. In the streets there were no lamps; vehicle headlamps were covered over save for one tiny strip. They gave out so little light they might as well have been switched off. Traffic lights had just one small cross showing in the centre. Torches were permitted so long as they were covered with tissue and pointed downwards. In the first few weeks of the blackout some 4,000 people were killed in the UK as they stepped in front of traffic, fell off rail platforms, into bomb craters, or even fell and drowned in local canals. It was not uncommon to see crocodiles of people all holding on to each other, being led by someone at the front who knew where they were going.

One late night, unable to see a barrier across the road in Belfast until the last minute, the driver of the motorcycle on which Alex Irvine was the pillion passenger managed to duck and avoid injury. Alex Irvine, unsighted, did not. As the bike went under the barrier, Alex, with no view at all, hit his head against the pole and sustained a serious injury. He recovered but suffered from constant headaches and some time later he died. Willie has always believed he died of a resultant brain haemorrhage. He was not yet 50. A footballer himself, who had played for the Irish League club Distillery, he would never see his son Willie play for Northern Ireland.

The blackout lasted until September 1944 and it thus contributed to the death of Alex Irvine when his son Willie was just eleven months old. Not surprisingly Willie remembers nothing of those eleven months. But by 1944 the war was beginning to draw towards its inevitable conclusion. In Belfast and Eden, life returned to normal, and in the Irvine home there was a routine and stability in spite of losing his father.

At school as he grew older Willie never had a father to watch him play or to talk about the game when he came home. These were the father/son conversations that he could never have. He had no father to follow his progress or to share his triumphs and successes. The loss of his father has always affected Willie Irvine. More than once he will ask his own three sons, "have I been a good father, have I done all right?"

The game is over. Burnley have not won. The crowd of people inside the main stand, in what is basically a gigantic matchday restaurant, collect their belongings and some of them slowly make their way down the wide, carpeted stairs, into the ground floor reception area and then out onto the car park where their transport awaits. Some stay for a while longer until the crowds outside have dispersed. There is still the buzz of conversation. Some of them wander over to the bar again. They thank and say goodbye to their host. He signs a few programmes, converses readily and easily, and is as pleased as they are that the team haven't been beaten, but in truth home draws need to be wins. He must sometimes wonder just what these modern players do to earn the money they are paid. Most of them are a shadow of the great players he used to know. He doesn't leave until the last guest has gone and he loves these days, which are now such an important part of his life. He is 62 years old and descends the stairs, content with what he has, comfortable and at ease with his life.

It wasn't always that way and today, when the Paul Gascoignes, George Bests and Stan Collymores of this world can pour their troubles and problems into a best-seller and make yet more money on top of the fortunes they earned as players, Willie Irvine still works in a factory to earn a living. He doesn't begrudge one penny of the vast fortunes modern players earn. It's just the way it is, he thinks. At his own peak he never earned more than a basic £60 a week at Burnley, £75 at Preston and £85 at Brighton, yet his talent was such that were he to play today he would command a hundred times that and more. He had that priceless gift that comes with instinct – the gift of scoring goals, and this in an age of strength-sapping, gluepot pitches, and brutish, powerful centre halves. It was a physical age when a meeting between centre forward and centre half could be more like a ten-round boxing match, the immovable versus the irresistible. It was an age when what was important was who delivered the first kick or fist in the back. Referees then did not blow a whistle at the tiniest hint of contact and players often played on with blood streaming down their faces and shirts. It is often said that yesterday's players could never cope with the high pace and incessant demands of today's game or that today's overprotected players could not have coped then. Willie Irvine would have been one of the exceptions.

CHAPTER ONE

EDEN

My sisters tell me we called him "Da" but other than that there are no clear memories. I'd like to think he must have dandled me on his knees and hugged me sometimes. But I'll never know if he was as proud as punch to have another son or whether he just brooded and worried that I was yet one more mouth to feed in an already overcrowded house. I was only eleven months old when he died in 1944. I was brought up to believe that I was one of a huge family of 17 brothers and sisters and presumed that some of these, the eldest, must have left the house before I was born. I know that two that I never met were the twins that mother had, Lily and Billy, but Lily died as a very young girl and I've no knowledge of Billy at all. I also knew that my mother had been born in India because her father had been in the British Army. Certainly there were eight of us who lived together in Eden but in all honesty I'm none too clear about my family history and as I begin these pages there is a haziness about my past. In those early days it never really bothered me that there were huge gaps in what I knew about my family.

We weren't the biggest family in the village; the Hanleys had 23 children. In later years my sisters told me I was the double of my father; and Elisha Scott, who played for Belfast Celtic and then Liverpool, said the same when I once played at Belfast's Celtic Park as a schoolboy.

I've only ever seen just one photograph of him. They tell me the impact of his death shattered them all and mother was distraught but strangely enough calm at the same time, working out exactly what to do and how to cope. She'd known of the dangers he worked under all the time but could never come to terms with the manner of his death. To survive the dockland raids, the dreadful damage and destruction of it all, and then to hit a barrier in the blackout. You sometimes wonder if the blackout did more harm than good. It seemed ridiculous to her then and still does to me now.

If there were 17 of us in the family I always made the assumption that many of them must have left the house before I even knew them and for years believed that four of my brothers were killed in World War Two. But there were still eight of us in the house; Bobby, Peggy, Jean, Joan, Sandra, George, Joey and myself and my father's loss changed our lives forever. Before his death it was a happy, busy house in spite of the fact that we were as poor as church mice. But there was an order and a routine, and noise and laughter even if there were never two pennies to rub together. But how could I possibly know or understand at the time how or why it all changed so suddenly? What did I know then?

The strength of my mother, that extraordinary woman, was endless and yet she was so small, only five feet tall. I have hazy memories as a toddler of sitting on her knee and I have an image that she would cry telling me about how my sister Lily died when she was very young, and that on the day Lily was buried she received the news of the deaths of four of her other family in the war. I always assumed them to be my older brothers. Maybe things have got a bit jumbled up in my memory as the years have gone by. I never knew them, or where they fought or where or how they died. The footballer Bob Wilson writes in his autobiography of how his two much older brothers in the RAF were killed in World War Two. He can describe them as if they were beside him now. Even though he was only two years old he has a hundred memories of them through their letters, notebooks and photographs. I have nothing to remind me of mine.

Years later, when there was an IRA atrocity in Hyde Park, London, and a beautiful horse called Sefton was badly hurt, I was confronted by someone who berated me for being Irish. I told him I'd had four brothers who gave their lives in the war; he soon went away very sheepishly. Lily was a little angel, my mother used to say, but was always very weak. What I'll not forget are her tears when she used to tell me this story. How anyone can be so strong as to cope with all that life threw at her is beyond me, but cope she did and somehow worked to feed and clothe the rest of us. I hardly ever saw her; all she did was work.

She worked in the village, cleaning houses, and then did a shift in some sort of factory in Carrick. I'd see her fleetingly when she came back to the house after working in the afternoon somewhere and then she was out again to work in the factory in the evening. Sometimes, exhausted, she'd fall asleep on the wooden chair by the table as soon as she walked in.

In truth it was my sisters who brought me up and looked after me. Once I was old enough I fended for myself. They dressed me, walked me to school, tormented and teased me and taught me to swim. They dressed me in girls' clothes a lot of the time when I was tiny. They must have thought I was a doll. One Christmas they dressed me in a Santa suit and threw me out into the snow. On Sundays they made me go to Sunday school, which I hated, especially as one day they made me stand up and sing a song. I can still remember it. *Give Me Five Minutes More*, it was called.

Eden was a tiny, quiet place of just a few hundred people. There wasn't much more than one road in and one road out. If you were on the bus and closed your eyes for ten seconds you'd drive through and miss seeing it. It was by the sea and our house was across the road and railway line from the shore of the Irish Sea. It's on the main road to Carrickfergus and then on to Belfast. Carrickfergus was two-and-a-half-miles away – a 3d. bus ride in those days. Or you could get the train from Eden Halt down Lockharts Lane. Across the rails and you were on the beach and behind the house was farmland. Of course, when I was a lad we'd save the bus fare by walking into Carrick; then you had 2d. for the pictures and 1d. for a bag of chips. Belfast was eight or so miles further on. They must always have been cowboy films we saw because then most times we galloped home shooting imaginary guns at imaginary Indians. Imagine that; I was only seven years old, maybe only six, and I was running and walking to Carrick with my pals to go to the pictures. Could kids of that age do that these days?

Eden

You couldn't say Eden was a fishing village but a few of the blokes had rowing boats and would moor them offshore. We knew everyone in the village and they all knew us, it was that kind of place. The butcher was McNeil's. John McNeil was his son and used to feel sorry for me and give me a chop every now and then, or some scraps to make a meal. I didn't tell him that his father Bertie used to feel sorry for my mother and give her meat as well; "to feed us up" as he used to tell her. And of course she didn't tell Bertie that John was giving me chops as well. I'd watch him chopping up meat with his cleaver and wonder how he didn't cut his hand off. I'd look, wide-eyed with hunger, in wonder at the meat hanging on hooks from the ceiling. I'd look at the strings of sausages in the window and my mouth would water and my stomach would rumble. All in all we didn't do too badly from McNeil the butcher's. The Post Office belonged to the Coles and years later one of the sons became a BBC TV reporter and political correspondent and I've always wondered if it was John Cole, who became very well known. Fred Cole was in charge of the Post Office but unfortunately for him was very nasal and used to talk down his nose. Of course we made fun of him and many's the time he chased us out of the shop and if he could have caught us he'd have given us a wallop. McLean's shop was one of those wonderful Aladdin's Caves that sold everything you could ever want. I used to stand just inside the doorway sometimes and look in wonderment at the jars of sweets and bars of chocolate.

It was a bit like Arkwright's in *Open All Hours*, selling everything from mousetraps to mangles, from candles to cans of paraffin, from biscuits to brushes, flour, tea, sugar and bread. Every shelf was crammed with tins of this and boxes of that and all manner of things hung down from the ceiling. It was a treasure trove and for a penny, when I had one, I'd buy enough sweets to fill a bag.

Poor we might have been but we had some wonderful times and games in a place like that. Just half-a-mile up the road was a cluster of houses called "Boneybefore". It was the birthplace of the father of President Jackson of the USA and on the shore were the ruins of an old white house we used to

11

play in. It was supposed to be something to do with Jonathan Swift who wrote *Gulliver's Travels*.

All this was in the days of empty roads and few cars, just the occasional bus, Dr Loughridge driving round in his old banger, or a lorry and the horses and carts still used for transport. There was the coalman and his cart and the milkman. Farmers ploughed their fields by horsepower. It wasn't even 1950 yet. I hear the sound of horses' hooves now and my mind goes back to all those years ago. The Boyds had one of the first tractors. Fiona Boyd was in my class. I remember Tommy Creighton had a motorbike, and when it was haymaking time and the kids got paid to help, it was me Tommy took up on his motorbike. I used to love that and all the other kids envied me. But Tommy diddled me. The farmer paid him for me as well but I never got it all off Tommy. I reckon the money he kept helped pay for his bike. He later married my sister Margaret but he used to beat her so when she'd had enough she ran off and left him.

We used to love to watch the steam trains chugging through the village and the clouds of steam and smoke that came billowing out as they pulled away from the halt. They'd be on their way from Larne to Belfast or vice versa. We'd wave to the passengers and cheer if they waved back. There'd be snow in winter, the rainstorms and mists coming in off the sea and long, hot summer days playing on the shore.

Some things stick in your mind, don't they? Crawford, one of the Hanleys, was a good pal of mine and we were in the same class at school. Whenever I went into his house there was always a roaring fire, wood of course, and a huge kettle steaming away full of stewed tea. The Hanleys at that point had 22 children but as we went into the house one day we heard a lot of banging and groaning and gasping and there in another room behind the door were Mr and Mrs Hanley hard at it; hanky-panky if you know what I mean. But at the age of six, what did I know then? I thought they were fighting. Mrs Hanley yelled at us to get out. Mr Hanley just had a sort of glazed, happy look on his face; Mrs Hanley looked as if she'd just finished one of the chores she was obliged to do. Crawford, well used to it, knew exactly what was going on.

"Don't worry, Billy," he said. "They're making Hanley number twenty-three."

We lived in a little rented wooden bungalow called "Happy Days". It had just the one living room, a scullery and two bedrooms. It had stone floors and no carpets, or curtains either for that matter. We had a tin bath that we filled with hot water boiled over the fire in the big kettle. We shared the water and topped it up as bath night went on. It was usually me who was last. The living room doubled as a bedroom many a time. There was no bathroom. The bedrooms had double beds and the girls slept in one of them and the boys in the other. There was no running water even. We got water in buckets or jugs from a pump across the road.

There was no electricity so we had candles and paraffin lamps which smoked and smelled and made flickering shadows on the walls. Furniture was sparse – a table and wooden chairs on the bare kitchen floor, a big wooden dresser with what crockery and possessions we had. In the kitchen was a fire with the kettle always boiling away for mugs of tea. Sugar was a luxury.

We burned logs we gathered from the woods in the autumn and summer. We always saved enough logs to boil the kettle but we often went cold. Just occasionally we had coal, which had either fallen off the back of the coal wagon, and we ran out to collect it, or was gathered from the beach. This was the stuff that the tides washed down from Carrick from the coal pier where the ships unloaded their coal and sometimes it spilled into the sea.

In winter there was ice inside the bedroom windows and you huddled up to each other and shivered yourself to sleep. The toilet was down the bottom of the back garden and it was no joke going outside, more often than not in bare feet, and finding it in the dark when it was throwing it down and blowing a gale on a freezing winter night. When I was in digs in Brougham Street in Burnley with Big Jim and Dolly Haworth we had an outside loo there but the journey to that one was nowhere near as bad as the one at Happy Days. Happy Days? Not when you had that trip to the loo on a bitter January night.

Willie Irvine

As a child I well remember going hungry many times. At the back of the house were the farmer's fields and they provided us with many a meal when we went in and helped ourselves to sprouts, potatoes, turnips and cabbages. We never got caught and I smile now just thinking about it. If the farmer ever wondered why the corner of his field was always empty he should have looked over our garden wall and into the large pot on the stove. I'm not sure that he didn't always plant a bit extra in that field because he knew we were digging some of it up. If he didn't, he should have. Farmers should know that in a small poor village where most of the folk usually have empty pockets, they're going to have things dug up from the edges of the fields. Up the road was an orchard which we raided regularly for the fruit. Sometimes we were honest and paid for it – well sort of. We'd wrap an old halfpenny in silver paper and make it look like a shilling. Mrs Richmond, who owned the orchard, always turned a blind eye and took the shilling without saying anything. She knew what we were up to, bless her. We knew she knew what we were doing and we loved her for it. Pears came from the trees in the gardens of the better houses on the way to Carrick. We'd sneak in at dusk and help ourselves.

In Eden, we roamed the woods and fields and beach and played all manner of games. We would light fires on the beach in the nearby ruin of the old white house and cook fish we caught or scrounged from the fishermen. The house was supposed to be haunted and we were always frightening ourselves with stories of ghosts. Sometimes we'd call and see the lady who ran away from the convent. Lord knows what her name was, I can't remember, but she was a lovely kind person and her door was always open to us. She was a born storyteller and we'd sit and listen to her for hours. She'd tell us about her hard times in the convent when she was beaten and flogged by the Mother Superior to break her spirit because she was independent and rebellious. Eventually she decided that convent life was not for her so she ran away and found a small cottage in Eden. We loved that dear lady.

We would roam far and wide and I still remember tramping over the old salt works, up Trailcock Lonan, near

Eden. There were bees' nests there all over the place and you could hear the drone of them under the ground. So one day I got too inquisitive and poked a stick down one of the nests and out came the swarm. They chased me down the lane and one stung me inside my ear. I knew then what a thick ear was all about.

We swam a lot. I learned from my brothers and sisters the hard way. They taught me in the sea, holding me by the ankles and ducking me. It was supposed to teach me not to be frightened. All it taught me is that sea-water tastes awful. I swallowed half of Belfast Lough. There was me not even seven. I was terrified and learned to swim as fast as I could. If I cried they just ducked me again and said "fill up your lungs with air". It did me good though and eventually I earned pennies by swimming out to the fishermen's rowing boats and then pulling them back into shore. I used to get 2d. for bringing a boat in and one night I did four journeys back and forward. I thought the 8d. in my pocket was a small fortune. Sometimes when the fishermen got back they'd give us a few mackerel for supper. Eventually one or two of the blokes asked me if I wanted to go out fishing with them. I jumped at the chance but unfortunately the first time I went out in a boat for a three-hour trip, I had just eaten pounds of gooseberries after raiding someone's garden. Never have I been so sick.

I spent such a lot of time on the beach and soon learned how cruel the sea can be. One of the local families, the Cairns, won a lot of money on the football pools and bought a big fancy yacht. They took it out one day and got caught up in a horrendous storm and, being unfamiliar with the boat, sank and drowned. The whole village was in mourning because everybody knew the two brothers who died.

I used to hang around the boathouse regularly and often crewed for the yachtsmen. I was only seven but was always the first to be asked.

The other way we had of earning money was collecting all the timbers and props that used to be washed ashore on the beach at Eden after a ship was launched in Belfast. Whole families used to do that, dragging the stuff up onto the beach, cutting it up, making firewood, using some of it on our own fires and selling the rest. We'd go down to the beach as a family, all of us except Mammy that is. She was at work. We'd be up to our waists in the water, freezing in winter, to get the big stuff out. Many's the time there was a row with another family about who had got to a huge piece first. We had a little cart and wheeled it all back to the house, dragged it into the back garden to saw it up, and then used the axe to make small, short pieces all the same length. Then we'd tie them into bundles. The villagers bought them, or people passing through the village on their way to work.

We used to love July 12th when the Scottish bands would come over to play. They'd come over from Stranraer to Larne, climb aboard a coach and then drive down through Eden. They must all have had a few drinks inside them by the time they'd sailed over because they were always opening the coach windows as they drove through and throwing coins out to all of us children lining the road waving at them in their uniforms. I once collected four shillings and twopence. That was more than a fortune and since then I have never called a Scotsman mean. I gave the four shillings to mammy and kept the twopence for me and went straight to McLean's for the biggest bag of sweets you've ever seen.

July 12th was a big day in the village. It was Orange Day and my mother was Grand Master of the Women's Loyal Orange Lodge and very proud of that she was. We children were in the Junior Lodge but could only watch the parades on the 12th. Our parades were sometime round Easter I think, and we would have a wonderful time. We would go to Bangor, Larne and Ballyclare. What did I know about Catholic/Protestant differences then? All it meant to me was the games, the fun of the parades, the fairs and amusements and how we'd come home thoroughly exhausted with smiles as wide as the doorway.

One adventure I had was when I used to climb on top of the wall of Lady Baird's estate, outside of Eden at Kilroot. Well that's what we called her; Lady Baird. She had the most beautiful dogs I had ever seen. I used to watch them for hours. That wall seemed about 15 feet tall to me when I was only six and so small. I climbed it for a dare but when I got to the top, at the bottom on the other side I saw five beautiful dogs. I didn't know then they were Irish Setters but I just fell in love with them. So for several days I went back to see and watch them until one day I jumped onto a tree inside the grounds just by the wall, shinned down it and was immediately greeted by the tongues and wagging tails of those beautiful dogs. I made good friends with them and went back often for several weeks until I was eventually caught. No way could I clamber back up that tree and over the wall fast enough. A pair of rough hands dragged me off to see Lady Baird and explain myself.

I was terrified. I was still not yet seven and when she said she would call the police my heart sank. All I could do was blurt out how much I loved the dogs, was doing no harm, and only ever came in to see them and play with them. There must have been a touch of kindness in her. She relented. She pretended she was going to give me a good telling off, but instead, to my amazement, she told me next time to come in through the gates to see them. She was of Italian origin. Don't ask me for the details but Artie McGuckin who had the village chip shop fell in love with her. Artie McGuckin then married this small, dark, attractive lady, who then, believe it or not, helped in his chip shop. We must have had the only fish and chip shop in the world where your chips were wrapped in newspaper by the hands of a real Italian aristocrat; and Archie would smile when we called him Lord McGuckin.

Since then I have loved Irish Setters. Many years later I eventually had my own. The first one I ever had came from the wife of the Northern Ireland Prime Minister Captain Terence O'Neill. Her dogs were champions. After a game against Wales I was at a reception at their residence, Hillsborough House, when I told her about Lady Baird and her dogs. The Prime Minister's wife was a well-known dog breeder and she offered to give me one of her prize puppies. It was delivered to Belfast Airport and transported over on the same plane. Sat next to me on the way back was George Best, my Irish team-mate, and with him to keep me company, the time passed very quickly with a few drinks. A very irate wife Rita collected the dog and me, slightly the worse for wear to put it mildly. George, too, got both barrels.

At school in Eden my first ever teacher was Miss Emily Young. Maybe teacher is the wrong word, for my early days in school were spent wedged between her feet as she taught the class. I was only one year old when my sisters carried me up there. I had to go. With mum at work all day there was nobody to leave me in the house with, so as soon as possible I was carted off to the school. How she did a day's work with me stuck under her feet or crawling round on the floor, is a miracle. It gave me one of my first memories. Once I'd learned a few words I could always tell the class what colour knickers she was wearing. Not many toddlers include the word "knickers" in their small vocabulary at such an early age. She was big and masculine and had a moustache but she was still nice. Many a day we went up there without shoes, we had so little money, including on freezing winter days. The school was only 300 yards away but that was far enough in bare feet in the snow. But when you had no money like us, and the one pair of shoes you had was worn through, or had to be saved for best, you thought nothing about it. And we weren't the only ones.

They taught us gardening at Eden School and that was with Mrs Sloane, my favourite. She was blonde and funny and so nice. I remember one day she came in crying her eyes out when she announced that some member of the Royal Family had died. I loved the gardening and I must have been good at digging. Maybe it was all the digging we did in the farmer's field pinching his vegetables. One day I found a ring under the school vegetable patch I was digging and it was the ring Mrs Sloane had lost some years earlier. From that moment on she always said I was her favourite pupil.

Not so with Mr Barclay the headmaster. He was short, round, bald and pompous. Think of Captain Mainwaring in the TV sitcom *Dad's Army*. His face was so foul-tempered some days it looked like a bag of spanners. Why are headmasters always so cantankerous? Are they born that way or do they just practise? He was always on at me and made it quite clear he didn't like the Irvines one bit. He stamped around the school, always in a mood, always finding fault, always picking on me. The cane never left his hand. I can still feel some of the whacks he gave me. Maybe he was just the same with everyone else but it did always seem to be me he glowered at or found something wrong with. It went on and on until one day my brother George collared him and threatened him. "Leave the Irvines alone or else." Nobody witnessed it and Mr Barclay kept quiet about it. It did the trick. After that he was a lot better. He still wouldn't put me in the school football team though. It was all we did at breaks and dinnertime, play football. Even as a seven-year-old I was a good goalkeeper and the best in the school. That was my best position. But he wouldn't put me in the team. Wild horses wouldn't have made me play centre forward. I was a goalkeeper and loved it, throwing myself all over the place, tipping a shot round the corner, diving at someone's feet, always saving certain goals. Think about it. Here's me going to be an international footballer one day and Barclay wouldn't put me in the school team. When he saw my name in the paper years later he must have choked on his prunes.

I have a hazy picture in my mind of a building that was small, single storey, built of stone, with a slate roof and two or maybe three classrooms. We had wooden desks with lift-up lids and a hole for the inkpot. There was a long groove where you put your pencils. The big responsible job was being in charge of filling up the inkwells from the big container. The desks were in pairs and faced the blackboard. We sat there for hours; there was no moving around. We'd chant tables and recite spellings and read and write and do sums off the blackboard. I was reasonably bright and never found it difficult. At least the place was warm but the milk was left in front of the big old iron radiators. To this day I hate warm milk. I couldn't drink the stuff, it was so awful, but Mrs Sloane cottoned on to this and always took a couple of bottles out to keep them cold. Yes, I must have been teacher's pet.

As I say I was always hungry. Breakfast was porridge. A real treat was champ. We mashed the green leaves of spring onions into the potatoes and put some butter in, when we had butter. Lunch was a jam sandwich. We didn't eat too badly in the evening but there was never enough. Not when there were so many of us to feed. There were lots of stews with the veg we pinched and the meat we scrounged and conned from the butcher and the fish from the fishermen after I'd helped them. Peggy, who worked in McGinty's chip shop, sometimes brought great bags of chips home. By hook or by crook we always had something to eat.

Seven years I lived in Eden and "Happy Days" and, yes, they were happy days. Yes we struggled, yes we went hungry, and yes we went cold in winter. Clothes – we had few. Toys – we didn't have any. I remember my sister Joan taking me and brother Bobby to her works Christmas party one year when I was very small. We were given a stocking and in it was a Dinky car. That was the first toy car I ever owned and I absolutely treasured it. When I found it at the bottom of the stocking my eyes just lit up and I shouted "LOOK!" I had it for a long, long time and it was my most wonderful, precious possession.

Money was always scarce but when Christmas came there was always a stocking at the bottom of the bed, even if it only had some sweets, an apple and an orange. The village was a real community and everyone helped and knew each other. News and gossip passed round the place like wildfire. There were no secrets in a place like Eden and everybody mucked in, in times of trouble. I never knew anyone who locked their door day or night.

Sometimes today I can sit by the fireside when the house is empty and quiet and I can still picture my mother coming home drained and weary. She'd be up at 5am in the morning to start an early shift. Then she'd finish at 2pm and be straight into some big house to clean. The other shift was 2pm till 10pm. When that happened she'd clean houses in the mornings. But even on her days off she was never still. Cyclists used to come through our village and one day one of them called at the house for some help because he had a puncture. He didn't mend it. Mother did. And with the kettle always boiling away over the fire, she made him a cup of tea before sending him on his way. And from then on others called in and they always got a cup of tea and she just gave it to them; she would never have thought of asking for money.

Eden

She was short and rather plump though she never liked to admit that. She'd pretend to be cross when I said she had grey hair. "No, it's sandy," was the reply with a smile on her face. There was a kindness about her; she was never strict with us but trusted us to be sensible and good even though she knew we roamed far and wide. People in the village knew how hard she worked and respected her for it. I enjoyed helping – growing carrots, parsnips and potatoes in our garden, carrying the water across from the pump.

She never talked much about the older family I never saw, or the ones I was led to believe were killed. She never talked much about Da and his death. Until I started this book I knew hardly a thing about them. I always wonder, if she knew the dangers he faced, that she must have thought that one night he would not return. She must have expected it maybe, the knock on the door, the serious face of the warden shuffling his feet. As soon as he started with, "it's bad news I'm afraid"... I'd guess that's what he said... she must have known straight away.

I wonder sometimes was he a good man, a good footballer? I heard he played a bit for Distillery FC. Maybe if I'd not left home at 16 I'd have had chances to talk about him and find out a bit more about who I was and about the brothers and sisters I never knew. My sons and grandchildren ask me sometimes what it was like not to know my father. I can't answer them because I never knew what it was like to have one in the first place. I tell them you can't miss what you've never had. Though if it has affected me it's that I sometimes ask the question, "I haven't turned out so bad have I? Have I done all right?"

Sometimes I sit at home and look at my grandchildren and think how lucky they are. How many people these days must sleep four to a bed, go without shoes, fetch water from a pump, read by candlelight, have just one set of clothes, make do and mend like we used to do? But yes, in spite of all that, they were happy days in Eden, even if my sisters did dress me up as a gnome one Christmas, as a change from Father Christmas.

And then, when I was seven, we moved.

CHAPTER TWO

CARRICKFERGUS

It was brother Joey who came racing along the road and found me playing. There was a look of alarm and panic on his face. He'd run all the way, racing round all over the place until he found me. He was red faced and stopped just for a second to try and get his senses back and then he panted out his message.

"Get back to the house quick," he gasped, struggling for breath. "Something's happened. You've got to come back."

My pals all stood round wondering what was going on. Joey grabbed me by the arm and began to pull me away. We walked quickly.

"Mum's got to go away," he said.

"What do you mean, she's got to go away?" was all I could say for the minute.

"I don't know, but all I know is she's got to go away for a while and we've got to look after ourselves while she's gone."

I felt stunned and worried. Look after ourselves? I was only nine. Why should she want to go away? How long was she going for? When was she coming back? Was she ever coming back? She was Mammy; how could she possibly leave us? Who would look after us?

Joey must have known what I was thinking. "She's coming back but has to go away and isn't sure how long for."

We began to walk even faster. The house came into view. When we got there and went inside there was no sign of our mother. Sister Jean was there, Bobby and Annie one of the neighbours. They were all silent but kept looking at each other.

"It'll be all right," Annie said eventually. "She will be back.

We'll all muck in and help and keep an eye on things. Some of you are working so there's money coming in."

Another silence followed. Annie left. There were still six of us in the house. Joey and George were now in the army although Joey was back at home for a few days. We'd been here in Carrickfergus for only a couple of years. I was just nine. We just sat there silently. My head was spinning. She was the rock of the family, had seen us through thick and thin and worked her fingers to the bone to keep us in food and clothing. There were times when she came back to the house and was just too exhausted to speak. How could she possibly leave us now? It just didn't make sense. In truth, with her out at work every hour of the day it was my sisters who had virtually brought me up but there was always the knowledge that Mammy was there if we needed her.

She did come back nine months later and it was only then that I found out why she left and where she went. All I learned was that she was in prison for nine months for continuing to claim benefits to which she was not entitled. When she came back, nobody thought the worse of her for it. Not a single person didn't admire her for her efforts to bring us up; for surviving the tragedies she had suffered, and for working all hours that God sent her. When she came back I was shocked by her appearance. It seemed like she had aged 20 years. Her face was drawn and lined and weary. She had been sent to Omagh Prison but the other inmates had sympathised with her story and because of her age, they went out of their way to help and support her, even to the extent of doing her chores. The sum of £280 was mentioned as the amount she was imprisoned for. In the olden days people were transported to Australia for stealing a loaf of bread when they were starving. My mother was imprisoned for nine long months simply for trying to feed her family.

We'd moved in to 9 Knocklade, a little cul-de-sac on Sunnylands Estate and left Eden because Mammy had got the chance of this house where she worked in Carrick. Sunnylands was a big new estate on the other side of the railway line from the old part of the town. Before houses were built it had been the site of a US Army camp in World War Two and the birthplace of the US Rangers, an elite group of tough commandos. When we got there the estate couldn't have been built very long and was roughly split into three areas – the top, bottom and middle. Knocklade was somewhere in the middle. It was no distance to move and we all knew Carrickfergus well. If you move from a place as small as Eden everyone gets to know about it. There was great concern. "Ah but Mrs Irvine is it a good thing yer doin'?" they'd ask.

"Ah yer sure yer'll be all right in the big town, there'll be so many people yer don't know up there."

"'Tis a big change for yer. Are yer sure yer'll manage, will yer not miss yer friends here, who'll there be to give yer the help when times is hard an' we'll miss yer children and especially that rascal William? At least the apples and pears will stay on the trees a bit longer." Little did they know I went back many times and happily carried on eating their apples.

I knew I'd miss the tiny school with Mrs Sloane and Miss Young although in fact I continued to attend there for several weeks before changing to Sunnylands School. I certainly wouldn't miss Mr Barclay. He certainly wouldn't miss us either; when he heard the news the Irvines were leaving he probably skipped all the way home with relief and then groaned when he heard we'd be staying a bit longer. Then there were the Irish Setters in Lady Baird's garden to say goodbye to. I cried as I gave each one a last hug. They wagged their tails and looked at me with their big soft eyes. I swear they understood what I was saying. The sight of the five of them standing there watching me leave through the gates is still with me today. And then there was my best friend Crawford Hanley. We vowed to do what best friends do when they are separated. Carrickfergus and Eden were only a spit apart; of course we'd meet up and stay best friends. As for raiding gardens for apples and pears and gooseberries, weren't there twice as many gardens in Carrick? And in the new school I'd be going to I might get a chance to get in the school team at last.

The house was like a palace after the tiny bungalow we had been in. It seemed huge, with four bedrooms and the novelty of an upstairs and a downstairs. There was a bathroom and an indoor toilet. There were taps with running water. Press a switch and on came the electric lights. For days we ran water for the fun of it and switched lights on and off at all times of the day. At first we'd barely enough furniture to fill even one room and our feet clumped round the wooden floors. What few things we had we moved by horse and cart and then bought more furniture and carpets on tick. Carpets – we thought we were living in luxury. It never struck us that there were dozens of these houses, all identical, on the estate. This one was ours and for that reason alone it was special. The walk back and forth to school in Eden, for those few weeks I had to stay there, was a couple of miles each way in all weathers. The quickest way was to walk along the railway lines, with a few detours into the gardens that had fruit trees of course. My job was the garden again, flowers in the front and vegetables in the back.

We eventually got a TV as well. I remember it being black and white; there was no colour in those days. We must have had it in 1956 because Bobby and I bunked off school to watch England play Ireland on a weekday. My mother watched it with us and there was a conversation that went along the lines of:

"Bobby, which is Ireland?" she asked.

"They're in the dark shirts."

A little later; "But Billy, which is England then?"

The first thing we did after we moved in was get a dog and we called it "Guard" after brother George who was in the Irish Guards. It didn't last very long. A similar-looking dog from somewhere else on the estate was worrying the sheep in the fields beyond the houses. A policeman spotted our dog wandering home one day. He followed it and came up the garden to knock on the door of the house. He stood there with a face like you'd need walnut crackers to make it smile.

"Is this your dog?" he asked, none too friendly.

It was Joan who was in and of course she said it was. "It's been worrying the sheep in the fields; it must be this one, I've got a description," he announced. "It'll have to be put down." He made Joan, who was by now crying and protesting that it couldn't be our dog, hold him. The callous, cold-hearted man just shot the dog in the head. Without a word more he just shook his head and left. It was left to us to dispose of Guard. We wept and wept. There wasn't a dry eye in the house and we moped about for days. Joan was distraught. Meanwhile the other dog continued to spend his days worrying the sheep and infuriating the farmer, while we buried ours in the garden. Thank you, RUC. They never came back to see us to say sorry.

Not long after I had my tonsils out and my adenoids. Apparently they do serve some useful purpose, being the first line of defence against infections. Unfortunately mine also served the purpose of making me talk with a very nasal voice. They tell me as well that at the ripe old age of seven I snored like a geriatric. If I had a pound for every time someone had to say to me, "would you say that again slowly Willie", or dug me in the ribs in bed, I'd be a very wealthy man.

Mammy said the operation was so I could speak better as I had such difficulty being understood. Sometimes I wonder if it made any difference especially when I first arrived in Burnley and nobody could understand a word I was saying. Mind you I couldn't understand them either.

While Mum was away we managed but I often think my childhood ended on the day my mother was taken away for those nine long months. George and Joey sent money. Jean and Joan were working. Peggy still worked in the chip shop back in Eden. We almost felt wealthy. I had a paper round and later on was a delivery boy for Henderson's grocery shop. I had one of those bikes with a basket on the front, and I flew round the town like the wind. On another part of the estate was one strange, old woman who frightened the life out of all the kids and the neighbours. She was almost a recluse but was one of our customers. The first time I had to go there my knees knocked and trembled as I stood there waiting for her to answer the door. I must have been developing the Irvine charm by then because before long we were the best of pals and every time I called there was a huge piece of cake waiting.

By now Mammy was in her late 50s and working less and less because of angina. She was at home more and more, her body and health suffering after years of child-rearing and working ceaselessly.

In the cul-de-sac we all got on fine. There was Mrs Broad and Mrs Lucas and then there was Mrs O'Toole and husband Ernie. The latter were Catholics but it made no difference to any of us in this little community we had at Knocklade, except that they always quietly left Carrick for a couple of weeks when it was July 12th to get out of the way of the parades and the Protestant celebrations.

I had plenty of pals and there was lots to do. Saturday afternoon was the matinee at the pictures. There was *Flash Gordon* and another film I remember is *The Fighting Sullivans*. A family of boys join the navy and one by one lose their lives. It was too close to home for me, still thinking four brothers had been killed in the war, and I know I cried. I was in the Boys' Brigade and of course there was the football. We never stopped playing.

Football began seriously for me in Carrickfergus. There were long games at Sunnylands and the different parts of the estate would play each other. The games would last for hours. In those days you didn't spend hours glued to a TV screen. There weren't any near us until 1953 and the Coronation and just a few people who could afford it bought one. All the dads would take part in the football as well. These games were deadly serious and stopped only when it went dark. I was still concentrating on being a goalkeeper. There was me still a lad, and these great dads bearing down on me soon made me agile and quick although I'd come off covered in bruises sometimes. In school holidays we played from dawn till dusk day after day. We had a good Sunnylands Primary School team as well with me in goal. I did eventually move there from Eden School. It was so much bigger and felt so huge. With a dozen classrooms or more it took some getting used to. It had been newly built to serve the Sunnylands Estate. In those days you stayed in a primary school till you were 14. Our teacher was Mr Joiner and he always claimed to be related to Stanley Matthews. I've never been sure how an Irishman could be related to Sir Stan but then discovered that he was English so maybe he wasn't pulling our legs. He was a huge man, 6ft 5ins, and lived only a few houses away from us on the estate. Mr Joiner was the first teacher to have any influence on my football.

We were so good we got to the final of the County Cup. The other team was from the older Technical School where my brother Bobby went and played. He was good as well and went on to play for Stoke City and Northern Ireland. He was nearly two years older than me and threatened to kick the living daylights out of me, except the expression he used wasn't "living daylights". He meant it too so I chickened out, faked an injury and found an excuse not to play. We lost 3-0.

Sister Jean encouraged me all the time and in big games came to watch and gave me a shilling if we won. I made quite a bit. She'd treat us all to chips and pop after a game. I guess sister Jean was the one member of the family I was closest to.

Football, though, nearly killed me because after one game while still at primary school on a hot summer night we all raced down to the harbour and Fisherman's Pier for a swim. Of course we raced to see who'd be in the water first. We still had our kit on and I was way out in front. Down Barn Road we went and Taylor's Avenue till we reached the Marine Promenade and the pier. Without looking I just jumped in but there was no water. The tide was well and truly out. It was a long drop as well. If I'd dived in headfirst there is no doubt I would have seriously injured myself, probably would have broken my neck. As it was I landed feet first in the deep, soft mud and there was little harm done though it shook me up badly. I tried not to show how badly I was shocked and laughed it off. Looking back I was really lucky.

There was a Summer League team as well. We won it one year and that was the first of my medals. Tommy Reid, who was a few years older than me, was a great friend of the family. It was from him I got my first ever pair of football boots – and my first ever pint – even though it was only shandy.

William Donnelly was a great schoolfriend at Sunnylands School. His family knew that we didn't have much money so his dad used to pay for me to watch some of the international games at Windsor Park. I watched and hero-worshipped players like Jimmy McIlroy, Danny Blanchflower and Bertie

Peacock. Like any young lad mad on football I'd go home and pretend one day I'd play with them. Never in my wildest dreams did I think that one day I actually would.

At 14 it was on to the Technical School for woodwork, physics, chemistry and German. My German must have been good. With a score of 98% for one German test I was chosen to be one of the choir to sing *Silent Night,* in German of course, in some big Belfast concert. My singing was awful though; I was told to stand on the back row and not sing loud.

By now I had abandoned thoughts of being a goalkeeper, there was too much competition, not the least of which was brother Bobby. We played against the other Technical Schools such as Bangor and Larne. As a midfield player, in those days a halfback, I progressed to East Antrim Schoolboys and then the Irish Schools. A trip to Watford with the schools team was the icing on the cake. There was me, hardly set foot out of Carrickfergus and Belfast, going across to England for the first time on what seemed an endless journey.

Terry Venables was an early opponent when we played against England at Watford in the Victory Shield. Then there was Bert Murray who played for Chelsea, with whom I later played at Brighton and am still in touch today. Venables was impressive even then, and was the first to play at all levels for England. Today he is known across the world. He managed England, Tottenham, Crystal Palace, Middlesbrough and Leeds; his face appears in the media every day. I still work in a factory.

Joe O'Connell was the sports master and Wednesday afternoon was rugby afternoon. He'd let me out early so I could miss the rugby and play in the Wednesday afternoon football league. Most of the lads who played were older and on the dole but they paid my bus fares wherever we went. Joe gave me a school mark to show I'd been at school and had done the rugby.

Linfield signed me when I was 14 and I played for the Linfield Rangers, the junior team. Brother Bobby, only 16, was already the Linfield first team goalkeeper. While I played for the second and third teams Jackie Milburn was playing for them. The only thing I remember of him is his terseness with me one day. Of course he was a legend in England and a huge personality in Ireland. After enjoying 14 years at Newcastle, he continued to score goals by the bagful for Linfield. By the end of his first season at Linfield he had scored 55 goals and Linfield had won just about everything. Malcolm Brodie, one of Ireland's great soccer writers, described him as the biggest crowd puller in Ireland, guaranteed to put 5,000 on the gate. Jimmy McIlroy says that not a footballer leaves or enters Northern Ireland without Malcolm knowing about it. Anyway, there is the story that when Milburn first arrived in Belfast he took a drive around the streets. Huge crowds lined the streets cheering and waving flags. Mr Milburn waved back amazed at this adulation. It was later pointed out to him that it was July 12th and the crowds in the streets were waiting for the parades, not him. My only conversation with him was short and sweet. "How do you chest and control the ball so easily in one movement?" I asked him. He said he hadn't time to bother with me so I never bothered him again. His reputation in north-east England is sacred. In Newcastle he is a saint not just for his goals but also for being a gentleman. In Belfast people still talk of the dozens of goals he scored. You'll rarely hear anyone say an unkind word about him. I must have caught him on an off day.

Anyway, I left Linfield soon after. In the toilet one day I overheard some of the other players saying I was only there because brother Bobby was first team goalkeeper. "Bugger you lot then," I thought and never went back until I was a full international. Bobby stayed at Linfield and by this time was also an apprentice engineer.

For me it was Barn United who played in Carrick. They were the nearest local amateur team and I suppose that was where serious competitive football really started for me. In the morning on a Saturday it was play for school and in the afternoon it was play for Barn with the men. Two games a day every weekend. Years later at Burnley we'd play three games in four days every Easter and two games on consecutive days at Christmas. Today our pampered millionaires seem unable to play two games in a week without mentioning the word "tired". It was Tommy Reid who introduced me to

Bobby Dummigan, one of the Barn United committee men. He signed me on. I remember telling him I loved football so much I'd go anywhere and play for nothing. Years later when we met and I was getting paid as a professional he reminded me of that. Barn played in the Northern Ireland Amateur League, which consisted of several divisions. Being much younger than all the rest of them in the team; they were in fact grown men; I was well looked after. I had a minder called Boko McCullough, tall, ginger-haired, and woe betide anyone who gave me any rough treatment. Boko would immediately go and kick them six feet up in the air.

Joe O'Connell encouraged me in everything and nobody was more surprised than him when I turned up in my school uniform one day to play for Barn United and there was Joe playing for the opposition. "What the hell are you doing here?" he asked. He must have realised in that game that I could play a bit and should be encouraged. By letting me off those Wednesday afternoon rugby sessions he was actually risking his job.

If there's one man to say thank you to it is Jimmy Murphy. I owe him everything. He'd have a sandwich ready for me in between Saturday morning and afternoon games. Otherwise he knew I'd go hungry. He'd been a player himself and played for Fleetwood in Lancashire. It was Jimmy who got me the trials sorted at Burnley. There was another good player in the Barn team called Geordie Pritchard and Jimmy used to give us a lift home. After one game he was very quiet but after he'd dropped Geordie off he explained he couldn't say anything in front of Geordie but had to sit with his mouth tightly shut. That was when he said, "I've got you a trial at Burnley". He'd helped me, shielded me, guided and supported me. Other clubs were interested; Manchester United, Wolves, Everton and Arsenal but Jimmy chose Burnley. I'd never heard of the place and knew even less about it. But Jimmy insisted they were the best club in England for young players to learn their trade and develop with the best chance of getting into the first team, and, of course, he and I knew that Irishmen Jimmy McIlroy and Alex Elder were already there. I did what he said, trusted him implicitly and didn't argue. If Jimmy said

Burnley was the place, then that was fine. The trial was eight months away and for all that time the Burnley scout Alec Scott came to check on me, but when the grounds were heavy and tough Jimmy knew I struggled a bit, so he kept him away by telling him I was ill or injured.

The Belfast Telegraph did a big feature about the trialists about to embark for England and various different clubs. There was a pen picture and a photograph of each of us and a prediction as to which would be successful and signed on. The prediction for William Irvine was not a good one. Not ready, it said, potential and talent maybe, but not suitable. I sat and stared at the back page of that newspaper for a long time and felt depressed and miserable. The modern footballer's vocabulary seems not to extend beyond a few words, "gutted" being one of them. Whoever wrote those predictions for the *Telegraph* was way out. Maybe it was the gardening expert roped in to fill the space on a quiet day. Of all the predictions, not one was correct. Those with a yes were all sent back. The one with a no was signed on. William Irvine of Barn United was signed on and asked to return to Burnley.

I spent nine years of my life in Carrickfergus. I was as happy and comfortable there as I had been in Eden. It was a great place to be a boy. I was never short of friends and never short of something to do. When brothers Joey and George were in the army they'd come home on leave and always give me money. Mammy was so proud of them. George eventually became a Regimental Sergeant Major and was an army man through and through. Years later I visited him with my wife Rita at his barracks in Windsor. It must have been the hottest night of the year. We met in the Sergeants' Mess and there they all were in uniforms, ties, shirts, jackets and the full paraphernalia. He wouldn't let me take my tie off and loosen my collar so there was the mother of all rows. He relented and then everyone loosened their ties and took their jackets off. In gratitude I was made an honorary sergeant by the rest of them. Sandra, the eldest sister, joined the WRAF. I didn't know her too well and only remember being eight or nine when she got married and getting into real trouble for drinking all the pop at the wedding. Joey was in the Inniskilling Fusiliers. He loved them with a passion and was distraught when some of the regiments amalgamated. His love for the army, though, didn't stop him going AWOL several times. When he had the hump he'd pinch the nearest army bicycle and cycle home to Sunnylands. A day or two later the Redcaps would arrive in hot pursuit. They knew full well where to find him and back he went with them to spend a few days behind bars. Of course we'd tell them he wasn't at home but they always knew and would wait till he went out to go the pub, showed himself, and back he went to the glasshouse as he called it. It was quite a regular occurrence and of course all the neighbours thought it was a hoot and would laugh themselves silly when they saw him being taken away waving to them. They knew he'd be back. Twenty-one years he was with them and when they amalgamated he was so angry he bought himself out. Had he served just one more year he would have had a marvellous pension. But he was a real Jack the Lad. He couldn't read music but played the piano. He was up and down the ranks like a yo-yo because he was as daft as a brush and his daftness caused a rift eventually between him and me.

I never forgave him when we played Scotland at Windsor Park and we won 3-2. I scored the winning goal. I gave him my international shirt but learned from a friend that on his way back to England afterwards on the ferry to Heysham he stood on a table in the bar after a few drinks and offered to swap the shirt for a cabin berth. I never saw him again after that. He died of cancer at the age of 50. And if anyone who reads this book is the bloke who got that shirt off him, I'd like it back now. Jean, too, joined the army after working for a few years in the Gallagher's cigarette factory. She could sing like a lark and I loved her dearly and still do but she moved to Canada.

I loved Carrickfergus. I loved its history, its castle, the old walls and the harbour. At school I loved to read and learn about the place and all the characters over the years who raided, burned or inhabited the town. Its story goes back over 800 years and it gets its name from Carraig Fhearghus, the Rock of Fergus. Fergus was a sixth-century character who left nearby Ulster to found a kingdom in Scotland. He must have woken up one morning and thought "Ha ha, after breakfast why don't I go and found a kingdom in Scotland?" When he returned, the luck of the Irish deserted him and he drowned on the rocks. Carraig Fhearghus became Carrickfergus. The castle is Norman and it was John de Courcy who started it in 1180 but didn't finish. He must have been short of bricks. Later along comes Hugh de Lacy to complete the job. Then King John, of Robin Hood fame, arrived in Carrick and, not being the gently persuasive type, threw out poor old Hugh, claiming the castle for himself. Edward Bruce, brother of Robert the Bruce, landed in Larne many years later and spent a year besieging Carrick. Soon it was his turn to be booted out by the English, but the retreating Scots very kindly burned down the town. Over the next century it was rebuilt and burned down again with clockwork regularity. For the next few hundred years it was a story of bloodshed, ambushes, backstabbing, squabbling and arguing, a bit like *Eastenders*! As a solution the town walls were built in 1608. That didn't work. Even after that, Carrickfergus was embroiled in changes of ownership, and religious squabbles. For a small place it attracted an awful lot of fighting. It must have been something in the water. Catholic James the Second sent troops to occupy it. A year later the Protestant Williamites bombarded the town and took over. And then at last King William of Orange landed in 1690, marched off to the Boyne to defeat James the Second's Catholic forces and British history was altered and affected for all time. But peace at last? No. The French paid a visit in 1760 and attacked the place. The castle surrendered, the church silver was stolen. Never trust the French. The British navy caught the culprits somewhere near the Isle of Man. Don't ask me where the silver went. And that, apart from some years later the American privateer John Paul Jones scrapping offshore with the British HMS *Drake*, is roughly the story of Carrickfergus. John Paul Jones is regarded by us as a pirate but is fondly known as the Father of the American Navy on the other side of the Atlantic. Funny how we see things differently.

But I had to leave – Burnley beckoned. Alec Scott took me, Cedric Gilmour and Billy Mills on the overnight ferry to Heysham. I had the shoes I was walking in, the clothes I was standing up in, my boots and a blazer that was far too small; the cuffs just about reached my elbows. In the pocket was a couple of quid that Jean had saved for me. My mother and I had gone to the shop and bought this jacket specially, but it was the only one in the shop. It was that or nothing, so that's how I ended up with a jacket that didn't fit. When I got to Burnley my boots caused great excitement. The other players had never seen anything quite like them, they were so old and worn. Hannibal could have worn them crossing over the Alps. They were the old-fashioned sort with studs that you nailed in. You pulled the old ones out, or they fell out while you were running. You filled the hole the nail had left with a matchstick and then hammered in the new stud with the boot upside down on a cobbler's last. If you didn't have a last you used the doorstep. And then you dubbined them, and dubbined them and dubbined them some more to keep them soft and supple. I had these boots under my arm and when Jimmy McIlroy saw them he laughed and gave me a pair of his. The only other exotic place I had been to was Watford. Watford today is nothing to get excited about and then it was even worse. I was innocent, wide-eyed and just 16 and I knew nothing about Burnley. Perhaps it's as well I didn't.

CHAPTER THREE

BURNLEY

Funny how you find things out as you go along and thoughts occur that have never appeared in your head before. I've lived for over 60 years and never questioned the family history that has been handed down to me or that I have just assumed was correct. I know my mother was Agnes Irvine, I know my father was Alex Irvine and that he died so stupidly as a result of the wartime blackout. By stupid I don't mean that he was stupid, I just mean it was so stupid the way he died. I've always thought I had 17 brothers and sisters and that I've known some of them but not all; I've never questioned believing that four of them were killed in World War Two. I just always assumed that all the family were Irvines and that I was the last of them.

Then, when working on this book, I began to wonder just how much I knew about them. Was I sure I was one of 18, was I certain that four of them died in the war? And I began to think that if this book was to appear on the shelves of bookshops, especially in Belfast, I needed to be sure that all of this was correct, because, as sure as apples are apples, journalists and the media over there will want to know more, especially about the wartime deaths.

And up until this point it had never troubled me, I'd never questioned it, never bothered, never thought about it. Jean, Joan, George, Joey, Bobby, Margaret and Sandra were real enough and they and me make the eight that are mentioned in the newspaper clippings I have going back to the time I made my debut and my mother was featured in several of the newspapers. It never occurred to me to wonder why these newspapers said eight and not 18. And what's also real enough is the struggle we had in those early days, of schooldays without shoes, of making do with hand-me-downs, and of walking the nine miles into Belfast more than once because there was no money for bus fares.

Burnley

Of the family I knew were still alive, Bobby was somewhere in or near Stoke, Sandra was in Scotland, Jean was in Canada and far from well (she was to pass away before the book was finished), and Joan, now in her 80s, was in Carrickfergus. And Joan I hadn't spoken to for six years or more. I did know for sure that Joey died but that George was still alive in Windsor, I think.

And so the niggles began, the niggles of wanting to know just how many there were in my family, and did those four brothers really meet their end so tragically. So I decided to see what I could find out; and you have to understand how big a decision this was for someone who had never queried his past until now. What if I found that everything I had believed for all these years was incorrect? How would I cope with that? Did I want to know?

And so, quite unintentionally, this book takes a different turn. For sure when it was started it was to be a story of football, of scoring records, a broken leg, conflict and other disasters that came my way, one of which would have tested the strongest man. And then how it all came good again in the end. But then another chapter emerges which almost amounts to: just who am I?

Would sister Jean know more? Were there things she could tell me that I had never thought or bothered to ask before? The truth is I put off telephoning her in Canada several times. I had the excuse that she wasn't well, she wasn't strong, she mustn't be bothered and even though the telephone is so marvellous that she sounds like she is in the room next door, you still say "but she's thousands of miles away, how can she be of any help, what will she remember?" And I put it off.

Then there was Tommy Reid, my oldest friend from Carrickfergus, a few years older than me; maybe he would remember the other family members I never saw and know the truth of the wartime deaths.

I rang them both. Tommy was a blank but Jean had answers; not all of them, only some, and the first was shock enough. Jean Irvine, the older sister who had done so much for me as a growing boy and then given so much encouragement to me as a budding footballer at school and at Barn, told me simply and clearly, when I pressed her, "Willie, I'm not an Irvine".

I was stunned.

After the brief silence I asked her what on earth she meant. And she explained that the mother who did so much for us all had been married twice before, and I was taken aback again because this was something I never knew, and I never knew because I'd never bothered to ask. Then I went on to learn that Jean and Joan were born when my mother was married to a fellow called Herbert Hamilton. So they weren't Irvines, they were Hamiltons and only my half-sisters.

I sat back, momentarily numbed by all of this, especially when Jean added that her real name wasn't Jean, it was Sarah Jane, but that everyone called her Jean. All these years and I never ever knew her real name. This was my closest sister, the one who did so much. And I also knew she had cancer and was dying and lived so far away.

But before all that, before she became a Hamilton, Jean went on to say, Mother was married to a chap called Willie Black and they had children; Albert, Elsie, Sadie and others she didn't know the names of plus maybe the four lads who were killed in the war, but that she wasn't sure about. "I always called them uncles," Jean added. "I don't think I ever even knew their names. I can't think we ever saw them." It left me thinking, why call them "uncles"? Jean thought, too, that Lily, the sister who Mammy used to tell me died when she was 12, was a Black, and she went back to the time Mother was married to Willie Black and Lily had a twin brother, Billy.

It took a while for the effects of the phone call to wear off. It was an odd feeling. There was no upset. I was numbed, yes, but there were no immediate feelings of enormity or anger. It was an odd sensation. I sat there trying to work it all out and let it sink in.

Tommy Reid said he would call back. By coincidence he had met Joan in the street on the way to somewhere, the shops maybe, he couldn't remember. They both still lived a few streets apart in Carrick. Yes, he would ask her if she would speak to me after all these years because in truth we hadn't spoken for such a long time and in my own head I'd labelled it as a rift. When I went to Carrick with my sons on an emotional return visit, a treat they had arranged for me to mark my birthday, I had avoided meeting her. But yes, Tommy would go and see her. And all I could do was wait for him to call back to tell me he had seen her and we could talk and heal our differences.

Does it make any difference knowing these things? Does it alter anything? I think it does in some ways. It makes me think that maybe I was too selfishly wound up in myself and football and my own needs for too many years and maybe I should have been asking these questions a long time ago about my family.

Burnley

But I tried to put things in some semblance of order by saying to myself that I was still the same man; the one who became a footballer so close to achieving greatness, and I'm sure I would have done so, given the luck and freedom from injury that was needed to go on for years at the highest level.

So yes, I was shaken by what Jean told me that night. It didn't change anything but it did leave me wanting to know more. But I think the abiding reaction it left me with was one of regret that I left it all these years before beginning to question just who I am.

But Tommy hadn't rung back and if Joan didn't want to speak to me just where did I go from here?

From Carrickfergus to Lancashire – the home of Hotpot, Stan Laurel, George Formby, Blackpool Tower, Lowry, Gracie Fields, Kathleen Ferrier, Eric Morecambe, the Rochdale Co-op, Tom Finney, the Industrial Revolution, Hilda Baker, Chorley Cakes, Eccles Cakes, Nat Lofthouse, Brian Statham, Creamy Lancashire Cheese, tripe, Uncle Joe's Mint Balls, Fisherman's Friends, Victory V sweets – the ones that burned off the back of your mouth – the ferry terminal at Heysham, surely the most depressing place on God's earth – or at least it was when I landed there – Bob Lord and Willie Eckerslike. They used to tell me Willie Eckerslike was Burnley's finest ever centre forward till I cottoned on it was a joke.

Burnley. It was an immense shock getting off the train and seeing the place for the first time. From the green hills of Antrim, rolling fields and the sea, to grey houses, grey mills and smoke. It just seemed there was nothing but smoke everywhere you looked. The train station was set above the town at the top of a steep slope and you looked down on all the grime and shabbiness. From the station I went down Standish Street and up came this dreadful smell. There was a brewery and a boneyard and I just can't describe the smells. From the high viewpoint of the station the landscape was one of rows and rows of little houses and streets, each with a pub or a shop at the end. My senses were just numbed. I stayed above one of these pubs and it was run by an Irish couple. They were the only people I could understand in those first few days. Everybody else talked and used words I'd never heard before. I had to guess what they were saying. Somebody met me at the station, looked at me and smiled, and said hello. Then he said, "Ah'll bet tha's fair jiggered". I looked at him and must have looked puzzled. "Tired", he said, "I bet you're tired." I walked down the street and heard a mother shouting at her little lad. "Shurrup skrikin' or ah'll gi' thee summat ter shrike abart." It puzzled me all night so I asked what it meant. It means stop crying or I'll give you something to cry about. Some of them didn't say hello, they said "eigh up". But they also said "eigh up" when they wanted you to move out of the way so it was difficult to know if they were saying hello and being friendly, or saying get out of the way because they were being grumpy. Tommy Hutchison, a great player who later came to Turf Moor, famously labelled Burnley "Grumpytown".

I had to learn words like "sithee" and "owdonaminit", "uz'll" and "ast". I lost count of the times I'd say something and they'd reply with "tha wa?"

People would ask me, "Where ast tha' bin?" Where have you been?

They'd tell me to "tek it wom withee". Take it home with you.

And many's the time, if I spoke first, they'd look at me and say, "What is thi on abart, can't thi speak proper?"

There were lots of other young lads there just like me, all desperate to do well. I saw the ground, Turf Moor, for the first time and the huge training area at a place called Gawthorpe, a beautiful place of green fields and farmland on the edge of the town. I saw Jimmy McIlroy and Alex Elder training but was too shy to go up and say I was from Ireland and tell them who I was. I wanted to say I'd seen them play at Windsor Park and that they were my heroes. To put it mildly I was awestruck by everything and felt dreadfully homesick, missing Carrick and the family, especially sister Jean.

My great friend Jimmy McIlroy had the same problem with Lancashire accents and speech when he first arrived. On the field there'd be him in broad Irish talking to some of the other players talking in broad Lancashire. It usually ended with them shouting in exasperation, "Just gi' us t' bloody ball will yer?"

Burnley were also famous for all the Geordies they had on the staff. Can you imagine a team of Lancashire, Geordie and Irish accents all unable to understand each other? Throw in the odd Scotsman as well, an average crowd of 26,000 talking in a language only they can understand, and it's a miracle that somehow Burnley won a championship in 1960.

Outside of Burnley, in that year, Wolves beat Blackburn 3-0 in the FA Cup Final in a game spoiled by Dave Whelan's broken leg and poor behaviour by the Blackburn fans after the game when they jeered Wolves and pelted the referee with rubbish. Only hours before kick-off Blackburn's star player Derek Dougan had handed in a transfer request. Don't ask me how Burnley let a three goal lead slip in the cup game at Turf Moor against Blackburn. Blackburn scored three in the last 20 minutes and went on to win the replay. Wolves also became the first Division One club to score 100 goals in a season for the third consecutive season. At Hampden Park, Real Madrid beat Eintracht Frankfurt 7-3 in probably the most memorable European Cup final of all time. Never before had football of this mesmerising, breathtaking quality been seen in the UK. The game was televised and on flickering, grainy black and white screens throughout the land viewers watched with open mouths at the football played by the likes of Gento, Di Stefano and Puskas. I watched it some time later on film in the Burnley boardroom. Harry Potts and his staff showed all the first team and the reserves the copy they had. Sometimes they'd stop it and talk about something interesting or some brilliant bit of passing. I was in there as a privilege. I had been put in charge of cleaning the first team dressing room and must have been doing a good job. So there I was, at the club for only a short while, sitting in with the likes of McIlroy and Jimmy Adamson, Ray Pointer and John Connelly watching the film while my mates Ralph Coates, Brian O'Neil and Willie Morgan were outside sweeping the terraces.

Burnley's championship win was well deserved and everybody enjoyed the football they played. Not until the last game of the season at Manchester City did they clinch the title. It was the first time all season they reached the top spot. Stan Cullis, the Wolves manager, sat in the stands watching and squirming. Had Burnley lost, Wolves would have been champions. I actually set foot in Burnley for the first time on July 1st, 1959, just in time for the '59/60 season. It would be nice to say my arrival immediately coincided with them winning the championship. But not so. They clinched it on May 2nd, 1960, without me. My contribution was mopping dressing rooms and cleaning up their mess.

When Jimmy McIlroy had arrived from Northern Ireland and the clean, fresh, green hills of Antrim with the sea and shore never far away, he was shocked by what he saw. He had seen Belfast, but nothing quite like this. Driving from Heysham and the ferry terminal with manager Frank Hill, the approach to Burnley made him yearn for just one thing – a return ticket. He found himself surrounded by the shawls and clogs of Lancashire, which he thought existed only in the writings of Priestley and Cronin. The abiding colour was grey. He stood outside the old Empress Hotel in the market place and surveyed a street filled with a depressing assortment of rotten apples, straw, waste paper and the garbage left by stallholders. But while McIlroy arrived by car and was spared the worst of the early impressions, I had arrived by train at a station that even the Town Council described as a crumbling Victorian monstrosity. When you left the station, two busy hotels, The Reindeer and The Adelphi, confronted you. Now they are just boarded-up, crumbling shells. Faded Massey's and Webster's Ale signs still hang stubbornly to the walls. If two buildings sum up the plight and decline that Burnley has had to battle against, it is perhaps these. From the station today you still see gaunt, crumbling mills. I had the same reaction as McIlroy, Blanchflower and Greaves. The difference was, I was just 16 and felt utterly and totally lost and bewildered by it all.

The word depressed barely did the place justice. I learned another 20 textile firms were winding up their affairs under a Government compensation scheme. As I arrived at least 700 weavers had added their names to the long list of the unemployed with hundreds more expected to follow. Only one firm, the Barden Mill Company, was somehow managing to expand but that was because it was able to specialise. Some new industry had been introduced but in one case, that of Wilson's of Colne, which produced electric heaters, fire had gutted and destroyed the place.

Long gone were the days that Don Haworth described in his books about a childhood in Burnley when the place came to life on a Monday morning, when doors banged, clogs clattered, tramcars ran, the oiled pistons and flywheels of the great mill engines moved again, buzzers sounded, railway sidings panted and clanked, the wheels of pithead winding gear turned and a hundred mill chimneys smoked.

Nobody foresaw, or they didn't want to see, the decline and gloom that would come, the irony being that old Lancashire mill machinery was sold to factories in India, which then undercut the Burnley looms. The depression was almost self-inflicted, bringing hopelessness for many and suicide for others. Burnley in the 1930s was already like a sinking fleet, wrote Don Haworth. By 1959, when I arrived as a starry-eyed youngster, it was more or less sunk. The football club and the championship win was the one ray of light and success for this struggling town.

Looking back it's quite clear to me now that if I had an early childhood marked by lack of money, few clothes, shoes with holes in, and frequent hunger, then there were an awful lot of people in Burnley who must have endured poverty, shortages, conditions and a life far worse than anything I ever experienced. There must have been hundreds of them. At least I had the sea, and green fields, and open spaces to enjoy. I could earn pennies and collect wood and by hook or by crook find something to eat.

So, Mr Blanchflower and Mr Greaves, let me ask you a question. If you thought Burnley so dreadful, tell me why footballer after footballer, including me, who came to this town, chose to stay? Or, if they left because they were sold, came back later to settle in the town or in the outlying areas? There are a score or maybe double that and they returned like homing pigeons. Maybe it is because, as Jimmy Mac says, in truth, beneath the grey exterior of this industrial town lies a heart of gold.

Meanwhile, in the town in which I was about to settle, the local newspaper cost 2d., ten Park Drive cigarettes set you back 1s.6d. Cotton workers who did have a job wanted an extra £1 a week for men and 14 shillings for women; these were the days of unequal opportunities and wages. At Burnley Co-op Grade A eggs were 3s.6d. a dozen and a tin of pineapples was 1s.3d. Improvements in the town were in the early stages with new shops in the town centre in St James Street and 140 workers working flat out to finish the new and then prestigious Keirby Hotel. The football team beat West Ham 5-2 at Upton Park and goalkeeper Colin McDonald returned after a broken leg to the A team at Gawthorpe. You could buy a new Austin A55 for £801 and a cruise to Madeira would set you back £75. The Mullards and Lucas factories were in full swing providing some employment (years later they would shut down as well), 15 shillings of Savings Certificates became £1 in seven years. There were cries for more teachers in schools. In some places there were still nearly 50 kids in a class. You could go to the pictures at the Odeon, the Empire (there it was *Wuthering Heights* with Lawrence Olivier and Merle Oberon, "stormy as the windswept moors", said the blurb), the Palace, the New Roxy, Tivoli (*Tarzan's Greatest Adventure* one week and Brigitte Bardot the next), the Imperial, Empress, Majestic, and the Grand in Padiham (*Gunfight At Dodge City*) or the Queens in Nelson. There was dancing at the Astoria in Rawtenstall. The Imperial Ballroom in Nelson was where you could dance to Johnny Dankworth and Lita Rosa. You could go skating at the Star Stadium in Brierfield (with lessons from Joy Sugden).

1960 was the beginning of an amazing decade in the world outside. Maybe it was the decade when the modern world was born. The Soviet Union put two dogs into space in Sputnik 5 and there was the first weather satellite. It was the era of the Beatles, Kennedy and miniskirts and not for nothing did it assume the mantle "swinging sixties". Having fun was the name of the game and even though the world was on the brink of war when the USA and the Soviet Union clashed over Cuba, violence flared in Northern Ireland and the USA announced it would send troops to Vietnam, it was pop music and fashion that was all that mattered if you were not yet 20. Then, when *Lady Chatterley's Lover*, a book previously thought obscene and banned was published, our language changed forever and the four letter word "fuck" went public. For most footballers now it is their favourite word. National Service was ended in 1960 – thank goodness, said thousands of young lads. It wouldn't have bothered me joining up; the army was our second home.

The big films were *Spartacus, Ben Hur, Psycho* and Elvis in *GI Blues*. On records or at the dancehall we listened to Roy Orbison, The Drifters, the Everley Brothers, Ray Charles, Sam Cooke and Connie Francis. We had our own Cliff Richard and Tommy Steele. If you had a TV you watched *What's My Line, Dixon of Dock Green, Hancock's Half Hour, The Army Game, Bonanza* and *Gunsmoke*.

It took a while for all the new fashion and glamour to arrive in a still gloomy Burnley but arrive it did when Willie Morgan, who joined Burnley at the same time as me, opened his trendy boutique on Keirby Walk and sported his own Beatles hairstyle. My hair was still in Elvis mode with a quiff that made me at least a foot taller. I had to duck walking under low bridges. The other Willie, it can be said, was Burnley's first real pin-up and glamour boy. I still see him occasionally and, other than his hair being almost pure white, he hasn't changed a bit. There used to be a mirror we could look in before we got out onto the pitch for a game at Turf Moor. Willie always used to check that his hair was just right. The boutique didn't last long though. Drab Burnley wasn't quite ready for the glitz of Carnaby Street; it takes a long time for things to reach the North. When Ralph Coates joined Tottenham in the early '70s the story goes the Spurs players nearly died when they saw his clothes, the like of which hadn't been seen in London for a decade. Willie's boutique, by the way, was next door to a butcher's shop. Willie had a Sergeant Pepper's outfit in his window. The butcher next door had strings of sausages in his, which did tend to take off a bit of the gloss.

Burnley in 1960 was the place that inspired Danny Blanchflower to ask Jimmy McIlroy, "How on earth do you manage to live in a place like this?" This small industrial town, set in a huge saucer-shaped vale, was filled with cobbled streets, endless terraced rows of mill workers' houses and a Dickensian town centre. Another Tottenham player, Jimmy Greaves, surveying the scene from the team coach at the top of Manchester Road, a scene of mist and fog with the tips of mill chimneys emerging through it, simply asked, "Where are we – Brigadoon?"

But the Mecca was the hub of dance and social life and if there is another reason why so many Burnley players stayed on to live in the town, maybe it is because so many of them met their wives there. Monday was the night for all the latest rock records with admission at 1s.6d. Wednesday was over 21's night for 2s.6d. Thursday was record night again but only one shilling. Not many people went out on a Thursday; you saved your money for the weekend. Friday was private night for hiring and charity dances. And Saturday, the big night, was carnival night with balloons and hats. Five shillings – that set you back and with a football apprentice on £7 a week it was a big chunk of your money.

And on top of all that, Padiham in 1960 got a new fire engine. It was big news.

Billy, Cedric and I stayed in the Cross Keys Hotel on St James' Street. Billy and Cedric went out dancing every chance they got. Me, I preferred waiting and washing up behind the bar. We were there for a month and nobody at this time, and certainly not me, had ever thought of me playing at centre forward. But in the first game I scored twice anyway from my midfield position. It was the first time ever I came across Brian O'Neil. That lad was special and went on to become a legend at both Burnley and Southampton. Up to that game my name had always been Bill. It was Brian who called me Willie for the first time and it has stuck ever since. He was an incredible lad. He had a heart of gold and made many friends, or in some cases hangers-on because he was such a soft touch. It's funny how some of the hardest people on the field are so soft off it. Andy Lochhead, Gordon Harris and me protected Brian as best we could but when we weren't there these so-called friends of his would fleece him whether it was in the pub or the Mecca or scrounging tickets. He was happiest up on his smallholding at the back of Towneley Hall somewhere where he kept a bunch of pigs. What a mudbath it was up there and maybe that was why he was so at home in the mud on a January football pitch. But the smell; oh God, he'd come back into our digs some nights and the smell was awful and even in the fresh air at Gawthorpe it seemed to follow him round. What a player though... small, slight but just ferocious and how he was never capped by England is one of football's mysteries.

It was in the second game that we first came across a young, gawky looking lad who had us falling about in disbelief and laughter when we saw him standing on the halfway line waiting to come on. He looked like he wouldn't say boo to a goose. His hair was piled up and slicked back, early Cliff Richard style. His shorts were hitched up to his waist so they looked like a badly fitting old-fashioned nappy. His legs were as white as a sheet and looked like they hadn't seen sunlight since the day he was born.

"What the hell is that?" was all we could say. And then he came on and played like an angel. His name – Willie Morgan, and a better winger in my opinion never existed. We stood open-mouthed at some of his tricks as he put on a super-show and didn't give us a touch of the ball for 20 minutes. We knew we'd seen something special. Burnley, Manchester United and Scotland were all blessed by his genius. Years later in a tournament in Brazil he would be voted the best right-winger in the world. But according to him it was only an accident that caused him to sign for Burnley. Every club in the land wanted him but at Burnley he injured his foot. Then, because Burnley and Harry Potts were so good to him during the time his foot was in plaster, he abandoned his plan to sign for Celtic and stayed at Turf Moor.

Willie was, and still is, quite a character. One story captures this. A group of us used to play golf every Wednesday morning at Clitheroe, then we'd have lunch. Golf was Willie's passion and still is. After lunch we'd drive back. There was one time that I was in my car with someone else, I forget who, and Willie had Brian O'Neil and Sammy Todd with him. Now Willie was an arrogant so-and-so, and maybe that was what made him the great player he was, and this day he wanted to race back to town. I was in front and wouldn't let him pass and I knew how mad that would make him. When we got to Read, he pulled out but I put my foot down and for a minute we were driving alongside at about 60 along these little lanes with the trees and bushes whistling past in a blur. But then I saw a wagon in front of us coming towards us so it was me that chickened out, and, slamming on the brakes, I let him pass with seconds to spare. The wagon almost touched both our cars and mine was swaying from side to side. It seemed as if it was going to go into a skid and I and my passenger inside were as white as sheets. From there to when we parked the car at Turf Moor I don't think we said a word and we got out with our legs shaking. Truly that was nearly the end of five of Burnley's finest.

As for me, it was touch and go whether I completed the month's trial after I twisted my ankle while larking about in a five-a-side game. It healed in time for one final game. What the club had to do so they could have one more look at me was in fact to put me in the B team, which was playing against Blackburn Rovers. So, for a start I was taking part in a needle game and on top of that I was up against big strapping 18-year-olds a couple of years older and bigger than me. But I was OK. We won. I scored.

The following Sunday morning the trialists lined up outside manager Harry Potts' office, 20 or so lads who hadn't slept the night before wondering if they'd impressed enough to be kept on. I had played only three games but I had an advantage. I'd asked Ray Bennion, who used to be head trainer but was now an odd job man at the club and someone who I was close to, if he would find out if I was going to be signed on. Officially I wasn't supposed to know until Harry Potts said so. Ray gave me the news that I would be signed but told me to keep damned quiet about it. Even so I was still sweating when I was called in case Harry Potts had changed his mind. Willie Morgan went in and came out smiling. Brian O'Neil went in and came out smiling. And then it was me. Even though Ray had tipped me off, when Harry Potts offered me an apprenticeship I could have jumped up and hit the ceiling. My smile filled the room. I couldn't believe I had done enough to impress them but they must have seen something. For now it was back to Ireland for five days and then return to Burnley in time to play against Bolton on the next Saturday.

CHAPTER FOUR

HOME FROM HOME

The life of a football apprentice in 1960 revolved around training, playing in the A and B teams, a very small wage, praying to be kept on and the digs we shared with other young hopefuls. None of us in those days ever understood the word pampered. None of us lived a life of luxury where we were cossetted and spoiled in luxurious football academies. Our digs were basic; in some instances the word sparse would not go amiss. We shared rooms that were barely furnished and if we were really unlucky ate meals that sometimes would barely feed a sparrow. Ralph Coates was in digs with other apprentices and they were so hungry they were desperate. One day the smell of a roast chicken came wafting up the stairs, but they knew full well the chicken was not for them. "Bugger this," they thought, and when the landlady was out of the way and the kitchen empty, they tiptoed down, removed the chicken and took it back up to the attic. They nearly ate the bones as well. When the landlady demanded to know where the chicken was, all they could say was, "What chicken?" To this day she's probably wondering which of those lads pinched her Sunday dinner. I still shudder when I remember one digs I had with the outdoor loo; I thought I'd seen the last of them. But in Burnley at that time, if you had an inside loo you were either the bank manager, the doctor or Bob Lord.

There was another place where all we ever ate was things on toast: beans on toast; eggs on toast; jam on toast; tomato on toast; cheese on toast and then sometimes for a change – just toast. No breakfast – we got that from a greasy spoon café near the training ground. Today the team eat a diet-conscious breakfast and lunch specially made for them at the ground. There was one digs where the landlady used to leave notes under the dinner plate for me to join her in bed. There was another digs where the landlady was a fortune-teller, another where the landlord was an undertaker. We had a thousand laughs – and froze in winter in our attic bedrooms.

Homesickness hit me badly in the first few months and I tried to get home as often as possible. But on wages of just £7 a week it wasn't easy. Out of that I sent £2 home with a weekly letter; my digs money was £3 and 10 shillings, which left £1 and 10 shillings for me. When I ripped the sole off my one and only pair of shoes and I had to buy a new pair it took all bar a shilling of my spare cash. That was a tough week. I walked miles from my digs to the ground every day and back again.

During the trial month I had stayed at The Cross Keys, more or less in the town centre. Now I moved into something more permanent. I lived with Big Jim and Dolly Haworth on Brougham Street. Dolly was a local fortune-teller and her front room was where she had all her paraphernalia and where she took all her clients. We five apprentices were forbidden to enter that room. We'd see people going in and out of there usually looking quite embarrassed. As they came out the comments ranged from, "Well that were money for nowt ah must say," to a tearful, "Ah never thought ah'd see 'im again, ah'm just so glad 'e's 'appy, d'yer think 'e'll talk to me again?" We were tempted sometimes to tap on the wall while she was doing all this, or thump on the floor above. It was so tempting to stand outside the door and gently groan while she had a customer, or client as she always called them. She only took me in the once and read my tea leaves and I was tempted to ask, wasn't she supposed to wear a turban? She told me that I would travel a lot and meet people. Well, let's be honest, you could say that to anyone and it would be perfectly true. I came out thinking maybe I'd be a bus driver.

It was like a gypsy caravan in there, all drapes and candles and coloured lights. If you could only see some of the digs I've stayed in. Another one was with Flo and Jim. They were the ones where we only got something to eat at teatime. I don't think they'd ever heard of the words breakfast or lunch. Jim's favourite trick was to sit by the fire and smoke his pipe. Every five minutes he'd spit in the fire. When it was on target it was OK and there was this lovely sizzling sound. Trouble is, most times he'd miss and hit the mantelpiece. If he was doing this at teatime and we were all eating, it was a treat I can tell you.

The four other lads at Dolly's were: Arthur Bellamy, who went on to play more than 200 times and is now Burnley head groundsman; Freddie Smith, who also played a fair number of games; Alan Haspell and Colin Williamson, although the latter two never made it. The five of us were in one room, so privacy was an unknown word. They had girlfriends and I didn't, which didn't help my homesickness. The early days were a lonely time, which sounds a daft thing to say when you're rooming with four other lads, but there were times when I was really miserable. I was just 16, sending most of my spare money home, and more often than not, struggling with what was left for myself. Then there was the time I was accosted by a drunken sailor. Before you start thinking, don't be daft, Burnley is nowhere near the sea, let me explain. I was walking back to my digs one night minding my own business and I realised a bloke had sidled up alongside me. Before long he's telling me he's home from the navy and it's clear he'd had a few drinks inside him. The street was empty and before I knew it he'd dragged me into a shop doorway and had his tongue halfway down my mouth. Bloody hell, I thought. I kneed him in the groin so he was doubled up in agony and then ran off and didn't stop till I'd reached the front door. "What d'yer do that for?" was the last thing I heard him shouting after me. So this is Burnley, I thought. Carrickfergus seemed a million miles away.

This was the house that had no inside toilet so the routine we'd use was a pop bottle in the bedroom if we needed to and then empty it the following morning. This worked fine if you remembered to empty it. Well, there was one particular Saturday night. We'd been out and had quite a few drinks; and as usual we used the pop bottle when we needed to go. Naturally Jim and Dolly had no idea we were doing this. The following Sunday morning I forgot to empty mine. I'd gone up to Towneley for some reason or other when Arthur came up to tell me that Big Jim was going spare because he had found the pop bottle where I had left it and when he realised what it was he was going absolutely mad and that when he caught me he was going to give me a good braying. Now Big Jim, who, by the way, probably wasn't even 5ft tall, which is why we called him "Big Jim", was not a man to upset so I went straight back and met him and apologised to him and Dolly and explained that I just couldn't wait and the bottle just happened to be there and it would never happen again. Then I began to realise that neither of them had a clue what I was going on about and they were looking more and more puzzled. Behind them stood Arthur grinning and desperately trying not to laugh out loud. Suddenly I twigged as Arthur legged it out of the room before he split his sides.

Dolly, bless her, did once promise me a special tea. Knowing how I loved my Irish stews she cooked one for me as a special treat. So I came back after the game that afternoon and proud as punch she took out this plate of potatoes and meat draped with wet leeks and sad-looking carrots. I'd never seen such a sorry, soggy mess.

"Here, Willie, I've made you this lovely Irish broth," she announced.

"But what the hell is that?" I asked.

She looked really hurt.

I looked at it horrified and then just burst out laughing whereupon Big Jim came over to the table, grabbed the plate and hurled it into the bin.

"Bloody laugh, will you?" he thundered. "You get nowt else 'ere." Embryonic young footballers weren't treated with kid gloves in those days.

Poor Colin Williamson. His promising career was cut short when it was discovered he had brittle bones. A lot of players I knew finished with brittle bones; Colin started with them. Anyway, we got on really well and Colin found us some new digs on Bracewell Street. We decided that five of us all sharing the same room was just too crowded and if our landlord was going to hurl our food in the bin we needed to move on. £17 and 10 shillings a week they were collecting from us as well, a tidy sum in those days. Charles Dickens could have written about the room in which we lived.

After just six months the Bracewell Street digs didn't work out either.

I remember sharing with Brian O'Neil, Arthur Bellamy and Bill Poynton at the Hartleys' and I still laugh at the stunt Brian pulled on Bill when he pinched his new suit. Bill was a great lad but always fancied himself so he went into town and got a new suit, brought it back, and went to the bathroom to tart himself up, leaving the new suit on the back of a chair. When he came out, after about an hour because he had to spend at least 55 minutes combing his hair and being meticulous, the new suit has gone and we heard the most almighty scream and ripe language. In broad Geordie he was yelling, "Who's got my fucking suit then, where's my fucking suit?" He twigged straight away. "That bugger Brian, he's got it." In his old gear he dressed as quick as he could and legged it down to the Mecca where he knew Brian would be. Yes, there he was, wearing Bill's new gear. So in the middle of the Mecca dance floor Bill made him strip off and they changed clothes.

We always had a big breakfast on a Sunday at the Hartleys' as well. Their daughter Pat cooked it for us because she felt sorry for us. The rest of the week we were half starved.

Next it was on to Mr and Mrs Whitaker. John was an undertaker for the Co-op and they were both very strong Catholics and just at this time a new Pope was being elected. It didn't go down too well when in my youthful humorous immaturity I suggested they should choose King Billy. I didn't last there long either. John now has his own undertakers business in Burnley. He used to take me out with him on jobs when I was free. I remember the first time he took me out in the middle of the night to dress a body. "Come on Willie, it's dead easy, ho, ho," he chortled. I was so frightened I never got out of the van and just sat there in the dark terrified, praying to God he didn't need any help with this one and wanting to go back to bed.

Next it was on to Woodgrove Road and Mr and Mrs Thompson. They were a lovely couple but unfortunately Mr Thompson became a victim of a polio outbreak in Burnley. He never properly recovered and was confined to a wheelchair for the rest of his life. They had a young family and with Mrs

Thompson, who was Dutch, having a lot to cope with, her sister Minge came over to help. Minge was probably nearly 30 but she and I got on extremely well, if you know what I mean. Well, she was very attractive and I was a healthy, good-looking young lad with all the right bits and pieces so what was I to do? The upshot was it was nice while it lasted but her sister told me one day to find new digs as soon as possible.

It wasn't a problem. I had already become good friends with the Whalleys. Tom and his wife Nan invited me to stay with them. Also there was Les Latcham, another apprentice who went on to have a great career at Burnley, and is another who still lives in the area. The Whalleys had no children and my time with them was absolutely wonderful. It is true to say they became my second parents. Les and I were their substitute family. I loved them dearly and still do. When I was in the dumps they cheered me up and when I was in the limelight they kept my feet on the ground. Maybe it's true that Tom was the father I never had. Tom certainly kept me on the straight and narrow for the six years I was there, or at least he tried to. He had a strict curfew. We had to be in by 11.00pm from Monday to Thursday and 10.30pm on a Friday. Saturday and Sunday night was "free" time. I found a way round the curfew times though when I managed to buy a car. I'd get in late and say, "Sorry, Tom, but I had a puncture and it was a devil of a job to fix it." By the time I reported the 11th puncture he'd cottoned on to my little ruse.

Tom and Nan would buy us presents and take us out on Sundays for a meal. Funny, they'd take us out for a good meal and then Tom would moan about how much it cost for weeks afterwards. He was a sort of old-fashioned bloke who saw himself as the head of the household, so much so that he always had to have the first cup of tea out of the pot. Woe betide anyone else who poured their own cup first. At every chance I would pour mine first just for the fun of it, and it was always Nan who stuck up for me when he went mad about it. I was seventeen-and-a-half when I went there and for those years was thoroughly happy and content. I couldn't have had a better home. I wrote a letter home every week.

All this time I'd been playing and training in my usual

position of inside forward or halfback and went through a spell where I couldn't do a thing right because I was so despondent and dejected, missing home as much as I did. And then something happened that changed my life. I'd been there with the Whalleys a few months and somebody, somewhere decided that Willie Irvine might make a good centre forward – either that or they were a man short up front. Up till then I'd been playing in my normal place and scoring the odd few goals. What they were pleased with was my heading and speed. Maybe that's why they put me up front. Anyway, I was in the C team and scored a hat-trick against Liverpool. I felt terrific and the coaches and the C team manager were well pleased. What was funny about it was that Johnny Gibson had his dad there watching and when we came off after the game he didn't half give Johnny a bollocking for not playing better and said he should go out and play like that young Irish lad. He wouldn't believe me when I said it was the first time I had ever played centre forward.

Now I was on the groundstaff I was in charge of the changing rooms. It meant I got to stay in the warm while the other lads were out sweeping the terraces on a Monday morning in the cold and the rain. I can tell you I pulled their legs about it mercilessly but they got their own back one day. Around three sides of the ground where spectators stood there were metal barriers sunk into the concrete to stop too many people crushing forward. Every so often these had to be painted green. So we were all out there painting the barriers green when Ralph Coates, Willie Morgan, Mick Buxton and Brian O'Neil and some of the others decided to get their own back on me for laughing at them when they got drenched having to sweep the terraces in the rain. I hadn't time to get away before they grabbed me and painted my manly bits green. We all ended up laughing but it took me a fair while to get the paint off my legs.

Billy Dougal was one of the characters around the place. He was a dour little Scot but really likeable and looked after the injuries. You knew it was a bad injury if he said "fuck me pink." He had one standard cure for an ankle injury. It went into a wax bath but he always had it too hot as he never had any idea what the temperature was supposed to be; you usually got third degree burns as a result. Billy Morris was another character who helped me a lot until he left. Billy taught me a lot about running and finding spaces and taking passes but said he could never teach me what to do in the box because that's just a gift and instinctive. You can't teach that, he used to say. Joe Brown took over from him and he was a great bloke.

I'll tell you one job I'm glad I didn't have to do on a regular basis and that was clean out the chemical latrines at the back of the Longside. The job was to shovel out this ghastly mixture of excrement and piss and then throw it all on a pile of ashes. Unfortunately one day there was no escape for me from this appalling job and, on the day I did it, it was windy and when I lobbed the shovel load of shit onto the ashes half of it blew back in my face. I pretended to be violently ill and got sent back to the dressing room where Ray Bennion was waiting. "Don't go out there doing that again if it's going to have this effect on you," he said, to my great relief.

Ray Bennion was the bloke I worked under. Friday used to be the day we'd get out all the match balls and test them. If they weren't just right we'd have to deflate them and then inflate them again. Try doing that 20 times.

Tommy Danns was the groundsman. He could never understand a word I said when I used to help him with the pitches. He always said it helped if I sang the words to him instead of speaking them. Instead of asking, "What do you want me to do today," I'd sing the words. Tommy used to say it slowed me down and so he could hear me more clearly. And I believed him. No wonder the senior players, when they heard me singing to Tommy in the middle of the car park, looked at me as if I was simple. Tommy was a real Lancastrian and a real Andy Capp. It was Tommy I used to help in the summer getting all the pitches ready for the next season. One of my jobs was rolling with the motor roller. Nice easy job that but not the mowing with a push-mower. I worked it out one day that I walked 12 miles pushing this bloody mower. Then when Tommy did it out came a motor mower with a seat. "You old bugger," I muttered under

(top left) Joan, Willie's sister. (top right) Rita, Willie's wife, aged 10. (bottom) Willie is the goalkeeper, middle top row. Teacher on the left is headmaster Harry Morgan; teacher on the right is Mr Joiner who told Willie he was related to Stanley Matthews.

(top left) Joint sportsman of the year at Carrickfergus Technical School. Willie is on the right. (top right) Willie ready for the parade. (bottom) With Nan Whalley (Howard Talbot).

Burnley (1964/65) (left to right) (back row) Mick Buxton, John Murray, Sammy Todd, Stan Ternent, Chris Nicholl, Johnny Auchie, Les Latcham, Colin Blant, Len Kinsella. (second row) Willie Irvine, Adam Blacklaw, Andy Lochhead, Gordon Harris, Harry Thomson, Brian O'Neil, John Angus, Dave Merrington. (third row) Ray Ternent, Ian Towers, Willie Morgan, John Talbut, Alex Elder, Ralph Coates, Arthur Bellamy, Freddie Smith, Ray Pointer. (front row) members of the youth squad.

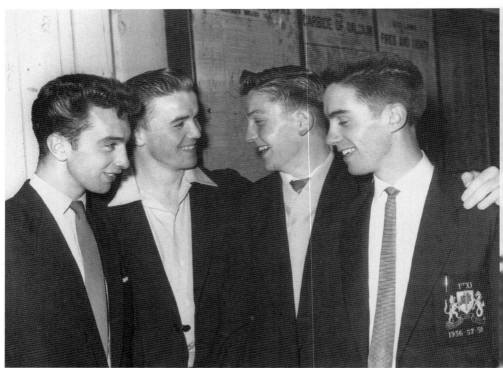

(top) Starting on the great adventure. Willie (second right) with fellow trialists just about to leave for Burnley. (bottom) Willie is on the far right with fellow apprentices (from left) Denis Crompton, Mick Buxton, and Albert Bird (Howard Talbot).

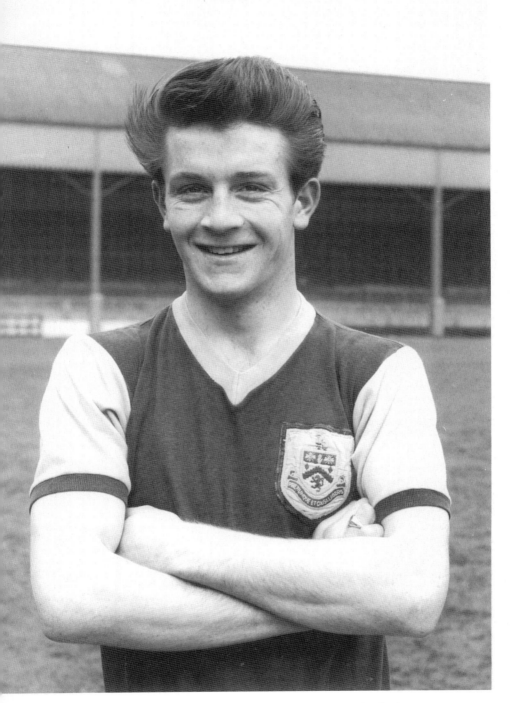

Elvis had a lot to answer for in the early 1960s (Howard Talbot).

At Burnley they even read about football. Ian Towers holds Brian Glanville's The Rise of Gerry Logan while Andy Lochhead (left) and Willie look on.

op) Bobby Irvine (left) and Willie pose with their mother Agnes when playing for Northern Ireland. (bottom) Harry Potts leads a public training run with Willie following closely. (Howard Talbot).

They didn't all go in. Willie follows in twice against Nottingham Forest at Turf Moor, a game in which he scored a hat-trick.

my breath when I saw him riding regally up and down the pitches.

When Tommy Danns died I was deeply upset, remembering the good times and fun we had keeping pitches in good order and preparing them for new seasons. He had me marching up and down those pitches with the mowers more times than I care to remember but he was a joy to work with. Was there anything more pleasant than walking the length of a pitch in warm sunshine under a clear blue sky at Gawthorpe, lost in your own thoughts and dreams? They were happy days and Tommy Danns was one of the people who made them so.

Just once I got a bollocking from the senior players. I was cleaning out dressing rooms at the end of the day and in the room were Colin McDonald, Trevor Meredith and Brian Pilkington, all recovering from injuries. I asked them would they hurry up so I could finish. Colin McDonald gave me a real telling off. You big-headed unpleasant so-and-so, I thought. Anyway they left and the next thing I know the lights go out and I'm locked in the ground. Somehow I got out by climbing through a window in the stand and then over the Cricket Field wall.

At this stage I was still in digs with Tom and Nan Whalley. Tom was an insurance company manager, and he enjoyed one thing above others and that was gambling on the horses. He sat up till midnight studying his paper and selecting horses night after night. Nan always told me off for wetting my hair with water in the morning so I could comb it. "You'll catch your death," she'd say. "It's OK," I'd tell her, "I'm using the hot."

Tom and Nan once took us out to Blackpool. Tom must have been in a good mood; he looked at me while we were having something to eat and he said, "I love you, Willie Irvine, and you are just the son I would have liked to have had." I had a big lump in my throat, I can tell you. They're special people. He was so proud when I had a game in the A team and scored six goals. Anyway in Blackpool they treated us to a slap-up tea. It came to £4.50. Tom paid and, laughing, said, "Your board's going up now." That's the kind of thing they used to do.

Tom and Nan did once throw me out, I have to say, and I

am ashamed about it now. I'd got in late once too often and told the usual story about having a puncture and Tom told me to pack my bags. Nan was really upset when I went to stay with somebody else. This time it was a widow who was very lonely and, well, let's just say the two weeks there were not without their compensations. But Tom came looking for me and told me he and Nan wanted me back. Perhaps he thought this voracious landlady was leading me astray.

There was never a shortage of girls either. There was a girl called Marjorie I saw on and off for a couple of years, three years older than me and taught me all I needed to know about you know what. There was a nice girl called Rita as well I'd been seeing but for the minute we didn't want to get serious. I was still seeing Olive back in Carrick when I got home. Mother really liked her and wanted me to get serious with her and thought I should give up all Burnley girls. She made it clear she did not want me to even contemplate marrying a Burnley girl.

We got to the Mecca quite a bit. Sometimes there was a bit of bother with the local Teddy Boys because they didn't like us young footballers when they saw us getting all the girls. There were three in particular, Cec, Dean and George who had a gang and always wanted to put us down. What Cec didn't know is that I was seeing his girl as well behind his back. It wouldn't have been the first set-to between the footballers and the Teds if they had found out.

Happy days they were. At that age you think they'll never end.

The first team players who formed the championship team of 1959/60 are now legends in Burnley. I looked at them all those years ago and felt a determination to follow them and to work my way up. There was fellow Irishman Alex Elder, a stunning left back of power and pace. He played 330 times for the club, moved to Stoke and then came back to Burnley to settle and run a catering equipment business. Jimmy Robson, who scored the Burnley goal at Wembley in 1962, joined at the age of 17 and played 242 games. He once scored five goals in a game against Nottingham Forest. Eventually he became a youth coach at Burnley and, now retired, still lives in the town. Centre half Tommy Cummings still does match day hosting work alongside me now at the club. He joined in 1947, scored Burnley's greatest ever goal, which is still talked about, played 479 times, went on to be a manager and then came back to the town. Adam Blacklaw was as good a Scottish goalkeeper as you will ever see and won three caps. He played 383 games before moving to Blackburn and then came back to live in the town where he still works. Brian Miller is known as Mr Burnley. A local lad, he joined in 1952 and served the club as player, coach, manager and scout. He played 455 games and won one England cap. He still lives in Burnley – where else could he live? Right back John Angus made an incredible 520 appearances. He was so quiet but so hard, giving great protection to the younger players when they appeared. When Steve Kindon made his debut at West Ham and faced the legendary hard man Billy Bonds, John did a canny thing. He went up to Harry Redknapp, then playing on the wing, and said, "Harry, this is my boy. If Billy Bonds harms him, I will do twice the damage to you. Now then, go and have a word with Billy." John Connelly was a right-winger who scored 20 goals in the title season. How many number sevens do that these days? He had the speed of a gazelle and the shot of a cannon. Some of his goals were stunning. He eventually moved to Manchester United but came back to Burnley to run a fish and chip shop. Bob Lord once said the average footballer would be unable to run even a fish and chip shop. John must have been above average. Twenty caps for England tells you how good he was. Jimmy Adamson from the north-east, tall and elegant, the best player never to be capped by England though he was assistant England manager in 1962. He was 1962 Footballer of the Year, played 486 games for Burnley and as manager of the "Team Of The Seventies" was so close to founding a new era for Burnley. Of course he still lives in Burnley. Centre forward Ray Pointer, known as the Blonde Bombshell. He still has all his hair and it's still blonde and he's still thin and fast as a whippet. It isn't fair. Twenty-three goals in that great season and scored in both his England games. Brian Pilkington at outside left. Small, tricky, scored some great goals, one cap for England, sold to Bolton and he always says the £30,000 transfer fee paid for Burnley's floodlights. And then there was the wonderful Jimmy McIlroy.

He played 497 games for Burnley and 51 games for Northern Ireland until he went to Stoke in controversial circumstances when sold by Bob Lord in February 1963 for unexplained reasons. He returned to Burnley where today, in retirement, he plays golf and paints and doesn't look a day over 60.

These were the marvellous players I looked at and watched on the training fields at Gawthorpe. They played football that was pure poetry, and were unlucky not to do the double in 1962. I had a lot to live up to.

I never kept very many cuttings or bits and pieces about myself. What I have now is old and battered and just about falling apart. My sons look after it and a lot of what I kept has vanished over the years. I had tears in my eyes I can tell you when at my 60th birthday get-together I was presented with a bundle of old programmes of some of the games I had played in. I sent a few things home with the letter I wrote every week and my mother kept cuttings that appeared in the Carrickfergus and Belfast newspapers. The newspapers over there followed the progress of any young Irish lad who went across the water to England or Scotland. One of them asks angrily why so many good young Irish players are signed up by English clubs to while away their time in reserve teams instead of being snapped up by good Irish clubs and given their chance.

The scraps of paper are faded, creased and torn; some of them are over 40 years old. I'm flicking through the pages now of this old and battered scrapbook and I can see me then as I was; youthful, optimistic, wide-eyed, learning all the time. Most of these tiny bits of newspaper are about the early days in the A and B teams with an occasional one about a reserve game. There's one about a game for Barn United. I could only have been 15 years old.

For the visit of the League leaders conditions were ideal and a fair-sized crowd were treated to some really good football. First to threaten danger, the youthful home attack had the visitors in trouble and Walsh from a Donely pass netted with a brilliant shot. Kennedy of Star of the Sea then equalized. Barn were not disheartened by this reverse and with Donely and IRVINE in sparkling form they soon regained the lead when IRVINE crashed home a terrific twenty-yard drive. Hitting back immediately the visitors equalized when O'MCauley netted with the home defence appealing for offside against two of their attack and from the touchline it appeared to be a fair claim. After the interval Star of the Sea took the lead. IRVINE then levelled matters but Star of the Sea however found the net twice more, the final result being 5 – 3 in favour of the visitors.

Today I smile at the pictures; me in my schoolboy international cap; youthful, grinning and cherubic face, life in front of me, no idea of what's in store, the glory and the pain that was to come. No thoughts of goal records, marriage, broken leg, smashed knee, money disasters, depression and an attempt at suicide. If I could choose one picture to keep forever, maybe this would be the one.

Here's me, and Cedric Gilmore and Billy Mills on the next page (William they call me and Billy in the caption). Billy Mills, the good-looking one, a dead ringer for Cliff Richard complete with little kiss curl falling over his forehead. My, don't we look smart in blazer, white shirt and tie; except the picture doesn't show my blazer was too small.

Off to Burnley for a month's trial these three Belfast boys give the thumbs up sign as they prepare to board the Heysham boat last night on the first part of a journey which could lead to soccer fame.

Fame would come for me, yes, but not for Billy and Cedric. There are some gaps in the scrapbook pages and bits of Sellotape mark where pictures and clippings should have been. Somehow it leaps on and here I am at 18. There's a picture of manager Harry Potts leading a group of players on a pre-season training run. I work out it must be early August 1963 and a gang of schoolboys in short trousers and school caps and jackets hold out autograph books and pens. It's me directly behind Harry Potts looking fit and sun-tanned.

A couple of days later we were officially welcomed by the Mayor and Bob Lord.

And next to this picture is a cutting that gives first mention of all the early goals I scored and a glowing report by Harry Potts that he wrote in a club programme when Burnley headed and dominated English football. How times have changed.

EYES ON THE CARRICK LAD AT BURNLEY

A Carrickfergus boy is attracting a lot of attention at Turf Moor, home of First Division leaders Burnley. He is 18 years old Willie Irvine, younger brother of Linfield goalkeeper Bobby Irvine. Willie, Burnley's third team centre forward, has cracked in over 30 goals in 16 Lancashire League games this season. Burnley manager Harry Potts is not given to over-praising young footballers but he singled out young Irvine who is in his second year at Turf Moor, for a special pat on the back in the last issue of the club's programme. Potts wrote that Willie deserved to be congratulated for he has just added to a remarkable record with a six-goal performance in the 8-3 victory against Blackburn Rovers A team. He said this was Willie's best performance to date and he has every chance of making a first class footballer.

"He is good in the air, packs a fine shot with both feet, and seems really dedicated in his ambition to become a league player."

Recently Willie had an outing with the Burnley reserve team against Barnsley and scored three goals.

I remember that first reserve team outing. Proud wasn't the word. Next to me was Andy Lochhead and that was a foretaste of things to come. But the Burnley staff put me straight back in the A team. Today, with talent in such short supply, they'd probably put me straight into the first team with a fat, money-laden, four-year contract. But then there were so many good players at this club you had to wait your turn playing in the reserves. They used to say that if a Burnley scout went up to the north-east and whistled down one of the pits, out would come half a dozen footballers. A scout called

Jack Hixon brought the very best of them to Burnley to feed the production line that chairman Bob Lord had set up.

The coaches were determined that I wouldn't go the same way as a young player called Ian Lawson. Ian had burst onto the scene at Burnley as a 17-year-old in 1957 and in his debut first team game scored four goals. He wasn't even a reserve team regular then but had been piling in the goals in the A and B teams just like I used to do. Three weeks later he scored another first team hat-trick. The word sensational would not go amiss. 27,000 spectators at the end of that game thought they had witnessed the coming of a new superstar in the Tommy Lawton bracket. It couldn't last and Ian Lawson joined that group of players who explode onto the scene and then fade, and long-term it just doesn't seem to happen for them. Maybe he was too young or maybe success came too early. The world seemed to be at his feet but he was eventually transferred to Leeds United and then drifted around from there to Crystal Palace, then Port Vale and then Barnsley. I wonder about him now, where he is and what he's doing. In the reserve team I played alongside him once or twice. He never quite lived up to that early glittering promise. Maybe you could say the same about me, even though I did enjoy some of the glitter in the early years, but an Everton player effectively ended any chance I had of sustained fame. I curse that player every time I think of him now. When my leg was broken I had another six years in front of me, maybe more, but they were never to be the great years that they could have been. How lucky Jimmy Greaves was never to sustain a serious injury. Mine stopped me from outscoring even Greavsie.

Even at 18 the Irish selectors were watching me before I'd played a first team game and Jimmy McIlroy was writing about me in his *News of the World* column. More reserve games came my way.

IRVINE IN CENTRAL LEAGUE SIDE

An interesting experiment is made in the Burnley reserve team attack to meet Bury reserves at Turf Moor. Regular centre forward Andy Lochhead moves to inside-right to give Willie Irvine his second run out with the Central League side. This Irish boy has been in terrific form this season with the A team hitting three hat-tricks in succession and scoring 44 goals in 21 games. In his debut with the reserve side on October 14th he got another hat-trick in Burnley's 6-1 win over Barnsley reserves at Turf Moor.

Keith McNee, the *Burnley Express* football writer, picked three of us out to go a long way – with me he chose Arthur Bellamy and goalkeeper Harry Thomson. What he didn't know about football wasn't worth knowing. He was right about all three of us.

Here's something interesting I've found. Did I really play in goal for one game during my month's trial at Turf Moor? If I did, I'd forgotten about it.

It is no rare occurrence for a footballer to find his best position by accident as records show that many famous players started off in a team position quite different from that in which they later gained international recognition. A Carrickfergus boy – Billy Irvine – who recently went to Burnley on trial may be the next player to figure in such a switch. Recognised in local football circles as an inside forward of great promise, young Irvine, who was on Linfield's books last season, accepted the invitation of Burnley's Irish scout Mr Alec Scott to go for a trial. He went to Turf Moor a couple of weeks ago and following an injury in one of the trials, he took over in goal and gave a display to quicken the interest of the club's officials who are giving him an extended trial as a goalkeeper. The result of Burnley's experiment will be awaited with interest as it would be an ironic twist if the injury led to this clever forward adopting the role of his elder brothers who are goalkeepers of ability – youth international Bobby who is a regular in Linfield's first team and George, who is in the army.

Me in goal? Now that's something I'd forgotten about and perhaps it's as well it came to nothing with the rivalry between me and Bobby being bad enough as it was.

My reserve team debut hat-trick gets another mention as I leaf through the album.

WILLIE IRVINE STARS IN DEBUT GAME

Irish eyes were smiling after this entertaining Central League game. They belonged to Burnley's Willie Irvine, the 18-year-old centre forward from Carrickfergus who cracked in three glorious goals on his debut for the Reserves. And young Willie might have had more, for he missed a penalty and had another goal disallowed. Burnley, weakened by the absence of regulars Towers, Lochhead and Meredith, took the lead through Lawson following a pass by Fenton. Not long after this Irvine scored his first goal with a great shot and at half-time Burnley were two goals ahead. Soon after the restart they went further ahead when Irvine smashed in another hard drive on the volley after good work by his fellow debutant Morgan. Bellamy got the fourth, Irvine completed his hat-trick for the fifth, and near the end Fenton made it half a dozen.

Towards the end of the album are two full-page team photographs. The first is the Central League side that was top in 1961/62. There I am on the back row, hardly a regular and the caption mentions "Irvine (who has scored close on 50 goals for the A Team)." At the end stands trainer George Bray, a man who gave all his football life to Burnley Football Club, joining them in 1937 when he was 18 and after serving as player, trainer and kit man, finally retiring in 1992. He was in the great team of '47, which reached Wembley and achieved promotion to Division One. How much I owe him. He played 259 games for Burnley and lost six years of his career during the war years. But for that he would have played 500.

On the next page is the A team photograph. Willie Morgan stands at one end of the back row and trainer Joe Brown at the other. Yet again a mention for me. "Irvine, who on Tuesday at Preston scored his 50th goal for the A team." Nobody has done this since. On the front row are Bill Poynton and Les Latcham, and a little pint-sized winger called Johnny Price who I doubt was much more than 5ft tall in his stockinged feet. But boy, could he play and there was no one braver.

How many memories can there be in such photographs? There they all are – the ones who made it and the ones who didn't. There they are, the lads I roomed with and had such good times. There they are – lads like Brian O'Neil, Harry Thomson, Andy Lochhead and Willie Morgan, terrific players who did such great things and played such great games. And there's Ronnie Fenton who went on to be number two to Brian Clough at Nottingham Forest. They say a picture is worth a thousand words. For me, when I see these pictures of over 40 years ago my head fills with a thousand thoughts.

Some of these pictures make me laugh. What am I in this one? Eighteen it says and I'm putting a record onto my Dansette player. Sure it mentions 44 goals in 24 games so far that season and I sure was a damned good-looking lad in those days with a head of hair that even Elvis would have died for.

TWISTING HIS WAY TO SOCCER SUCCESS

Irvine thinks about football first and last; he has not a lot of time for other interests. But with what time he has, he enjoys popular music, crosswords and dancing – particularly the Twist. "It helps keep me fit", he says in a strong Irish brogue. We saw him doing the Twist on Saturday afternoon as he attempted to increase his goal tally in the key Reserve clash with Wolves. He didn't manage to twist a goal home but he looked to have a rosy future for all that.

I haven't forgotten that game either. 10,789 people watched that ding-dong end-to-end game which we won 2-1 though sadly I didn't score. That's nearly as many as watch the first team today. On a wet and cold January Tuesday night people, who once flocked to Turf Moor in their thousands, now prefer to stay indoors and watch TV where there's so much football to watch in armchair comfort. Sometimes you can watch seven days a week with Carling Cup, Champions League, Premiership, Championship, Spanish League, Italian League and UEFA Cup games.

In that reserve game in 1962 we were top at the time and Wolves had some great players in their side. They scored first but we put our 95th and 96th goals of the season in the back of the net. Both the first team and ourselves were well on the way to 100 goals for the season. No wonder people came to watch us play. In 2005 Burnley had scored just ten goals in 11 games and that was enough to have them in ninth place because they had let in only seven. That's the modern game for you. No wonder people like Jimmy McIlroy have fallen out of love with football and can barely bring themselves to watch.

Meanwhile I was back into the A team again. My time hadn't come for regular reserve team football even though

I scored goals as easily as shelling peas. These were the days when Burnley would have had somewhere around 50 players on their books, from the young apprentices to the established stars.

Three teams played in the Lancashire League; the reserves played in the Central League; the big boys in Football League Division One. It was likened to a conveyor belt, almost like a factory, and that's what it was, pure and simple. You learned your trade, worked your way upwards from one team to the next – if you weren't good enough you were weeded out – and one day four or five years later you made it into the first team.

There was a natural order and progression to things and for me, even as a regular in the A team, the paltry wages kept all our feet on the ground. I look at the Rooneys of this world today and my head just can't get round the size of the money they receive. I hesitate to use the word "earn". Then, when the timing was right, the star players or the ones not quite good enough but who had tasted first team football, were sold to fund the system. Burnley were a byword for all that was good in nurturing young players. George Bray, Ray Bennion, Joe Brown, Billy Dougal and Harry Potts schooled us and cajoled us and it was like one huge family.

1961/62 and the A team, with me scoring goals by the hatful, won the Lancashire League. The reserves won the Central League with me scoring goals there as well. The first team almost did the elusive double of League and FA Cup. They were heady days. My days of fame and record breaking in Division One were not far away. Harry Potts continued to say good things to the press about me, especially after scoring yet another A Team hat-trick in the opening game of the 1962/63 season. Every other clipping in this ancient album seems to say hat-trick.

Potts says in one of them:
We haven't had a more consistent goal getter than Willie for a very long time. He certainly knows where the goal is. He's even better than Ray Pointer was at the same age. Willie is a born opportunist and has proved that he knows where the

goal is. Over the past few years no other player on our books has scored with such consistency. We have not wanted to rush him into senior soccer yet because he has plenty of time and should, without doubt, eventually reach the top.

On the next page it says:

IRISH STAR SHOOTING TO THE TOP

Where are all the outstanding young Irish footballers? Many who could be big names in the Irish League are serving their soccer apprenticeships in the limbo of second, third and fourth teams with clubs in the English League. Snapped up as kids straight from school, these lads disappear from the headlines for years before either emerging as first team stars or returning, rejected and often dejected, to their own country. Take the case of Willie Irvine. Few folk apart from Burnley fans have ever heard of Willie. But at Turf Moor this centre forward from Carrickfergus is being methodically groomed for star status. Last season he scored 50 goals for Burnley's A team. And last week after Burnley's regular reserve leader Andy Lochhead was called up to the First XI, Irvine moved to the Central League side to score a hat-trick in his first match. Turf Moor regulars rate Willie Irvine one of the most promising youngsters they've seen for years: they go as far as to forecast international stardom for him in the Jimmy McIlroy, Alex Elder tradition. Incidentally competition for team places even in the 'stiffs' is as keen as ever at Burnley. The Turf Moor reserves won the Central League last season, scoring 113 goals in the process. No wonder Burnley's average reserve gate is a useful 7,500.

I close the pages of the album and sit quietly thinking about how things have turned out. Images of goals scored and chances taken, celebrations and triumphs, dance through my mind. The book, almost falling to pieces, ends with the torn strips of newspaper celebrating a first international cap before I'd even played a first team game. Staring at the flickering blue flames of the fire I can turn and see behind me on the wall in the glass case the shirts, caps and mementoes of a past where I was known and feted. I'm over sixty now and can look back on good times and bad, and successes and failures. Sixty, but still having to work for a living, unlike the new breed of footballer who earns ten times what we did in my day, with less than half the talent.

The album containing so many memories ends in the spring of 1963. Less than four years later I was lying on a stretcher at Goodison Park with my leg broken, and to my dying day, I'll never know for sure whether it was an accident or not. Mine was one of five broken legs at Burnley Football Club that season. From that day on my life changed, but the years from 1963 to 1967 were just the best a man could want.

CHAPTER FIVE

THROUGH THE RANKS

There's another crowd of people for me to take round Turf Moor today. I love doing this job and always will. I love the contact, telling my stories, answering the questions and, yes, lapping up just a little of the attention.

There's a dull drizzle and the day is overcast. As I lead the group out around the perimeter of the pitch it's possible to see at close hand just how shabby the oldest stand at the Cricket Field End really is. I tell them that in its day it was hailed as the best of its kind, with warm air heating blown from vents under the seats. But today the concrete is showing signs of age and the roof girders and stanchions are rusting rapidly. I tell the story that Bob Lord, the tyrannical old chairman who initiated this stand, was justly proud when it was completed. When he got the first electricity bill, however, he ordered the heating to be turned off.

In the Bob Lord Stand, which the far-sighted man built with foundations strong enough to build a second tier at some later stage, my group squeezes into the Chairman's Lounge. The huge table is laid for lunch: crisp white cloth, napkins, printed menu, the best cutlery, a well-stocked bar in the corner and around the walls framed shirts and memorabilia of the great days when this club produced a string of international players, and won trophies and championships. The panelled walls tell a dozen stories. One of the shirts belongs to Jimmy McIlroy and was worn by him in a European Cup quarter-final game against Hamburg. He swapped it with an opponent and the shirt vanished to some distant corner of Germany. Forty years later it has arrived back at the club, tracked down and bought by a Burnley man anxious to return it to its spiritual home. McIlroy is revered in the town. One day, when he is gone and his magical performances are just distant memories, his shirt will be an icon.

I feel at home, at ease, telling my stories and jokes and I usher the crowd back into the corridor, then down the stairs, back again onto the wet pitchside and finally back to the warmth of the James Hargreaves Stand where lunch awaits. Another tour over, but not before I have managed to fit in a quip about there being real centre forwards in my day who never got tired. I feel proud to be able to tell the group what it was like to play in the atmosphere that was generated by the old Longside terraces where thousands of people bellowed their noise, waved their rattles, and roared the team on. It was the same for any team at any ground in the country when the din a crowd could generate could both inspire the home team and terrify the visitors.

An intoxicating drug, I call it, and the louder it got, the more the adrenalin flowed and the more you increased your effort and performance. And the more you did this the better you played and the more goals you scored: The roaring, baying crowd and the team: a bond, a partnership; unison and accord with one purpose.

Today football grounds are often like morgues because the design of these all-seated stadiums doesn't allow for that basic requirement needed by all passionate fans – to be able to stand and in unison create a wall of noise so deafening that an opposition player can often be reduced to a nervous wreck. Stand up, and in seconds an eagle-eyed steward will be on hand to order you back to your seat. I can remember seeing Alan Ball reduced to a dithering wreck by the ceaseless baying and heckling that followed his every move during a game against Arsenal.

"When was your first game?" asks one of the group.

"May 11th away at Arsenal in 1963," I reply promptly. "Scored as well and three days later scored a hat-trick in my second game against Birmingham."

At such times I beam; there isn't much I have forgotten about the good times.

August 1962 – I was still in the A team but with Andy Lochhead banging them in for the reserves I knew it wouldn't be long before he got his chance in the first team and that would mean me moving up to the reserves to take his place. In the very first two games of the season he scored four times while I was carrying on where I'd left off the previous season, banging them in for the A team. There was a hat-trick in a game at Bury almost as soon as the season started. Meanwhile the club had sold a record number of season tickets and old Bob Lord was as pleased as Punch, claiming that the club was one of the wealthiest in the land.

Only months earlier they'd been at Wembley (losing to Tottenham) and just missed out on doing the double. The truth is that they missed out on the double because their legs had gone. They were drained and they'd be the first to admit it. The average gate had been over 27,000 and there were plans to replace the old Brunshaw Road Stand, the directors being ashamed of it. Bob Lord had sleepless nights worrying it would collapse, its condition was so bad.

At the AGM Bob Lord sang the praises of Harry Potts, and quite rightly so, and then went on to say what a jewel Jimmy Adamson was. At this time there had been a lot of speculation that Adamson would be leaving the club to take up management elsewhere. He had been elected Footballer of the Year, and had also acted as coach and assistant manager to Walter Winterbottom with the England team in Chile for the 1962 World Cup. When Winterbottom later resigned Adamson was offered the position of England coach but declined. Even though he was a fully qualified FA coach he said he lacked managerial experience.

At 33, maybe he knew his playing time was coming to an end. Bob Lord clearly had plans for him though, and at the club's annual dinner in Blackpool told everyone that Adamson would have a place at Burnley be he 33 or 63 and that nobody else was going to get him. Maybe it was at that point that Adamson realised the managership of Burnley would one day be his. Perhaps he already knew he would be retained as first team coach when he finally finished playing.

He would play a big part in my career. I wish I could say that all of it was good but sadly there was a long period when we never got on.

By mid-October Andy Lochhead had indeed got himself a first team place. It meant of course I moved up into the reserves. While Andy scored two in a derby against Blackburn Rovers at Ewood Park, I rammed two home for the reserves and had one disallowed. His time had come in Division One and my time had come in the Central League. He had served his apprenticeship; I had a little more time to do. No matter, my day would come with the sort of natural upwards progression that the club was now famous for.

By January '63 I was doing well and just couldn't stop scoring – but then I had to stop – the weather was so bad that all games were postponed. These were the worst blizzards here that anyone could remember and that was on top of the freezing weather that had been causing chaos in Lancashire. The piles of snow and blocked roads stopped coal deliveries so that around the town coal was running out and many people had no water supply.

Even water pipes under the ground were freezing up. Roads around the town were blocked and up on the moors there were drifts that were ten feet deep. Cars and coaches were stranded and only two miles out of the town 50 women were stranded for hours when their coach was trapped on the way to Nelson. They were on their way to some big function and were from a catering firm. The van behind them was full of food so they wouldn't have starved but eventually the police got them out after ploughs cleared the road. The locals said that this was far worse than even the 1947 blizzards.

So, for the moment we were neither training nor playing and when we were managing to do some work it was on a field covered in snow. We could do some running and general fitness work but we really were kicking our heels rather than a football. At least Burnley looked clean and picturesque with everything white and crisp and covered in snow. The most enormous icicles hung down everywhere you looked and on a blue-sky day it really did look beautiful. But the sheep up on the moorlands were trapped in deep drifts and the farmers

73

couldn't get to them. Some of the farms right up on the tops were marooned for days and conditions were dreadfully dangerous for them.

The last league game at Turf Moor was on December 29th, when the first team beat Sheffield Wednesday 4-0. The cup game at Tottenham went ahead on January 16th and Burnley won 3-0, revenge for the FA Cup final defeat. In my 15 games so far for the reserves I'd scored eight goals and couldn't wait to get started again. It looked like I was a regular by now and Andy Lochhead was doing well in the first team. There was a home cup game to play against Liverpool as soon as possible and all the other fixtures were piling up. It was a mess; snowball fights are great for the first couple of days but the novelty wears off and then boredom and frustration take over.

Despite the temporary halt, the Irvine career soon gathered pace and in the Central League the goals flew in. I received an even bigger boost with the news that I was selected for the Irish Under 23 team to play Wales at the end of February. Having played just 22 games for the reserves and not even a sniff of the first team the Irish selectors must have decided that I was the embryonic answer to their prayers for a successor to Derek Dougan, who with his strong views could cause a punch-up in a monastery. The word "surprise" was an understatement. The newspapers now said I had scored 53 goals in the A team last season. The total seemed to go up every time it was mentioned. But while for me things looked rosy, for the club and Jimmy McIlroy events were to become front-page news.

Some say the origins of this lay in the cup game on January 26th when Burnley could only draw at home against Liverpool. It was a month before the weather relented enough to allow the reply at Anfield and Burnley lost 2-1. Within days Jimmy McIlroy was placed on the transfer list and the town of Burnley was affected as if an earthquake had hit the place. It could probably never happen at any club today the way it happened then. Players today rarely stay at one club for the whole of their career and today the big city clubs would snap up a player of his calibre and quality at a small-town club like Burnley very early in his career. Never mind the Arsenals and the Manchester Uniteds, today he would have been on his way to Real Madrid or Barcelona. The man was an institution, a living legend, and there were many who said he was Burnley FC. He was the epitome of the loyal one-club player and the service he had given to Burnley was inestimable. Of course it affected me. Jimmy and I had become very close.

The game at Liverpool could not have ended more dramatically. In the very last minute of extra time goalkeeper Adam Blacklaw took a back pass from full-back Alex Elder and decided to boot the ball upfield from the edge of the area. The ball hit Ian St John, standing just a few yards away. He collected it, rounded Blacklaw and was on his way to scoring when Blacklaw brought him down.

Ronnie Moran scored from the penalty and Blacklaw is still no doubt having nightmares about that goal 40 years later. All of us at the club, from the team that had played to the youngest ground staff lad, were stunned at the manner in which the game was lost and Turf Moor was like a morgue the following day. Football can be a cruel game when you lose in the last minute, but to lose to a freak incident like that was heartbreaking.

It was a game in which McIlroy actually came in for criticism over his performance. It was described as "disappointing" and "ineffective", the result of him spending too much time in "no man's land" as the report put it. Later, Mac was to refute this, saying he was simply playing to instructions.

Whatever, he was placed on the transfer list and it is no exaggeration to say that the town of Burnley was rocked and shaken to its foundations. There was elation for me with the news of my Under 23 cap, but bewilderment for Jimmy McIlroy when he was called in to Harry Potts' office and given the news. I had become good friends with him by now and was as stunned as he was.

One old cutting I came across expresses the mood of the town.

MAC, ANGRY FANS WANT TO KNOW WHY

There have been many controversial issues involving Burnley Football Club in recent times, but nothing to match the storm which has broken out following the club's sensational McIlroy-to-go decision. In homes, workshops, pubs and clubs, in cafes and buses, there has been but one talking point – "What lies behind it?"

Up-in-arms fans have launched petitions, including one in which the signatories threaten to boycott games at Turf Moor until the football club's board of directors give an explanation of its action.

The board's decision to give no explanation of its action taken at a specially called meeting has angered the fans more than anything else.

Only 10 months earlier fans had stood by the Town Hall steps after the cup final chanting "We want Mac". Now he was on the transfer list with a reputed £40,000 price on his head. Only months before this the club had rejected an £80,000 offer from Italian club Sampdoria who had tried to tempt him with a fabulous salary and a wonderful villa.

To this day no one accepts that the Liverpool game was the sole reason for the transfer. Rumours abounded of friction between Mac and Bob Lord, or Mac and this director or that director. McIlroy himself thought it was to do with a friendship of his with one particular director called Cooke and his family, and that this was a director whom Lord could not abide. That, too, seems a flimsy reason unless there were things going on that were kept quiet.

Transferred for lack of effort was one reason given but if they'd valued him or wanted him to stay, wouldn't a spell in the reserves have been the best course of action until he regained his appetite? Or did they just want rid of him for reasons never made public? It was so sudden, so unexpected, and so immediate. There was no warning, no premonition, and no sign of anything impending. It hit me almost as hard as Mac himself because of our good relationship.

In not much more than a week he was shipped out for a paltry £25,000 when only months earlier they had refused £80,000, an enormous amount for the early '60s. It just didn't add up. We all wonder now if it was a personal thing between him and Bob Lord, but whatever the reason was Lord took it to his grave.

Jimmy signed for Stoke City although Preston were also interested. McIlroy was attracted, however, by the Stoke manager Tony Waddington and the other great players he would play alongside, one of them being the incomparable Stanley Matthews. The club was ambitious and could pay First Division wages.

When Jimmy signed I couldn't believe he had gone, with him and me being such good friends. I loved being in his company and I'd spent a lot of time driving him round Burnley when he had functions to attend or people to visit. I knew Mac was happy to have got things sorted out after days of just feeling confused and bewildered. He decided to go on living in Burnley, which I was really pleased about because I could continue to see him. He and his wife just didn't want to live anywhere else. I did a lot of babysitting for him and I drove him to various places to which he was invited – we called them "shoving-over-halfpennies" functions because that's exactly what one of them was. Some club or pub collected hundreds of halfpennies, piled them all up on top of each other and the high spot of the evening was Jimmy knocking them over. Well, that's what made a good night out in Burnley in those days and after that, every trip out became known as "shoving over the halfpennies". When he knew I was taking a girl out anywhere he grinned at me and said "shoving over the halfpennies, are you?"

I think fondly to this day of Jimmy Mac who I occasionally bump into in the town or at a function at Turf Moor. "Oh no, not you again," he'll say, to which I usually reply, "Have you heard the one about the…" He says he'll put that on my headstone.

It's to him that I owe my first Ireland game. He knew I was scoring goals in the reserves; we played against each other every week in training, either full team games or five-a-side. Bertie Peacock, then the Ireland manager, phoned him to ask about me and I know Jimmy recommended me and in his newspaper column he wrote to the Irish selectors, although in my own mind I never thought I was ready. He'd tell me I was a natural goalscorer and we'd often talk about goalscoring. Some players just have the knack of being in the right place at the right time, of knowing instinctively where to be. We might be useless at making a forty-yard pass or a crunching tackle but give us the ball in the penalty box and we know what we are doing; or in truth most times, in fact, the ball is in the back of the net and we don't know how we've done it. We don't think about it, we just do it.

Jimmy used to tell me that I reminded him of the great Brian Clough, playingwise that is. I was always much better looking. He only played alongside him once and that was in a testimonial for Jimmy Hagan at Sheffield sometime in the late '50s. Jimmy made a short pass to Clough and waited for the return. Clough's attempt was abysmal so Jimmy looked across to Danny Blanchflower, who was also playing, and said something to the effect of: "Just who is this bloke with this great reputation; he can't even make a four-yard pass." Shortly after, the ball was in the six-yard box; Clough was onto it in a flash and scored. The same thing happened again later with Clough making a hash of a routine pass. Blanchflower and McIlroy looked at each other and Jimmy Mac in amazement said to Blanchflower, "the lucky so-and-so." Blanchflower smiled at Jimmy and replied, "Yes, Jimmy he's been a lucky so-and-so 40 times already this season." Five minutes later he scored again. He could head a ball, was lightning sharp, was onto any chance in the six-yard area but couldn't make a pass to save his life. He was just a natural goalscorer, and that's what McIlroy used to say to me about both of us.

Jimmy tells people a couple of stories about me that I don't remember. Is he telling true stories or am I telling the truth when I say I don't remember? Do you believe him or me, or can you ever believe any Irishman?

I'm in Ireland and we're training with Bertie Peacock and the squad for an international. He's got them doing lap after lap of the field and the sun is beating down and the sweat is pouring off them. This is hard work and I'm thinking I'm having none of this malarkey. I'm sat on a wall near the edge of the field and I'm swinging my legs and relaxing and whistling away, catching up on my tan watching them. And Bertie yells across in a blue fit, "What the fuck are you doing there while we're doing this?" And I call back, "Well, when you've just broken the Burnley scoring record you can all come and sit on the wall with me and sunbathe." I don't remember that, but if Jimmy says so then it must be true I suppose.

Then there's the other story I'm supposed to be in the middle of. I've gone home to Carrickfergus for the summer and it's July 12th and as well you know that's the big day of the year and there's parades and marches and all the lodges come out with their bands and banners. The streets are lined with folk and by and large it's carnival time. So Jimmy tells this story that I was so pleased to be back and there's a march coming down the street, and of course folk there know me well by now, so out I leap to the front of the parade and grab the mace off the parade leader and I start to lead the march and lob the mace up and down in the air like you do. But then there's a disaster. I'm really getting in the swing of things and throw the mace too high and the bloody thing gets stuck in the telegraph wires. Pandemonium. That was the last time Willie Irvine took part in an Orange Day Parade.

Today Jimmy and I don't see each other that often, even though we still both live in Burnley. We were once reunited at a dinner at the club when a number of players were voted by the fans to be official legends. Our names are up there on a plaque somewhere. At the dinner, though, he was a guest of honour up on the top table in the end seat, and this top table is on a raised platform and all I kept thinking was, "well, I hope you don't fall off the end Jimmy, it's a long drop." He's a very dignified man and when he speaks you listen. But I laughed when he began his speech up there on the top table with the words – and don't forget he's up there with all the dignitaries and there's 400 people in that room – and don't forget Bob Lord is the man who put him on the transfer list, and said the average footballer couldn't run a fish and chip shop... and Jimmy, with a twinkle in his eye, says, "If only Bob Lord could see me now... " It brought the house down.

He was always grateful for all the babysitting I used to do for him, but to be honest the reason was that his house was where I took all the girls I used to know for a bit of hanky-panky. It was very handy; there's not much you can do with a girl in your digs when the landlady is in and your fellow lodgers are around the place. So Jimmy's house when he was out was very convenient once the kids were in bed. His children still tell me nobody does Yogi Bear better than me.

Anyway, he went on to have two good years with Stoke City and they won promotion with him. Then he was manager of Oldham, and finally Bolton. But then he got weary of football, I suppose, and I'm not sure he even visits Turf Moor too often these days. He became a journalist and a very fine writer and now he's retired from that he's a wonderful painter and plays golf as often as he can. Jimmy McIlroy is just a great man and a pleasure to know.

April 3rd, 1963 is a date imprinted in my mind. The goals were going in for the Central League team, and the season would end with us top of that league. Then at midnight one night I was asleep in my digs when there was a banging at the door downstairs that woke up the whole house. It was Noel Wild, a reporter from the *Nelson Leader*, shouting, "Does Willie Irvine live here?"

I stuck my head out to see what all the commotion was. "You've been picked for Northern Ireland," he shouted. By this time just about the whole street were hanging out of their doors or windows, and don't forget this was a row of terraced houses in which you could lean out of a window and almost reach across and shake hands with the person opposite. I nearly fell out of my window when Noel Wild shouted again. We let him in to stop him from shouting any more. At Gawthorpe the next day most of the players seemed to have heard. "How many books of Green Shield Stamps did you have to collect for an Irish cap then?" somebody yelled. Then George Bray really took the smile off my face when I heard him say, "Sorry, Willie, we can't release you, there's an important reserve game coming up." I was devastated and then saw the wide grin spreading over his face.

I hadn't played a first team game, nor did I expect to just yet, but then I saw it confirmed that I would play for Northern Ireland against Wales. BILLY AND BOB IRVINE

Through the Ranks

IN IRISH TEAM said the headline. Of course Jimmy McIlroy would be in the side and so, too, would Alex Elder. And, as if to add more spice to the occasion, it would be against Blackburn centre half Mike England.

Just about the whole of Carrickfergus seemed to travel to Windsor Park for the game and it felt marvellous. In my own mind I didn't feel ready but generally the papers were kind and made allowances for the fact that I hadn't played a first team game at all. Just one or two said my selection was too rapid but that I couldn't be blamed for that. What it did reveal, they all agreed, was just how much out of favour Derek Dougan was. I told the press before the game that not until I had a regular place at Burnley would I consider myself fit to play for Ireland. I've got this old cutting from just after the game. I'm saying all the proper things – we didn't deserve to lose 4-1, the criticism was unfair, I've time to improve and learn. I was still homesick then as well, even after so long in Burnley. I had a girl in Carrickfergus and given the chance I'd have been playing in Ireland. But England and Burnley was where the money was.

The truth is that in that game the Welsh played like backstreet, roughhouse brawlers. They won few friends that day. The rugby team had finished bottom of the Five Nations championship and national pride was hurt. It was felt that a Welsh football win over the Irish might restore a little of that pride. So, they came and kicked us all over the park. As reporter Malcolm Brodie said at the time, they played more like bulls at a gate than soccer players. Their conduct was unbecoming of players of such high repute. They chopped our legs, pushed, shoved, tripped and committed many unforgivable sins as if it were a dogfight. It was a deplorable performance and George McCabe, the referee, should never have allowed it to happen. A draw might have been a fairer result; both sides were abysmal and neither deserved to win. But Brodie was very kind to me, saying that I deserved a pat on the back and was no failure. Not a bad debut at all, he wrote, and prominent in his report was the fact that Mike England had chopped me down at every opportunity. Twice, or maybe three times, I was carried off for treatment during the game. I came off at the end black and blue. I could have had three goals in the first 20 minutes but it wasn't to be. On another day they would have gone in.

I did learn one thing from that game and it was simply this; that instead of thinking about what I'm going to do with a shot, from now on I'd just hit it first time without thinking. I think I missed a few chances in that game through being too careful and that was because of not doing what I'd spent the last couple of years doing – just hitting the ball first time. There certainly weren't any rave reviews; the nearest thing to a bit of praise was that from Brodie and another report saying I had put up a good show with limited support.

The proudest moment though was knowing my mother would be there watching. Of course the press made a big thing of her and how she'd struggled to bring us all up. We stayed at the Abbeyland Hotel in Newtownabbey and she made the trip to see us there. Her face beamed and I can't imagine what she must have felt as she sat watching the game, especially as we came out, and then as we lined up for the kick-off. Looking at her two sons in the Irish team she must have felt a million miles from Armagh Prison. "It's what your father would have wanted," she said to me once when I said I was unhappy at leaving Carrick to live in England but I'd have left Carrick anyway I suppose. If the early trials at Burnley had been a failure I'd a job lined up to go back to. I'd been to see the job exchange people and had signed up to be a galley boy on one of the Cunard liners. Then I had to tell them about the trial at Burnley. "Don't worry," they said, "if you come back here the job will be here for you."

The euphoria of my debut didn't last long and for the reserves the goals kept going in. Willie Morgan was becoming an absolute star; Ralph Coates was coming through in the A team. At that time he was a little barrel-shaped centre forward thumping goals in just like I did. And then there was Brian O'Neil who was such a dynamo. So much talent coming through and Keith McNee wrote, *"The most exciting prospect is Irishman Irvine. His display against Blackpool was a real eye-opener. Taken off the field with a badly cut face in the first half, he returned for the second and scored the finest goal I have seen..."*

Through the Ranks

The big thing we all talked about though was the punch-up between first-teamers Gordon Harris and Jimmy Adamson. Such a thing at Turf Moor was almost unheard of. Adamson by now was approaching the twilight of his playing career while Gordon Harris was a tough, powerfully built ex-miner who tolerated no nonsense from anyone, on or off the field. His thunderous shots from his tree-trunk legs were said to be the hardest of any Burnley player ever. He was born in Worksop and Burnley found him playing for a colliery team. The press were fed the line that nobody was too sure about what happened in the gym during a five-a-side session except that Gordon well and truly thumped Adamson after they had both been into a tackle.

What happened is still crystal clear in my mind. For a start the two of them weren't getting on very well and in the five-a-side which ended that particular day's training, and in which some of us ground staff lads were playing, matters came to a head. Adamson body-checked Harris. They had words. Jimmy Adamson laughed. Adamson body-checked him again and brought him down. Nobody could say that Jimmy wasn't brave but Gordon was not pleased and you could see he wanted retribution.

He kicked the ball hard against the gym wall and in the same movement kicked Adamson up into the air. As he came down Gordon caught him with a solid punch. It was at my feet that Jimmy landed with the blood running from his nose into his mouth. I stood wide-eyed at him lying there with the blood making funny little gargling noises in his mouth. Gordon turned and walked straight out of the gym without a word. The newspapers said that Harry Potts took Gordon to Jimmy's house so he could apologise. To my knowledge Gordon never did apologise.

Gordon became a very accomplished player with one international cap and his eventual partnership in midfield with Brian O'Neil became the bedrock of the mid-60s team that did so well. But his temper was well known and his altercations with referees frequent. You didn't mess with Gordon 'Bomber' Harris. If you did, basically you got walloped for your trouble. The fracas was sorted but not forgotten. Harris was transferred years later in 1968 and he went on to play 120 games for Sunderland.

The season reached its end. The reserve team won the Central League and the Northern Ireland versus Wales date was a milestone in my life. But May 11th, 1963 was doubly so. What happened on that day was totally unexpected.

CHAPTER SIX

FOOT ON THE LADDER

The first team were due to play Arsenal and I was asked to go down with them. As boot boy I went down with Ray Bennion the day before with all the kit and helped him with it. We went down by train and stayed in the hotel the night before and it was our job in the dressing room to lay all the kit out and check everything was OK. Going to Highbury and London was a huge thrill. I knew Bob Lord made sure the players and staff stayed in good hotels and were well looked after and we were staying somewhere in Kensington. Arsenal was a great club and just going down and staying overnight I knew would be a marvellous experience and so I was really looking forward to it. I'd be in the dressing room with the first team and it would be the first time I had done this. The first team were a great crowd and they were all pleased I'd made my Ireland debut. I got my leg pulled as well – Ray Pointer and Andy Lochhead telling each other they'd better be looking over their shoulder for this new wonder-kid coming along. I told them not to worry – it wouldn't be for another six or seven months – and they had a good laugh.

I had laughed that week when I saw an old local paper. They thought they might find oil in the hills around Burnley at a place called Widdop Moor so an American firm was given permission to drill. Oil, my foot. There was about as much chance of finding oil round there as finding the Pope in a Protestant back yard. The only thing they'd find up on the moors that's black were the sheep. Still, it brought much entertainment to the locals in a town where cloth caps were still the height of fashion. They all jokingly dreamed of being oil millionaires.

Willie Irvine

I was the last to find out that I was actually playing at Highbury. The local Burnley newspaper knew it the day before so therefore half of Burnley knew it, the management knew it and the players knew it. Andy maybe knew it because he knew he wouldn't be playing with an injured nerve in his leg. Everybody but me knew it. It was a well-kept secret, kept so that I wouldn't have any sleepless nights worrying about a league debut.

Highbury was in fact a good ground for Burnley who hadn't lost there since August 1958, and Arsenal had already been beaten at Turf Moor earlier in the season. Also at the hotel were the Wakefield Trinity team due to appear in the Rugby League Cup final. They were supping pints like there was no tomorrow. I remember seeing *The Black and White Minstrel Show* in the evening somewhere. How times change; political correctness was unheard of way back then.

How Ray Bennion managed to keep quiet about things I'll never know. It was his job to make sure I didn't eat too much on the Saturday morning other than a good breakfast, that I didn't pile up a mountain of chips on my plate at lunchtime, without telling me why. I can still remember what he said.

"Willie, keep off the chips; if the other players see you eating chips they'll all want some. Have extra chicken instead."

At lunchtime I felt what a treat and an honour it was to be sitting at the same table as all these great Burnley players. The one piece of boiled chicken did not last long. I left the room starving.

In the dressing room we laid out the kit, put the boots under each seat, cut the laces for tying up socks, laid out all the embrocation and checked the first aid kit – not much more than a sponge and a bucket of water in all honesty but there might have been a roll of plaster in there as well. It was my job to check that studs were fitted securely and that none were missing, and that all the boots had laces. There were little things to do like check that the baths had soap and that the hot water taps worked and that hot water did actually appear. As this was Highbury we had no worries about that but a cold bath after a game was not uncommon at some grounds. Then it was lay out the mugs for the half-time cuppa.

With the time running out, Harry Potts asked for quiet and announced he'd quickly run through the team even though everyone knew what it was. John Connelly was back in the side to replace Trevor Meredith and then I had a vague recollection of hearing my name mentioned. It didn't sink in at all. It just didn't register.

"You OK, Willie?" a voice asked.

I looked around at the grinning faces. "You're playing, didn't you hear me? Get changed; you're playing."

I looked at the number 9 kit hanging up on the peg. The same kit I'd just laid out, never thinking twice about it, having no idea that Andy would not be fit. Blacklaw, Angus, Elder, Adamson, Talbut, Miller, Connelly, Bellamy, Irvine, Towers and Harris were the team to play. Arthur Bellamy I knew well; we had learned, trained, and had been in digs together. His face grinned across the changing room at me. So did Harry Potts. Harry was never known for giving detailed, complicated, technical team talks. This one consisted of something along the lines of, "It's been an age since you've won an away game and the way things are going it'll be another age so please go out there and do something about it."

You're just 19 years old and you're running out in front of 23,000 people and playing against stars like Joe Baker and Laurie Brown at one of the most famous football grounds in the world and you score in your first League game. It was like yesterday and in my mind I've saved that moment forever. I can still see me intercepting a pass, pushing the ball on to Gordon Harris who then gives it to Arthur Bellamy. Bellamy beats somebody, crosses, and up I go, soaring like a bloody eagle, and put a bullet header into the back of the net. I'm having a great game, running rings round Laurie Brown, collecting every Blacklaw clearance, roaming wide, covering every bit of grass. I have another almost identical header saved and then another header is cleared off the line. Mine was the first goal in a 3-2 win and I'm the man of the moment.

And the next game was even better, at home to Birmingham City in the last game of the season. I kept my place. A hat-trick. It doesn't get any better. John Connelly says he sent over inch-perfect crosses and that I couldn't miss. I say they were awful crosses and I made them good. The last goal I had in the net before anyone could blink. Feet faster than Cassius Clay. The Irish selectors were there to see it and it made them keen to retain me in the side for Spain in spite of pressure to bring back Derek Dougan. Burnley ended the '62/63 season with three straight wins and finished third. For me it was four goals in two games. I went back to Carrick for the summer and basked in the adulation. People stopped me in the street and asked me how things were going. Heads turned and voices whispered, "Hey, that's Willie. He's doing well, he's in the Burnley first team now, he's Ireland's number 9... "

I always was a confident, brash kind of bloke, not like Tony Cascarino. Dave, to whom I'm telling this story, says he's read Cascarino's book and that he's full of uncertainty and doubt and played his career without any belief or confidence in himself even though he was the Republic's number 9 for donkey's years. I was never like that. I can't say I heard voices in my head like Cascarino says he did when he was one on one with a goalkeeper, or had just missed a sitter of a chance. Good job I didn't, although the chance I missed in Spain at the end of May would haunt me forever. The minute doubt creeps into your head, the minute you start to dwell on mistakes and misses, then your skill, talent or effectiveness as a striker, call it what you like, is halved. If ever now I am asked for advice about being a centre forward that advice always remains the same; keep moving, never stand still, keep that centre half dizzy, wear him out, run him ragged so that all he can say in exasperation is "Where's that bloody number 9?" and he comes off the field with a stiff neck because he's been constantly turning his head this way and that looking for you.

So I came off that field at Highbury, and then at Turf Moor a few nights later and my whole career was in front of me; the goals, the records, the caps, the fame, but I'd no idea of what was to come – that shattered leg at Everton, broken in the Johnny Morrissey tackle, the rows with Adamson, the eventual need to get away from Burnley, and then the gloom at the end that was Halifax Town.

But then I was 19 years old and being 30 or more didn't

enter into my thinking. It wasn't ten years away, it was a hundred. I watched Jimmy Adamson nearing the end of his career but he knew what he wanted to do, which was stay and coach. The job was his. But for me there were no thoughts that some day this would come to an end. You lived and played for the moment and loved every minute of it. Sure there might be just the vaguest thought that this was a job you couldn't do the other side of 35, but what path you might take after that, or what job you might do; those thoughts were a million miles away. You were about to enter a world of hotels, travel, good meals, and being looked after. Some of the shops you went into wouldn't take money, the butcher slipped you the best cut of meat, you found yourself at the front of a queue and not the back, the drinks flew faster. You began to notice that people wanted to meet you, they stopped you in the street, the girls in the dance halls started to give you that bit more attention and looked at you more. The days of struggling on £7 a week were over.

And then there was a first international goal. It was Bilbao, Spain in a European Nations' tie. We might have been humiliated by the Welsh a few weeks earlier but the display in Spain was one which had Northern Ireland in raptures. The Irish FA President, Harry Cavan, said it made him feel six inches taller. Spain had a brilliant team and they hammered us. We held on but at last, in the 58th minute, they scored. Their fans thought the floodgates would open but brother Bobby brought off save after save and the two full-backs Elder and McCullough were world class. Bit by bit we clawed ourselves back into the game and at last the chance of a lifetime came my way. It was so simple, so straightforward, I could have blown the ball in with my eyes shut. A three-man move worked the ball to the right wing. Braithwaite put in a perfect cross. The goalkeeper was nowhere; the goal was wide open from just yards away. All I had to do was tap it over the line. But no, what do I do but blast the ball over the bar. The crowd was astonished at this unbelievable miss. If this had been the age of videos and instant replays it would be shown over and over again on programmes like *They Think It's All Over* and my humiliation and embarrassment would have been broadcast across the nation. It was that bad. Malcolm Brodie was quite clear about it. *"All that eager Billy Irvine had to do was tap it over the line. He did not need his feet for the job; his breath would have done equally well. Irvine hung his head in shame..."*

I can still see it. If the ground had opened up I would have jumped in. There's a sickness you feel in the pit of your stomach. But, for me, it was over in an instant and all I could do was turn away and get on with the game so that when the next chance comes I would do better. And I did. Bingham slipped the ball to Crossan and then the pass on to Braithwaite again. The cross came over, Vicente fumbled the shot and at the second attempt I rammed it home. I stood on that goal line, arms raised, and basked in the moment of glory. We had almost been given a football lesson by the artistry of the Spaniards, but we had held on, defended like tigers and it was ME who equalized. Ireland has had many nights of glory and this was one of them. Somehow that night we had fire in our bellies and we extinguished the flames of Spain. The goal I scored was ample revenge for the kicking I got from the Spanish centre half. He kicked me black and blue, including the private bits, which turned the colour of a plum and twice their normal size. My evening was ruined as I sat in agony.

I cursed the broken hand, though, that put me out of action at the beginning of the next season after just a couple of games. It wasn't till the back end of '63/64 that I got a regular place: the last seven games and four goals. The very last was a 7-2 thumping of Tottenham at Turf Moor. It masked the mediocrity of that season with Potts and Lord excusing it as transition. By now Jimmy Adamson was coach but it was the first season for years without Jimmy McIlroy. But when he had come back to Turf Moor with Stoke, he had been anonymous and almost a passenger. There was a kind of sadness to it. But in the game at Stoke, when he had played against Burnley for the first time ever, he almost did have the last laugh. At half-time Stoke led 3-0 and he had had a blinder of a game. As he walked off he looked up at the Burnley directors' box and smiled at them. Nice one Jimmy. With minutes left Stoke led 4-2 but somehow Burnley pulled it back to 4-4 in a game that was generally agreed to have been one of the best ever at the Victoria Ground.

The weeks drifted by with me on the sidelines. In those days the Imperial Ballroom in Nelson was one of the biggest in the north; big enough to attract the Beatles and 2,000 screaming teenagers including two coachloads who had come over from Belfast. For one night Nelson was the centre of the universe as people came from all over Lancashire. The streets outside were packed with kids who couldn't get in and afterwards the Fab Four were wheeled away in a police van to avoid them being mobbed. I didn't get to see them but we talked about it for days at the training ground. The Beatles in Nelson…it seems an age away.

Though it was six months since Jimmy Mac had been transferred, the town had not finished having a go at Bob Lord. At the AGM there was an angry exchange of views when one of the shareholders harangued Bob the Butcher and demanded to know why Mac had been transferred. He referred to McIlroy being blamed for the cup defeat at Liverpool, that he was Burnley's best ever player, that he had been given away on the cheap and that the decision had been ill-thought and made hastily. It became a shouting match. Lord insisted Burnley would always have to sell players. He never mentioned McIlroy by name but said the player concerned had admitted he had become complacent. The club had some difficult problems during the year, he added. The McIlroy saga was certainly one of them.

Survival for so many clubs today is about cost-cutting, staff-cutting, and keeping heads above water. Lord forecast all this years ago. Impoverished clubs today often have just two recognised forwards to choose from. Back in 1963 there was a little headline in the paper to say the Clarets had eight to select from – Pointer, Morgan, Connelly, Harris, Meredith, Robson, Lochhead, Bellamy, and Willie Irvine if you count me as well, with my broken hand. Any one of us would have walked into a team today on one leg.

September and I was still out. But there was big news:

world heavyweight champion Sonny Liston had been in town. It was the publicity stunt to end all stunts – the world boxing champion meets the world bingo champion – and I have a hazy memory of a few of us being there at this event. Bingo was big in Burnley but avid fans at Burnley's Palace Casino put down their pencils and stood up as the Big Bear sauntered down the aisle. They cheered as he climbed into a makeshift ring, answered a few simple questions, posed for photographs and handed the world bingo champion a huge bundle of fivers. Sonny Liston in Burnley – it was only a few weeks since he'd flattened Floyd Patterson. Gordon Harris would have lasted longer. In fact it was tempting to suggest to Gordon that he should go and challenge him. My money would have been on Gordon, having seen what he did with one punch to Jimmy Adamson. It was explained to the famous visitor that bingo was the number one social game in Burnley and that there was big money to be made. "Then I'm gonna quit boxing and play bingo," he replied. He should have done that. It wouldn't be long before Cassius Clay whupped him good and proper. The big moment: Liston was to present £7,000 to world champion Malcolm Heap, actually £7,339 17s. 3d. His huge hands scooped up the fivers, maroon-jacketed guitarists broke into a strum and the magic moment was done. For an encore, weightlifter Mr Heap asked if he could try and lift up Mr Liston. This he duly did, grasping him round the thighs and hoisting him a couple of feet into the air. The razzmatazz over, a clearly by-now bored Liston was whisked away into his Cadillac and then to the airport for a flight back to London. He'd only been in town half an hour. Mr Heap announced with the money he would buy a house in Nelson. Today he'd have the Burnley chief executive asking him to "walk the extra mile" and donate it to Burnley Football Club's survival fund.

The town of Burnley, and certainly all of us players, talked about the Liston visit for weeks but as in all things in this part of the world football matters took centre stage again and an up to now indifferent Burnley won back the love of their supporters with a 4-3 victory at Goodison and that 4-4 at Stoke.

Manager Harry Potts took centre stage for a short while; no mean feat with Bob Lord around; and blasted football in general following two contentious Spurs goals at White Hart Lane in a game Burnley lost. "Our players obey the rules," he announced. What he would have made of David Beckham neatly deliberately getting himself a yellow card in the World Cup game against Wales, so as to get himself a one-match suspension while his ribs were cracked and he would therefore miss the next game anyway, will never be known. Bob Lord, I am sure, would have hung him in his nearest butcher's shop window and left him on display for a while in among the sausages and pig's trotters, with a sign round his neck saying "dimwit".

Never far from trouble, Bob Lord was in the news again after the Birmingham game, having seen four Burnley goals disallowed. I repeat – four. The referee allegedly got the sharp end of Mr Lord's tongue as they left the field. Not long after that – never one to speak softly – he announced that there was no crisis at Burnley Football Club and that while other small Lancashire clubs might be feeling the pinch, all was rosy at the Turf with no end of reserve players coming through. The reserve team was top of the Central League again and almost invincible. "I hope the day never comes when we will have to buy a player," he said. "Our policy of finding, grooming and selling players is paying off well."

"There'll be no bingo here," he thundered. I don't think Gordon Harris would have been the only bloke in Burnley able to give Sonny Liston a good hiding. I reckon Bob Lord would have had him on the floor even quicker.

March 30th, 1964. Maybe that's the day I can say I had both feet in the door, coming into the side for the final seven games. It was the closing game of the season and Tottenham had come to Turf Moor knowing that a win could get them second place for the second year running. They didn't know what was about to hit them. Burnley fielded their youngest team of the season, the homespun against the millionaires, and the latter had Jimmy Greaves in their side. It was a known fact that Greavsie was bemused by Burnley the place, and thought it was the end of the world. The display put on that day was maybe a sign of things to come at Turf Moor. Only a handful of players remained from the great championship side. To fill the other places Burnley had people like me, Willie Morgan, Andy Lochhead, Brian O'Neil and Gordon Harris and we were raring to go. Our teamwork, power and poise was all too much for the southern softies who usually turned their noses up at the sight of Burnley as soon as they reached the top of Manchester Road and looked down at the drab streets. On a greasy surface we produced some brilliant attacking football to go three up in the first twenty minutes. O'Neil rocketed home a twenty-yarder to make it 4-0 before half-time. As we walked off we could hear the crowd vibrant and buzzing with excitement and pleasure. There was nothing a Burnley crowd liked more than to send a glamour team packing back to London. Burnley v Tottenham games had been a feature of the FA Cup for the last few seasons with the Londoners taking the honours.

I can still remember it rained that day and Spurs were non-existent. The second half began where the first left off and we seemed able to do as we pleased. We could have doubled the score. I thought if there was a heaven then this must be it, scoring twice in front of nearly 17,000 people. There would have been more but for the rain. The dressing room buzzed afterwards and we knew we had the beginnings of a good side. After a result like that – and we'd won the previous game away at Nottingham Forest as well – you ended the season on a high. You knew you could enjoy the summer and look forward to coming back. Me – I couldn't wait. I regarded that number 9 shirt as my own.

Brash, cocky, impetuous, confident, full of youth and vigour, Irish international, Burnley number 9, faces smiling at you in the street, programmes thrust at you for autographs, newspapers writing about you, girls looking at you. A tough childhood in a huge family, a father I'd no memory of, a mother who'd worked her fingers to the bone and been to prison for her children. I'd earned my fame and deserved it. The best and worst was yet to come.

At the beginning of the next new season I was in the first team for the start and scored. We drew 2-2 at home to

Blackpool and it was disappointing not to win a home game. I was pretty sure I'd done my last chores as an apprentice. No more getting to the ground for 9 o'clock on a Monday morning and laying out all the kit and towels for the first team. Now someone could do it for me.

CHAPTER SEVEN

NEARLY THE RECORD

1964/65. I remember the season beginning with optimism but it ended in mid-table: 12th. Injuries, frequent team changes, transition – there's that word again, just like the previous season. But the talent was there and so was the potential. Having clattered Spurs 7-2 in the final game of the preceding season no wonder we were raring to go and it was assumed we'd get maximum points from the first two games which were at home. Not so, they were both drawn. Bob Lord's pep talk to us all concentrated on poor away form. Only three away games had been won and that was even less than relegated Bolton. On top of that John Connelly was sold to Manchester United before the end of the season.

If only Connelly knew what sort of place he was joining, maybe he wouldn't have been so keen. We'd heard on the grapevine about how things were run at Old Trafford and in later years Connelly expressed his own surprise at what he found. Manchester United then was a club where organised training and coaching was minimal, where practice games really did take place on a car park behind one of the stands and if one day they were five-a-side, the next they could be 20 a side depending on how many turned up. It was a place where players like Noel Cantwell and Maurice Setters, who were also bought, were highly critical, if not contemptuous, about the state of training and how factions undermined the dressing room and morale. Add to that it was one of the lowest paying clubs in Division One and all this at a place where the Busby myth grew and grew. It really was a club where tactics were unheard of and the only instructions players ever got when they went out on the field was to keep it simple, find another red shirt and express themselves. And yet they achieved such great things. You wonder exactly how? There was one simple answer, I suppose. It was that they had such great players and somehow Busby instilled in them a love of that red shirt and the name "Manchester United".

But at Burnley, Harry Potts talked about team spirit and new players coming through; although one of the older ones, Alex Elder, was at odds with the club in a confrontation about money. No player blamed him for that; good luck to him, we thought, an experienced world-class regular international player. He wanted paying what he thought he was worth and he wasn't asking for the moon.

The months between the two seasons went by faster than you would imagine. I saw Olive a lot in Carrick when I went back home, but back in Burnley there was Rita. We'd met in a pub initially and then bumped into each other again in the Mecca.

Anyway I'd asked a pal of mine, Tom Skelly, to go over to Rita and ask her could I walk her home from the pub we were in. The cheeky sod went over and asked her could he take her home. She said no to him and yes to me; that was the beginning of a relationship that's lasted over 40 years. For a while it was on and off and we'd go our different ways but at some stage we'd always come back to each other. There's a time when you don't know what's best, when you want the best of both worlds; burn the candle at both ends so to speak. Olive in Carrick and Rita in Burnley; if there was a choice to be made I wasn't ready yet. If there was a choice it was simply carry on with the arrangement, a girl in every port as they say. My mother made her feelings clear. She did not want me taking up seriously with any English girl. It was to cause big trouble later.

If I couldn't make up my mind about which girl I wanted, neither could the club seem to make up their mind about Jimmy Adamson. He was to continue as club captain but in a non-playing capacity. Would he leave to take up a management role or be kept on as coach at Turf Moor? None of us knew. Uncertainty filled the club especially as Ray

Pointer had injury troubles which had dogged him for nearly a year.

But no uncertainty clouded the number 9 spot. It was mine. There was a goal for me in each of the first two games, one of them illustrating perfectly the goalscorers' maxim that all goals are good goals. A scruffier goal you couldn't wish to see than the one against Spurs. Cyril Knowles half hit the ball back to his keeper Pat Jennings. I nipped in; collected the ball and it hit Jennings, then hit me on the rebound, bounced around a bit and bobbled over the line.

After the first game of the season it was as if black clouds hung over the club and the supporters. We finished the game against Blackpool struggling against a side that a couple of seasons earlier would have been trounced by the likes of Adamson, McIlroy, Pointer and Connelly. The crowd of fewer than 16,000 was the lowest in the First Division and a far cry from the 26,000 average of the championship season. One thing stood out in the Blackpool game and it was a little player with ginger hair called Alan Ball. He was everywhere and it came as no surprise when he became a great player.

I can still picture the dejected dressing room after that game. You feel you have let people down and you feel the disappointment of the whole crowd as you walk off and disappear into the tunnel. First game of the season at home and you want to win it. Elder and Morgan had played with injuries they had even before they began the game. After two games there was the feeling already that this was going to be another mediocre season.

Gloom is maybe too strong a word for the general air at Turf Moor in that early part of the season, but the club, sensing economic uncertainties, shelved all plans to build a new stand that would have seated 17,000 people. Things like that do filter down to players and we did talk about it. The reason given by Bob Lord was that this was a plan born before the maximum wage was abolished but now nothing would happen until there was greater financial stability. The club weren't happy about the shelved plans. As ever Lord got short shrift from shareholders at the AGM where the announcement was made, but one answer he gave to one questioner certainly had us players sitting up taking notice. When he was asked what was club policy on buying players, instead of saying we never buy players, he answered by saying that if they had to they would buy – but if we do buy we will do it carefully. With a declaration like that several of the players felt just slightly uneasy as their ears pricked up. A statement like that makes players feel the management might just think they're not good enough. On top of all that the club had lost money the previous season for the first time in years and gates were down. To be a club losing money meant one thing – further players would be sold to balance the books.

Alex Elder remained unhappy. He had shocked the club and fans by refusing the new terms he was offered, saying he wanted to get to a city club where he could earn more money. Lord was quite clear in his answer, saying that the club had stood by him while he had been out injured for four months on full pay. In all honesty most of us regarded him as the best left back in Britain.

My turn to argue with Lord for more money would come later. Elder's row with the club, though, was messy, involving appeals to the Football League. Lord seemed to be rowing with everybody. There was hell to pay when it became public that Sunderland wanted to approach Jimmy Adamson and interview him for their vacant managership. Rumours had even linked Harry Potts with the job. Lord told Sunderland that next time they came they could bring just eleven players and a trainer and their directors would never set foot in the ground. Adamson, at 35 and knowing that this would be his last season as a player – and an infrequent one at that – professed ignorance about the whole thing while Lord just went on ranting and raving at everybody and everything.

And me – I was dropped. Four points from six games. In a nutshell yours truly wasn't doing his job in the eyes of management. WANTED – A FORWARD WHO CAN SCORE said the newspaper headline after yet another defeat, this time 1-0 to Leeds United with me back in the team again. Leeds left the field wondering how they had won after we had plastered them. For me, it was the first meeting with the likes of Johnny Giles, Norman Hunter and Billy Bremner. Jack Charlton was missing from this game. But for all the reputations of the former, if there was anyone harder than Bobby Collins in the game then I have yet to meet them. It was he who took Leeds by the scruff of the neck when he first arrived and he was the foundation for all their play and competitiveness. There's a story that once when they were playing Manchester United, as they came down the tunnel, George Best suddenly felt a sharp pain at the back of his leg. He turned round to find Collins grinning at him. "And that's just for starters, Bestie," said Collins. "Wait till we get on the pitch." But Collins, who they bought from Everton, could take it as well as dish it out; he was irrepressible. In maybe the same game Nobby Stiles took Collins aside on the pitch after he had clattered into him and is said to have told him in no uncertain terms that every time he hit George, he, Stiles, would hit Collins even harder. Collins got up, dusted himself down, continued to harass Best and then scored the winning goal. You had to admire him and he appeared to be indestructible, but not quite. It was only an Italian jumping on his leg and shattering the bone during a European game that ended his career. Apparently even into his middle '50s in amateur games his opponents came off black and blue.

They were tasty games with Leeds, no quarter given and none asked. Mass brawls were commonplace. Revie produced teams which would stop at nothing to gain an advantage. They were mean, vicious and underhand. Collins was only 5ft 3ins. Thank God he wasn't another foot taller; at that height he was bad enough. Contrary to popular opinion Jack Charlton was a gentleman, hard but fair. The others I mention were just assassins: foot over the ball, raised studs, niggles, trips, shoves, pushes, insults – all part of the game in those days. Our own John Angus, Brian O'Neil, Andy Lochhead and Gordon Harris could certainly dish it out a bit but they were never "dirty" while Leeds brought a new dimension to gamesmanship and rough stuff. There's more physical contact in a convent than there is in football today. You just sneeze, the player next to you goes down and the referee blows his whistle.

Nearly the Record

Fourth from the bottom of the table in early November and we had a trip to charming Chelsea who certainly had their hard men in those days – Ron Harris and Eddie McCreadie tackled first and asked questions later. Andy Lochhead was flattened over and over again and when he came off he was black and blue all over. Adam Blacklaw was out cold for two minutes after a knee in the face, Willie Morgan was kneed in the back, I got a whack on the leg that was no accident, my boot was torn in half by one tackle and at one time two players were simultaneously laid out in our penalty area after being on the receiving end of Chelsea thumps. Trainer George Bray was on and off that field more times than in the whole season put together.

It was before this game that Bob Lord gave me the benefit of his wisdom on the way to London. As usual we travelled by train the day before and as we journeyed south I was in the gents when Bob Lord squeezed into the cubicle beside me. Now Bob Lord was not the smallest of men so how we both got in there I've never quite worked out. Anyway, he implored me to score – "Willie you can do it, do it for me" – and as we stood there he gave me several tips and hints about why he thought I wasn't quite firing on all cylinders. Believe it or not we won 1-0 and it was me who scored. I was deadly from three yards and a cross came over that several players missed. I didn't. Bang, in it went. Pick that out, Harris. On the journey home Lord again squeezed into the gents beside me. "Told you, Willie, didn't I, told you how to score and what you were doing wrong didn't I?" I would have touched my forelock and humbly bowed and scraped, but in a speeding, swaying train, in a cramped cubicle, with one hand holding the rail for support and the other hand holding my manhood aiming for the urinal, it was all I could do not to fall over in it.

The Irish press hammered us for losing against Switzerland in a World Cup qualifier but at the end of the month, even though we lost again in Scotland, there were two goals for me and terrific praise for the team as a whole. Malcolm Brodie was unstinting in his tribute. By now George Best was in the side and he ran them ragged in the first half. In the second he vanished. But Brodie sang our praises loud and clear – *Glory in defeat, entertaining, action packed, fighting qualities, magnificent defensive play, full blooded, competent, Billy Irvine opportunist supreme, striker and scorer of the two goals, his second from the Magill cross was one of the best seen at Hampden Park for years..."*

The first was courtesy of Georgie Boy. He cut in from the right and cracked in a great shot. At the last minute it clipped my head and screamed into the net. Was it a great header or fluke? Great header of course, what else am I going to say?

But, meanwhile, mother was fuming because I was seeing Rita the Burnley girl. She was letting me know in no uncertain terms what she thought of me maybe ending up marrying an English girl and thought I should be marrying Olive. I knew I was causing a real problem for her. It was a bit unsettling and alongside that I was having a bit of an up and down spell, mostly down I should say. I missed a few games because I'd been injured in the Scotland game and later I injured the wrist I had broken during the previous season but fortunately an X-ray showed it wasn't broken a second time.

Liverpool hammered us at home earlier in the month. Bill Shankly was their manager and it was interesting hearing stories about him. There are stories that he and Busby worked together to keep their players' wages down by paying the same. But after they beat us at home 5-1 it was as if the roof fell in on the club and town. It was the worst home defeat since 1942. People were talking about relegation and that this was the biggest crisis ever at the club and asking just where did we go from there. But maybe things clicked after that. After two defeats we won four on the trot with seven goals from me. In the Fulham home game I got a hat-trick. The next game two days later at Fulham it was me again who got the winner. I felt good, sharp, the injuries had cleared, the place was not so gloomy; we didn't think for a minute we would finish anywhere near the bottom. There was talk of me breaking Ray Pointer's post-war scoring record of 27 league goals if I kept up this rate. Sometimes I just felt I couldn't miss, couldn't stop scoring and I was so confident I thought every chance would go in. I started games just knowing I was going to score. In one of the four games we won, a young lad called Ralph Coates made his debut. We knew he was going to be a great player even though he was the funniest shape for a centre forward, very short and built like a barrel. Alex Elder would be staying as well. His differences with the club seemed to be sorted out. George Bray was now reserve team trainer. Jimmy Adamson was chief coach and I wondered if it would change him in any way because you can never tell how people are going to react when they move from player to coach or coach to manager. As a player he had always been good with me and had taught me a lot.

I really thought the scoring record was in the bag after two more goals against Blackburn Rovers at Ewood Park. There was only one thing better than beating Blackburn, and that was thoroughly beating them on their own ground. The history of Burnley v Blackburn competition and aggravation is long and pitted with controversy, confrontations, and supporter rivalry. There was the time when Burnley fans in a fit of pique set fire to one of the stands at Ewood. There was the time a Rovers fan paid for a plane to fly over Turf Moor with a less than complimentary message towed behind it. There was the dreadful penalty decision in a cup-tie at Burnley in the early '60s when Burnley were leading 3-0 and from it Blackburn went on to beat Burnley in the replay. And there was me scoring twice in the 4-1 win at Blackburn in '65. Nothing controversial about those goals – just sweet satisfaction and pleasure. It gave me 18 goals with 11 games left to score another ten. With luck and no injuries the record was perfectly possible. The 4-1 win was, as usual, a niggling, foul-ridden game where the ill temper and squaring up was non-stop. Things calmed down a little in the second half but the annoying thing was I could have had two more quite easily but missed two sitters, one of them from almost right under the crossbar. From this game onwards all thoughts of a bottom end of the table finish were banished. Burnley turned on the style and dominated everything. The journey back to Burnley from Blackburn is short; this one was short and sweet.

It's funny how some grounds seem to be good for Burnley. Leicester certainly was. The Clarets won a cup semi-final there, won a League game 6-2 around about the same time and rarely ever seemed to lose. This one was a game I remember because of probably the softest goal I ever scored. One of their defenders, with Andy Lochhead breathing down his neck, passed back to the goalkeeper. It stuck in the mud. What was I supposed to do? I thumped it in and said thank you very much, another one on the way to the possible record. Twenty goals scored, eight more needed in seven games. Ralph Coates scored his first ever goal at Leicester in the 2-0 win, and all of us knew that here was a player destined to go on to do great things. I can remember little Ralphy making some great runs in this game and being unlucky not to score more than one. He would be transferred years later for a record sum to Tottenham Hotspur. What a mudbath it was, though. Modern players should watch old films of what we had to play on. How lucky they are now to play on grassy pitches that stay green all year. A muddy pitch and a heavy ball in those days made twenty-five-yard screamers a rarity so most of my goals were headers or from inside the six-yard box. Today the lighter ball dips and swerves, sometimes as much as a beach ball in the wind on Blackpool sands. We argue long and hard about how today's players would cope 40 years ago in our conditions. The arguments rage similarly about how us old timers would cope today. We would cope fine; they would struggle.

Any hopes I had of bettering Ray Pointer's record slowly faded with games missed through injury and then a fairly lean spell before two more goals came in the last two games of the season. Ironically, for the second time an injury came in an international game, this one in a game against Wales. By the time the last two games of the season arrived there was no chance at all of the record. The penultimate game against Stoke was notable only for the one goal I scored which won the game 1-0. Jimmy Mac was back again at Turf Moor and was unrecognisable as the player who had teased and tormented us in the game the day before at Stoke when Stoke won 2-0.

The final game against Chelsea was at home and Andy Lochhead scored five and not for the first time either. We have argued good-humouredly for years that one of his five was actually scored by me. Seven against Tottenham the season before in the final game and now six against another London team to end the season and a final position of 12th. Looked at from any angle it was an ordinary, average season but for me there was a total of 25 goals in League and Cup.

There was a two months' break to look forward to and some time in the clean air of Carrickfergus. The problem remained though of my mother's dislike of the idea of me marrying an English girl.

CHAPTER EIGHT

JOAN

As I'm writing this book I continue to be dogged by the questions that float through my mind about my past. Tommy Reid did call to say he hadn't as yet been round to see my sister Joan in Carrickfergus. He was full of apologies and explained he had spent some time in hospital, and was now confined to the house for the time being. I'd been telling myself I wasn't too bothered about finding out anything else but really it was an excuse not to make the effort. I've lived for all these years quite happily knowing what I know and never really questioning it, but when he told me that, I felt a sense of disappointment and I knew then that I needed to know more. He told me I should ring her, let bygones be bygones, make the call, make the contact, speak to her. That, plus this growing sense of curiosity made the decision for me. OK, I would ring her. But it took a while to do it. How easy it sounds to pick up a telephone and make a call. Pick it up, dial the number, wait for the ringing tone, and then speak when you hear the voice at the other end. And then you start to think. What if she doesn't answer, what if she does answer and then hangs up, what if she is angry and blasts me with some kind of tirade that has been building up for years?

But what if she has been thinking the same things as me; wants to call me but won't, can't summon the courage to dial the number. What if, what if... How many more times would those words go round my head. She's 75 and I decided this couldn't be put off; it had to be done.

After two or three days of this indecision I picked up the phone, dialled, heard the tone, and waited for what seemed an age. The phone was picked up at the other end. "Joan, this is Billy," I said and waited. She did not hang up and I knew straight away that things would be fine. I told her everything that Jean had said to me from Canada, told her what I was doing now with this book. When I had finished speaking I felt drained, spent, and then, as she spoke to me, as I listened I just felt more and more tired and surprised. She spoke for what seemed an age and I listened with my eyes closed to what she said.

"I've such a lot to tell you, Billy," she said with kindness in her voice. "But I'm glad you called. Our mother Agnes was an amazing woman, hard with us but very fair. Life taught her to be hard, but underneath that hardness was a devotion to us and a determination to bring us up and feed us as best she could. And she did. And she did a fine job bearing in mind the merry dance you led her most of the time. You were always in trouble. There was the time the landlady came round to the house to ask where you were. 'Tucked up in bed,' she said, thinking that's where you were. 'Oh no they're not,' said the landlady, 'they're in my orchard pinching my fruit.' Then there was the time you came in from somewhere with your shoes all ruined and your breeches covered in mud. She took one look and reached for the strap and you ran off with her chasing you down the street. Then someone stopped her and said, 'And what's that strap for?' So she said, 'to teach that Billy Irvine a lesson.' 'Well not with a strap,' the stranger said and took it off her, and that was the last time she ever used a strap. She never got it back.

"The Irvines were always in trouble and always got the blame for everything in the village, and that was long before you were even born. We all used to meet and gossip by the water pump across the road from the house. There'd be the Bowens from the top end of the road, then the Hanleys, from the middle, the McMurteys were from near the bottom end and we were from the very bottom. And even in 1939 we got the blame for things. Everyone is waiting to use the pump and Mother puts down her bucket. Up comes Mr Acheson, a real busybody, and asks have we heard the terrible news, the terrible news that the war has started? And quick as a flash mother replies, 'Ah and it is terrible indeed and it's certain that the Irvines will get the blame for that as well.'

"But look how well we all did, those of us who were in the army and you and Bobby, international footballers. I'll not forget the pride in her face and eyes, the day you and Bobby played together for Northern Ireland for the very first time. I thought she would burst.

"She was born Agnes Quinn in 1896 or '98, I'm not certain, in Belfast, one of a large family. I can't say how many there were in

Willie Irvine

the family as I'm not sure but I do know that there were several of them. They were poor, and scrimped and scraped to make ends meet, and as soon as she was old enough she was packed off to go into service. I think she worked in one of the big houses somewhere, don't ask me where, but she started at the bottom, working all hours on the dirtiest jobs, cleaning grates, laying fires, emptying commodes; general dogsbody. Up at five in the morning and lucky if she was in bed before ten. It was soul-destroying work. But she stuck at it, she had to, and what money she earned was sent back home to her parents. It was probably there that she learned the meaning of hard work and fortitude. She was able to visit home just once a week on her one day off. Her room was shared with other girls in the attic of the house where she worked. She froze in winter and washed in cold water and had little more than the clothes she worked in. At least she was fed regularly in the kitchens down below and then spent hours scrubbing and cleaning pans. She was the lowest of the low in that house but she was a survivor.

"When she was old enough she volunteered to be a nurse in the Dardanelles during World War One. Maybe that would put her birth date in '96. The Dardanelles was one of the big campaigns against the Turks. She must only have been 18 years old. The whole thing was a fiasco with the troops more or less pinned down for nearly a year on the beaches and in their trenches. Hundreds of them were killed and injured as they tried to cross the minefields. Everything had to be brought in by sea and landed at night. The hospitals were full of wounded men and hundreds of cases of dysentery and later in the year 15,000 cases of frostbite. The conditions were even worse than in France. Out of all the deaths something like 145,000 were due not to fighting but to sickness. It was horrific. And there was Mother doing what she could and not much more than 18 at the oldest. It's a miracle she survived all the sickness.

"She always maintained she had brothers who were killed in World War One. Over time that became jumbled and hazy and that's why somehow you thought you had four of your own brothers killed in World War Two. No, they were her brothers, your uncles, and she said they were killed at the Somme. They were in the Royal Inniskilling Fusiliers and I seem to think there were four of them but we're not sure. That was in 1916. Whole families of young men were wiped out; whole streets had their menfolk massacred in that stupid

battle. Most of those men literally walked to their deaths, ordered to advance by foolish old men sitting behind their desks a hundred miles away. It was cruel, relentless and shocking, and it went on for months. There were 60,000 casualties on the first day alone. Those men didn't have a prayer and I can't imagine the suffering they went through.

"One of them was your father. You've never known until this day that he joined up to fight in World War One when he must have been about 17 years old and somehow he survived the trenches and the bullets. Lots of young lads joined up underage and nobody asked questions. He survived because he was wounded in the arm, came home and had a metal plate inserted. You told me you've always thought he was killed in an accident in the blackout of World War Two when he came off the back of a motorbike. Well, he did have an accident but died a few years after that in 1944. I suppose you could say it was the blackout that killed him because it was that caused the accident and the head injury and all the terrible headaches he had afterwards.

"They called it 'going over the top' in World War One when the troops climbed up out of the trenches and advanced. A whistle blew, they climbed up the ladders and were just mown down as they moved forward; it's as simple as that. There was always heavy bombardment of the German lines before they got the signal but that was largely a waste of time because the German trenches were dug so deep. What chance did they have against the lines of machine guns that opened up on them?

"How true it is I don't know, but Agnes always used to say that her family received the news of her brothers' deaths on Christmas Day. I think she used to tell me that Lily, one of her early daughters, also died on a Christmas Day. So it's easy to see how it all got hazy and jumbled up over the years and became the story that Lily was buried on the same day that she got the news that her brothers had died.

"Your mother said they used to send the troops parcels full of chocolate and fruit, dry socks and gloves. It was dry socks they were desperate for. They lived in mud and water, covered in lice and plagued with rats. I shiver just to think about it.

"So it was not your brothers, Billy, it was uncles who were killed in World War One. You never met them, never knew them, they died

long before you were born, but they were your mother's kin so they are ours as well and we should remember and be proud of them."

She stopped and there was a pause of several seconds. She had spoken for several minutes and I could sense she was tired and wanted to stop even though there was probably more to tell. The conversation resumed when I began to talk about my own sons and grandchildren. "Your sons are fine boys," she told me every now and then as I told her about them. "Stephen, Jonathan, Darren... they're fine boys. You can be a proud man, Billy...and proud of yourself. You've done all right, Billy. In truth there is more to tell you but I'm tired now and I'll be glad to talk again and tell you more whenever you want."

I sat back, head spinning just a little, and mulled over all that she had said. There was nothing to shock me, nothing that was hurtful, but nevertheless there was so much to digest and take in. "More than sixty years old," I thought, "and known none of this till now." I thought of my mother for a while; the struggles, the sacrifices she made and a part of me regrets now that I never bothered to talk more to her about her own life and family. So much I could have asked her about, so much she could have shared with me. Too late now, far too late.

The following day, not for the first time, as I left the house and stepped out into the early morning dampness and drizzle, I mused wistfully on the fact that here I was, still having to work for a living. The memory of that Everton tackle which broke my leg remains with me. On days such as this the leg aches badly. My hips aren't too good either. On days such as this the last thing I want to do is leave the warmth of the house. Sometimes I do feel bitter and angry about the premature end to my career. I ought to have been playing well into my thirties, still scoring goals with panache and ease. Yes, there are days of resentment, and the day after the long talk with Joan was one of them.

CHAPTER NINE

ON THE WAY TO THE RECORD

At the beginning of season 1965/66 in Burnley you could buy a detached three-bedroomed house for £3,775, a three-bedroomed bungalow for £3,435, or a three-bedroomed semi-detached house for £2,415. A two-bedroomed bungalow at Ridge Avenue would have set you back just £1,750.

At Jackson and Hanson's garage at Barrowford you could buy a used *de luxe* Ford Anglia for £495 or a Zodiac for £750.

At Safeway's supermarket the special price of just one shilling applied to tins of beans, peas, apricots, packets of biscuits, tea and tins of dog food. You could buy a cabbage for 3d. A 5lb bag of washed potatoes was just one shilling and three pence; that's not quite 8p in today's money.

At the new Crazi Cutz shop on Accrington Road three pairs of nylon stockings were just seven shillings (35p), a man could buy a quality striped shirt for just under twelve shillings (60p) and a bottle of tomato sauce was a mere one shilling and twopence (6p).

In August 1965 the *Burnley Express* reported that the town was cut off from the rest of the world for 30 seconds as the town's 6,300 telephones and telex machines went silent in the switch-over to direct STD contact with Britain's 943 other telephone exchanges. The switch-over was not without its glitches.

A retired Burnley businessman while having a quiet afternoon watching TV, spent the afternoon answering more than 30 callers who thought he was their new bookie. The population of Burnley was asked not to make any phone calls at all between 12.55pm and 1.05pm on August 17th, which was a bit of bad luck if you really did need to ring your bookie with a certain winner.

At Turf Moor, season ticket prices ranged from £9 for the best Bob Lord Stand seats, to £3 3s. to stand. A juvenile could watch a full season's football for just £1 10s. It was cheaper for women to watch in any of the areas of the ground. These were still the days of gender inequality but as far as Turf Moor was concerned it worked to the female advantage.

The *Burnley Express* jobs page for August 14th, 1965 advertised for a whole range of workers at the Lucas factory and Mullards. Lilford Weavers at Veevers Mill, Brierfield, wanted loom weavers, sweepers and loom overlookers. Presumably these must have been the last twitchings of the once great cotton industry.

On TV BBC *Grandstand* showed real sport and not just the left-overs from Sky as it does today.

Wayne Fontana and The Mindbenders were appearing at the Imperial Ballroom, Nelson; The Animals were at the Astoria, Rawtenstall. Alan Whicker was judging "Rimmels" Miss UK '65 at The Locarno. Kathy Kirby was the star attraction at the Joseph Lucas Star Cabaret Dance. The big films were *Major Dundee* with Charlton Heston, *Genghis Kahn* with Stephen Boyd, and *Hercules Against The Moon Men. Carry on Cleo* was showing at the Empress.

And at the beginning of 1965/66 Burnley FC had put together a team that midway through the season many would think was just as good as the great championship side of '59/60. It was a mixture of the old and the new. From the "old" there still remained Adam Blacklaw, Brian Miller, John Angus, Ray Pointer, Gordon Harris and Alex Elder. The latter, however, was still only 24. Added to these names were the "young 'uns"; Harry Thomson, Willie Morgan, Ralph Coates, Brian O'Neil, Andy Lochhead, Arthur Bellamy, Sammy Todd, Les Latcham and yours truly.

We were hungry, eager and raring to go. The new captain was a trim Alex Elder who had shed 7lbs. In my own case I had seen in the previous season how close I had been to setting a new scoring record. I wanted to do it badly and couldn't wait to try again. There was optimism and confidence and there were forecasts of a top six finish. We felt that the transitional period of the last two seasons was over. In Harry Potts we had a manager we all loved. In Jimmy Adamson, we had a coach who knew what he wanted and how he wanted us to play. But there was also a realisation that fans and supporters wanted a return to the good times and that expectations and demands were high. With a settled team we were up for it, we were buoyant and had a spring in our step.

You'll forgive me if I dwell on this season and bask in its glory. By the end of it, yes, I did set a new record but it was a peak I would never reach again. I was only 23 by the end of the season; ten more great years should have followed but it would never happen.

We began with a 1-1 draw at Chelsea. Arthur Bellamy scored. An away point you don't consider to be too bad but it was the next game at home to Blackpool where we displayed all the skills and excitement that would characterise the rest of the season. It was a sparkling curtain-raiser for the new season, said the local paper, with some deadly finishing and a first half where we romped home in rampant, unplayable fashion. There was the first goal of the season for me, and another two from Bellamy and Lochhead. I can remember the pouring rain before the game but it stopped by the time we started. The wet surface helped our slick and accurate passing; we shot on sight and could have had six.

Up against that big Scotsman Ian Ure in the next home game, I came off decidedly worse. It took him only 37 minutes to lay me out in the penalty area with a tackle so high he would have still got me if I'd been on stilts. To say that the tackling from Arsenal in this game was X-certificate stuff would be the understatement of the year. Let's just say it was a game typical of the era. You dished out the clog and you took it. The one good thing about the mud we played in then was that when you were kicked six feet up in the air, at least you had something soft to land on.

I lasted until half-time and then limped off, the bruising on my upper thigh from Ure's attempted decapitation looking like a modern art painting. Two goals up by half-time, me unable to continue, substitute little Ian Towers dwarfed by the 9ft tall Ure, continually thwacked and upended by crude Arsenal martial-arts tackles, without any protection from the referee, Arsenal took control, allowing the couple of footballers they had, Joe Baker and George Eastham, to assert their influence and equalize.

Two goals for me in the next game, the return Blackpool fixture at Bloomfield Road. Funny how things seem to go; eight of our nine goals had come in the first half of the games we had played so far. Again there was another brilliant first half performance and we ran them dizzy. Willie Morgan was in mesmerising form; the press described us as slick, speedy and reminiscent of the side of '62, sparkling like vintage claret. Four games gone, early days, but we were top of the division. You have no idea how good that looks and feels, even though it was so early. You come in the next day for training and feel on top of the world. Confidence grows, you know that at the very least you can stay with the leaders, you know that at your best you can match anyone; you can't wait for the next game.

And you lose it 1-0 at Everton. Down to earth, lesson learned.

But it was back to business in the next game at home to Northampton and how we didn't score ten in this game will remain a mystery forever. The final score of 4-1 was hard to believe. First Harvey in the Northampton goal had one of those games where he made save after save, and even when he was beaten, his defenders three times cleared shots off the line. At half-time even our own goalkeeper Harry Thomson joined in the applause for Harvey. Willie Morgan was again outstanding, teasing and tormenting the Northampton defenders at will. None of us could believe the half-time score was only 1-0 and it wasn't until the last ten minutes that the scoreline assumed some semblance of reality. By the end of the game I had a hat-trick and it was no less than we deserved.

The Northampton win was the first of three consecutive victories, the next one being at home again to Manchester United. They came as champions with a forward line, including John Connelly, that had cost nearly £400,000. They left looking like they would win nothing. Were we good or were United bad? We were good; it's as simple as that. 30,000 saw us win 3-0; we were fitter, more determined and afterwards, back in the dressing room, we were buzzing with the sense of achievement. And this was against a side that included the likes of Crerand, Law, Charlton and Best. The third of the three consecutive wins was the return fixture at Northampton. There was another goal for me and then a thunderous volley from Alex Elder that nearly broke the net. This was another game we should have won by several goals. We hit the crossbar, the post, we missed sitters. Elder's goal came only four minutes from the end but the star of the game was the dynamic Brian O'Neil. In this game he was magnificent, ruthlessly determined, a destroyer of other teams but at the same time able to create things and drive the team forward with his energy and passes. He was laid out twice, once by a kick to the stomach, which left him with huge bruises. We were convinced it must be a stretcher job but up he got after treatment and then in another incident the shirt was nearly ripped from his back by one of the Northampton gorillas – for that is how they seemed to play the game at times. We came off the field on top of the world. Here was a collection of players that ran and fought for each other and brought the best out in each other. The words "team spirit" can be bandied about far too often, but this team of '65/66 had it in abundance. We covered each other's mistakes, we encouraged each other and were beginning to think: this is it; this team can do something.

As for me personally I had just got engaged to Rita Berry and Mother back home in Carrick was not pleased. My goals were making me a star; sure I was a good-looking lad, people sat up and took notice, and onlookers and autograph hunters would inevitably interrupt a meal out in a restaurant. I would be stopped in the street, people shouted and called out, and there were interviews and features. Fame had arrived. A feature in the local newspaper said if I lacked anything it was not confidence. In other words I was a cocky so-and-so and full of myself. Unlike Andy Lochhead who gave opponents a hard time and let them know he was around with his sheer physical presence and muscle, I was lippy and wound players up with cheek and brashness. The day was coming ever closer, however, that it would cost me dear.

I recently came across a page from an old *Burnley Express*, September 22nd, 1965. There's me and Rita, faces beaming, she's a head wages clerk, says the caption. Many of my goals are headers, it says, because of a natural aptitude and hours of practice when I was teenager. Apparently I preferred hard hit crosses from the right and, full of the brazenness of youth, I thought I could break Ray Pointer's post-war scoring record. In those days Andy Lochhead and I were a pair off the field as well as on it – favourite pastime; snooker. Then when I pulled on the green shirt of Ireland I was like a madman and would stop at nothing to score, willing to run forever and through a brick wall if necessary.

We lost at Newcastle and the run of three wins was ended but the story behind the game was that it was, to put it mildly, adults only. It was a demonstration of how hard the game could be in the '60s, of how bruising and physical it could be. There used to be an instruction to full-backs then "to show the winger the touchline". It was a polite way of saying, "kick him into the stands". After the Newcastle game, which we lost 3-2, Bob Lord stormed away from the ground saying Newcastle were the roughest team Burnley had ever played against. Their tactics would win them nothing, he raged. They should be playing in a menagerie and next time Burnley visited them he would take a team of elephants. The rough stuff had Harry Potts asking what football was coming to if we had to contend with this? The Newcastle manager claimed his own player Jim Iley was injured by a Burnley tackle but this was nonsense. Iley hurt himself attempting to "show Willie Morgan the touchline", or rather the back row of the main stand.

On the coach home we looked at ourselves and grimaced. Gordon Harris was covered from head to toe in bruises. I had a black eye and a broken nose and looked like I had done 15 rounds with Rocky Marciano. There was a general assortment of ankle, knee and calf injuries. The dressing room looked like an ambulance station. Harris and John Talbut had to be helped to walk to the coach. Newcastle were sickeningly vicious; our players were flattened and chopped and whacked systematically. Harris was brought down with a tackle nearer his head than his waist. I was knocked clean out twice. The referee was weak and ineffective. If you have been brought up on modern football, watching the game today and seeing the referee blow the whistle for the slightest contact, you can have no idea what it was like 40 years ago. For the record Andy Lochhead scored both our goals. In a game like this, Andy was in his element. He was never deliberately "dirty" but he could give as good as he got.

The high feelings caused by this battle lasted for a long time. Burnley's board of directors mulled over whether to send pictures of the bruised players to the Football League and ask for their observations and comments. Harry Potts insisted that the pictures be published so that the public could see the graphic details of the injuries sustained. Former head trainer Ray Bennion said that he had never seen a collection of bruises on one player like those on Gordon Harris in over 40 years. "He is black and blue," said Harry, "with stud marks from his legs to his shoulders." And as for me, my face was so bad I had to see a specialist to put it straight again. I look in the mirror today and I think, "hmmm, Newcastle, September 18th, 1965".

If that Newcastle game did one thing, it showed that Gordon Harris was indestructible. He was explosive, had a real temper, was hard as nails, blunt as a shovel and as a result had more than his fair share of brushes with officialdom. If he didn't like something, he said so. He didn't like playing outside left, so he asked for a transfer. Moving to inside forward saw the best of him and his partnership with Brian O'Neil was superb. He didn't like being called the new McIlroy; he didn't like being a marked man with referees. But off the field you couldn't meet a nicer chap. Gordon Harris played just one game for England. Had he been at a "glamour" club I'm sure he would have played more.

Jimmy Adamson, meanwhile, sang our praises, saying we were potentially better than the '62 team. We had skill, aggression, courage and determination. "They're going places," he said. His coaching was respected by all of us. But respect Adamson though I did for his coaching, he was a hard man to love. There would one day be a major row between us. Harry Potts was loved by all of us. At that point in time they made a real team.

And in the next game, a win at home to West Brom took us top again. The month ended with four wins in three weeks, 14 points out of 20 and in those days it was just two points for a win. In full flow there wasn't a weakness in the side, Brian O'Neil was seen more and more as the best half-back at Turf Moor since the war. Our 4-2-4 system with O'Neil and Harris as the middle two was almost unstoppable at times. On song those two were a sight to behold, searching, probing and running, passing, controlling and hard as nails to boot. Then on top of that there was Andy Lochhead scoring goals in the games that I didn't. Our partnership was becoming the talk of football. Elder at full-back was playing the best football of his life. On his day he was world class. Willie Morgan was a magician. The camaraderie and spirit: you could have put it in a bottle.

If there was one problem, however, it was a lack of consistency. Of course there were games we lost, sadly at Blackburn by 4-1. It knocked the stuffing out of us and brought us back down to earth. Mike England and I renewed our sparring. One of the happiest days in any Burnley supporter's life was the game when Lochhead left England in a largely unconscious heap in the penalty area while Andy trotted back to the centre circle as if nothing had happened. But then came a run of ten games where we only lost once and ten goals came my way.

It was in this period that more and more attention came Brian O'Neil's way and there was talk of a World Cup squad place. That's how good he was. He was the equivalent of Nobby Stiles at Manchester United or Dave Mackay at Tottenham. If there is such a thing as perpetual motion, he was it. His energy was boundless, his skill unending; the ground he covered in a game just astonishing and this was where he scored over Stiles and Mackay. Only Billy Bremner at Leeds was perhaps his equal. He was certainly twice the player Stiles ever was and yet Stiles took the World Cup place. Perhaps Stiles was seen as a better out-and-out hatchet man. Brian was more than that. His trademark was the way he always pulled his sleeves down over his hands: that plus being covered in mud. As a lad he was a Newcastle United fanatic and modelled himself on the great and legendary hard man Jimmy Scoular. He modelled himself well.

Willie Morgan, meanwhile, now had his own official fan club. It must have been official because it actually had real live secretaries and applications for membership. Linda and Liz, the two secretaries, claimed to have more than 30 members. For four shillings members got a card, two signed photos of Willie, an information sheet and a newsletter which told them all his likes and dislikes, what he did before and after a game and even his car registration number. We used to pull his leg mercilessly about it and tell him if it had more than 30 members he must have joined it himself at least a dozen times. Brian O'Neil was an honorary member. He had to be honorary, because he refused to pay. Willie was a wonderful ball player and could dribble in his sleep. He was individual, unique and there was nobody quite like him other than George Best. Eventually his fan club had 200 members all over Britain. His philosophy was simple. He said it was his job to get to the byline to get crosses over. If there were three men in between him and the byline then he had to get round them to do his job. Even at an early age his passion was golf, and in one book it is claimed, perhaps a little tongue in cheek, that it was during his Sunday morning rounds of golf with Matt Busby when he was a Manchester United player that all the big decisions at Old Trafford were made.

By the time we had played Sheffield United towards the back end of October we were in third place and had won seven of the last nine games, one of which was a League Cup game. Two of the wins were against top of the table teams. The national press praised us to the skies. At Sheffield there was just one criticism from one national – that we didn't score six. Little Ralph Coates was beginning to make people sit up and take notice. I say "little" with some reservation. He might have been on the short side but certainly made up for that in other areas.

And then came Leeds at Elland Road. As ever, this was the usual rough, hard, tough game, against the likes of Hunter, Reaney and Bremner. But even referee Kevin Howley joined in the applause at the end, and though it finished as a 1-1 draw it was described as one of the best games ever; a fantastic, tremendous, end-to-end game, as exciting as you could wish to see. This was probably the game where Don Revie decided that Willie Morgan was the best thing since sliced bread and he had to have him at Elland Road. Willie never got there, eventually going to Manchester United. Bob Lord didn't like either club but when Willie was eventually sold, Old Trafford was seen as the lesser of two evils. After the Leeds game the press were ecstatic about him, likening him to Stanley Matthews at his best, inviting tackles like a matador entices the bull to come in close before despatching him. Andy Lochhead was missing from this game and Jack Charlton probably breathed a sigh of relief. Nobody liked to play against Andy, but for this game he was dropped for being a naughty boy in training during the week.

These days, teams jet off to La Manga for team bonding but in our day it wasn't quite so sophisticated. We went to the Norbreck Castle Hotel at Blackpool. The most expensive thing we did as a team was a jog on the beach. One night we were there, all of us headed into town in the evening to the bars and pubs. Some of us came back in the early hours of the morning well and truly plastered. Well, let's face it, without the wives to keep us in check, it was too good a chance to pass up. Once back in the hotel we behaved less than properly and a few pranks took place up and down the corridors. (The Norbreck manager must have been fed up to the back teeth of footballers: on a similar training break involving a Manchester United goalkeeper the hotel ended up with a door kicked down.) Eventually all this ended up with Andy being locked out of his bedroom with very little on, in fact he might well have been starkers. The other guests woken up by all the commotion came out of their rooms to see what was going on and our bad behaviour was reported to the hotel manager. The following morning Harry Potts got us all together and demanded to know who the culprit was,

Rita and Willie at Carbis Bay.

Against Arsenal at Highbury.

The first photo of Willie after he joined Preston North End (Howard Talbot).

Willie kicking in before his first match for Preston (Howard Talbot).

Lining up for Preston. Willie is second from left on back row. Front row third from right is a young Archie Gemmill.

Early marketing. Willie's signed photograph when with Brighton.

Brighton and Hove Albion (1971/72) (left to right) (back row) Ian Goodwin, Willie Irvine, Steve Piper, Terry Stanley, Stewart Henderson, Brian Powney, Alan Dovey, Alan Boorn, Peter O'Sullivan, John Templeman, Alex Sheridan, Kit Napier. (middle row) Glen Wilson (trainer), Norman Gall, Eddie Spearritt, John Napier (capt), Pat Saward (manager), Dave Turner, Alan Duffy, Bert Murray, Mike Yaxley (coach). (front row) Ricky Sopp, Kevin Worsfold, Stephen Barrett, Julio Grato, Tony Paris, Tony Towner, Mark Douglas, Billy Wylie, John Rodkin.

Leaping like a salmon, but foiled by Plymouth's Jim Furnell.

out in the corridors without any clothes. Andy owned up, was fined £100 and dropped into the reserves for one game. Andy still laughs about it, and claims he got more grief from his wife Carole than he ever did from Harry. Footballers out on the town... what goes on today certainly went on 40 years ago I can tell you. The only difference is, it didn't make the newspapers.

It was only by accident that Andy arrived at Burnley. A prolific scorer in his younger days, he would have almost certainly signed for Sunderland but for injuring himself in a practice match and being sent home. Burnley's scout Jimmy Stein saw the next game he played for Renfrew and invited him to Turf Moor. What a player he was, and it's thanks to him taking a lot of the attention away from me that I scored so many goals. Just sometimes two characters come together who dovetail perfectly – Giles and Bremner, Bruce and Pallister, McIlroy and Adamson, Morecambe and Wise, Ant and Dec – Andy Lochhead and me. We still work together today on matchdays at the club and do our double routine in clubs and pubs around Burnley. What do they say – old footballers never die, they just find ways to relive their glory days.

I remember the game at Leeds for two other reasons. Firstly my attempt to con the referee to avoid a booking failed miserably. I'd reacted to little Bobby Collins launching himself feet first, horizontally, kung fu style towards my midriff. I leapt up and flattened somebody, probably Collins though I don't remember clearly.

"Please ref," I implored him. "I've never been booked before, I want to go through my career without a booking, I want to be able to tell my grandchildren I was never booked... this will be my first ever booking..."

The referee looked at me and grinned. "You bloody scoundrel," he said, "I think you're forgetting one thing... it was me who booked you last year."

The second reason was my goal. It was a peach. Leeds went ahead but straight from the kick-off Willie Morgan advanced to the byline, beat Willie Bell for the hundredth time, and I got on the end of the cross and headed it quite tamely towards the goal. Gary Sprake bent to collect this most mediocre of headers, legs apart, and let the ball go through his legs. On his day he could be superb, but throughout his career Sprake was prone to dropping some awful clangers. "Thank you very much," I said and notched up one more goal on the way to the record.

Burnley 3 West Ham 1, back to the top of Division One, Lochhead and me having scored 23 of our 36 goals this season so far. Poor game though and we played badly. We were described by one paper as a £1,500 shoestring team, which in truth is what we were. The only highlight was the superb individual goal scored by Irvine (the *Sunday Mirror's* words, not mine). Did you know my eye for an opening was lethal? (*The Daily Mail's* words, not mine.)

If there comes one game in a season when a performance is so sublime as to be indescribable, it was perhaps at Sunderland on November 13th. "The people of Burnley should be over the moon with delight," said Keith McNee after the game. Keith was so fanatical about Burnley FC that it was many years later during the Orient game that he had a heart attack. He died shortly afterwards.

The Sunderland display was fabulous he said, adding that this was a team better than that which won the 1960 championship. At Roker Park that day we were a team without a weakness, strong in every position, and could have been five ahead by half-time. O'Neil, Coates and Morgan were supreme with Harris not far behind. My goal came when the Sunderland players were so mesmerised and confused by the bewildering attacking play that I was left so unmarked it was untrue. Their defenders literally didn't know which way to turn – until turn they did and saw me firing the ball in without one of them in sight. They must have been dizzy that day.

It was a game in which yet more talented reserve players came in, Dave Merrington and Mick Buxton, and played like they had been there all season. It was a team that cost nothing except for £110 signing-on fees, an incredible tribute to the youth policy. The national press waxed lyrical about brilliant man-to-man passing demoralising and tearing Sunderland to ribbons. This was near perfection.

If we were not champions that season, the reason came just days later, not in a League game but in a League Cup game where lowly Peterborough beat us 4-0. If one word gave the reason, then the word would be "inconsistency": brilliant one game, poor the next. This was a quarter-final and winning the cup would have ensured a place in Europe. That would come anyway but at the time we were not to know that. None of us could say we had a decent game and their win was no fluke. It hurt, especially the critical reports the following day. Peterborough were then in their infancy as a club and loved for being giant-killers. Against us they had little to beat that night. And yet three days later we clouted Aston Villa 3-1 with two goals from Andy and one from me – explain that. Football; just so unpredictable – and that unpredictability would cost us dear by the end of the season.

It wasn't until early December that the press pointed out that Ray Pointer's record could well be broken. Not only that but his record of scoring in eight consecutive games was in danger of going as well. With another goal in a 1-1 draw against Tottenham, if I could score in the next two I would equal that record.

For the seventh consecutive game I scored; this time three more against Fulham at Craven Cottage. Alf Ramsey was there to see another wonderful display, particularly from Harris and O'Neil. The latter scored with a thirty-yard rocket shot. Willie Morgan again spent the game going past defenders like they weren't there. The legendary Johnny Haynes was a spectator for most of the game.

There was no one more dejected than me though in the dressing room after the next game. It was another win this time by 4-2, but I didn't score. When the game began I needed just one more goal to equal the record. Alex Elder took the penalty that would have given me that chance. Alex had a difficult decision but he made the right one. As captain it was up to him to decide who should take it. At the moment he had to make that choice we were losing 2-1. The penalty area was a mass of mud, you couldn't even see the penalty spot, and the goalkeeper was Gordon Banks. This was no time for anyone to miss. He took it. He said afterwards that even up until the last moment he debated whether to let me take it. It was a captain's decision. He scored.

Twenty-one games played, the air of confidence and optimism was enormous. We had twice as many points as the previous season at the same stage, and had taken more points than the championship team of 1960. The team was a marvellous mixture of the young and the old, and even the "old" were not even 30 except for good old John Angus who we all kidded was at least 40. We were up alongside Liverpool, Leeds and Manchester United; already we looked at the games against Liverpool and Leeds at the end of the season as deciding games. Christmas was just a couple of days away – on Boxing Day we would thrash Stoke City and my brother Bobby 4-1. My goal was a stunning thirty-yarder. Jimmy Mac didn't play in the Stoke side owing to injury.

If you were a Burnley footballer Christmas was wonderful that year. Not so good if you were a Burnley miner though with the news that five local pits appeared to be doomed. It was only in October that the area's 3,000 miners were praised for showing the way in the battle for increased production. Bank Hall, the biggest pit, employed nearly 1,000 workers. Hapton Valley had recently set a new record for production in one week. But now only Hapton Valley and Thorny Bank were to be classed as continuing collieries. Bank Hall was now classed as having a doubtful future. Some pits might continue for another two to three years; for others it was a matter of months. It was the old story. Pits that had ample reserves were described as not being worked economically. Men would not be made redundant but moved to other pits as the need arose.

"But where do we go when the last pit closes?" was the loud, frequent and obvious question. Bank Hall, Fir Trees, Thorny Bank, Hapton Valley, Huncoat Hill, Hill Top, Old Meadows and Deerplay were names with a long and proud history. Along with the town's cotton mills, today they are no more.

CHAPTER TEN

GEORGE BEST AND ME, AND A NEW RECORD

There are inevitable questions whenever I take a group round the ground. It was one of the proudest moments of my life when the club asked me to return and become a matchday host. It was perhaps the final piece of the jigsaw of my life that somehow I managed to put back together after the difficult years. And as that record-breaking season took its course, it simply took me ever closer to the day and the one incident that would hurt me, change me and alter my life.

Someone will always ask, "Did you know or play alongside George Best?" Someone else will ask if there was just one magic moment out of all the many I experienced that is still vividly present in my mind. I love both these questions and have probably been asked them a dozen times or more. The answer to both questions is ready. "Yes, I did know George Best and yes, that one moment is Northern Ireland 3 Scotland 2, October 2nd, 1965."

George and I played in that game. We were about the same age, coming up together, roomed together, and maybe I can claim to be the first person he ever slept with. Jimmy McIlroy, at the ripe old age of 34, played in that game and Danny Blanchflower said he was the best player on the field. Georgie had a great game as well, running the Scots ragged with some of his footwork. You never knew what to expect with him, whether he'd keep the ball and try to beat every man on the pitch or just sometimes take you by surprise and actually pass to you. There were some games when I thought I might

125

as well take a seat on the touchline and just wait for him to finish what he was doing. Mac and Bestie more or less ran the game in the second half, the crowd roared, there seemed to be green shirts everywhere and we pushed that ball round like it belonged to us. And then in the last moments came what every player dreams of – scoring the winner. With the score at 2-2 the ball came over and with an overhead kick I got the goal. The ground, the players, everyone went mad. Don't forget in those days the Home Internationals meant something, the rivalry was intense. And Scotland had some great players then – Jim Baxter, Denis Law, Dave Mackay, Willie Henderson... Did I get the man of the match award? I think I did but if I didn't I should have. If I could put one moment into a box and carry it round with me forever that would be it, maybe.

Something else I won't forget, and neither will my wife Rita, is the trouble she got into for being at the game. She had told her boss she was poorly and then came across to watch the game. Unfortunately, guess whose photograph was on the back page of one of the newspapers when we got home? "Feeling better?" asked her boss on the Monday.

After the game Bob Lord came into the dressing room. My God, you could have knocked us down with a feather. He got special permission to come in and the first thing he does is approach Jimmy Mac, shake his hand and congratulate him and tells him he hasn't played as well as that for five years. Jimmy said afterwards he wanted to say "How do you know? You haven't seen me play for five years", but didn't.

But back to George Best: what a talent. Who will forget the way he destroyed Burnley at Christmas 1963? On Boxing Day Burnley beat Manchester United 6-1 at Turf Moor. I was still basically a reserve team player though I did break into the first team at the end of that season. Andy Lochhead got four of the goals and Willie Morgan the other two. This was back in the days when there were back-to-back games at Christmas so just two days later the return game was at Old Trafford. George had played a game for the first team in September but was well and truly on the fringe of things and after that hadn't played again. Come Christmas and he was told he could go home for the holiday which was bad news for any player because it simply meant that you weren't even wanted for a reserve game. United lost at Everton 4-0 and then came here and we hammered them 6-1. Panic set in at Old Trafford. Matt Busby sent for Best, who by this time was in Belfast. He got the next flight over and played outside left in the return fixture against Burnley. I've mentioned that Manchester United did their training in their car park when they had games that varied from five-a-side to twenty-a-side. It was no more organised than kids playing in a school playground at playtimes. Anyway, it was in these car park games that George Best used to get the ball and no one could ever get it off him. This is just what he did in the Burnley game. He used to be called the car park genius, and once that genius got into the team on that day against us, that was it; he was there to stay. He ran John Angus ragged. Bobby Charlton had been playing on the wing up until then; what a waste. He moved inside and was reborn so that George could take his place on the wing. Big John must have cursed the day. Charlton once described the occasion. "John Angus was playing right back for Burnley, marking George. John was a good pal of mine; we came from the same part of the country. He was hard and fast. He'd kick you; he was like an oak tree and brave. George murdered him, stuck the ball through his legs, and turned him inside out. We'd all heard about this great young player from the youth team but I'd no idea he was this good." I don't think John Angus ever really recovered from that match and George Best more or less leapfrogged the reserve team straight into the first team. The rest is history.

Another international game we played in together was in November 1965 against England at Wembley. We lost but he was just outstanding. To this day I remember one thing he did. There was a spell of mickey-taking when he had the England players chasing after him like dogs after a sheep. Then when they were tired of that he just stood there juggling the ball in his own penalty area and then when he had done enough of that he just impudently flicked the ball into the hands of Pat Jennings. It was to show his complete disdain for the English attempts to contain him. Didn't do much good though, wonderful though it was. We lost even though I scored. England had scored but within a minute I had the ball off Bobby Moore and hit it home through the legs of Gordon Banks. We had them ragged and left them like tattered rags but two lapses gave them two goals. If you'd seen them that night you'd never have believed that just a few months later they'd win the World Cup.

Funnily enough, George didn't play in a game where we played really well and won 4-1 against Wales. That was earlier in March '66. We'd blown our World Cup chances, and had a patched-up team. The goal I got was the fourth in four games for Ireland. "Top goal snatcher and most accomplished leader for years," said the *Belfast Telegraph*.

There's one story I don't tell on a Saturday afternoon though. It was about 1.05pm and all of us were sitting on the coach outside the hotel waiting for the ride to Windsor Park, though to be honest I've forgotten who the game was against. We were supposed to leave at 1pm on the dot but there was no George. "Where is he?" shouted one of the selectors in exasperation. I volunteered to go and look for him, seeing we roomed together. I had a fair idea of what he was up to and sure enough when I barged into the room there he was with the maid, giving her what every woman wanted with George. "For God's sake, hurry up, get a move on," I yelled at him as his trim little backside pumped happily up and down. "What do you think I'm doing?" he answered. "He was still in bed," I explained to the coach in general as we got on and they all sat there waiting for an explanation, which was true enough I suppose. Dear George, as nice a man as you could wish to meet, without an ounce of badness or malice in him and the greatest footballer I ever played with.

At the beginning of '66 we carried on where we left off with two more wins. The first, on New Year's Day at Blackburn, was marked by the usual rivalry in a foul-strewn game. The last, gruesome 12 minutes saw all the petty niggles boil over into a grand finale with players from both side laid out. Willie Morgan was sent off for fly-kicking Mike England, and a

Blackburn fan attacked goalkeeper Adam Blacklaw. Two-nil up and this was the game where Ralph Coates performed his legendary feat of sitting down on the ball for a rest. Trouble is, the game hadn't stopped and his act of showboating was highly criticised for inflaming an already overheated game. Not by the players and fans though – we thought it was wonderful. Blackburn had a player called Darling. With a name like that you expect to be ribbed. We duly obliged. My goal came with a lightning reaction to an Elder shot that came off the post. "How did you like that, darling?" I asked him. A voice from somewhere replied with something along the lines of "fuck off", I do believe.

A win over Fulham gave us five wins out of six but little praise. If things went off the boil that season maybe it was during this game. Somewhere, somehow we began to struggle and even though the Fulham game was a win it was unconvincing and way below standard. John Angus scored the single goal, a rare event for him. John was the model professional, didn't smoke or drink, didn't stay up late, and never used two words when one would do. A bigger homebird you couldn't wish to meet and on his first trip to Burnley as a boy he lasted just two weeks before returning home, homesick. Luckily for Burnley FC, though, he came back and made his debut on his 18th birthday in 1956. He was one of the best right backs ever to play for Burnley. In his one international appearance, England in their wisdom played him at left back.

The *News of the World* actually tipped us for the title after the Fulham game. We were Division One top scorers but the next six games produced not one win and just two points. The sparkle had gone. Brian O'Neil and Gordon Harris weren't quite as brilliant as they were before Christmas. Brian was frequently less than 100% fit after the hammerings he took. Maybe our passing football suffered on the heavy, muddy grounds. Maybe a small club like Burnley could no longer hope to keep up with the likes of Leeds, Liverpool and Manchester United. Liverpool were regarded then as one of the finest club sides ever produced. Leeds were coming up on the rails. Mind you, at the end of January we did thump Bournemouth

7-0 in a cup replay with Andy Lochhead scoring five. I only scored one. Andy just happened to get there before me every time. We were pleased about that win because in the first game at Bournemouth they had tried to kick us off the field and over the stands for most of the game. Jimmy Adamson was so incensed at what he had seen that either at half-time or full time, I can't remember which, he hurled a tray of glasses against the wall and couldn't wait to get Bournemouth back to Turf Moor. Brian O'Neil was the victim of some appalling treatment. I'll say it again. For football fans today who never saw any of the sixties stuff, they would be just amazed at some of the roughhouse games that went on. The difference between then and now is a bit like the difference between cotton wool and a Brillo soap pad.

It was after this game that Bob Lord had one of his apoplexies because the BBC had advertised the game as being on TV later on that evening. He was livid and cursed them for reducing the size of the crowd. The BBC vans even turned up outside the ground. He was so incensed that he swore he would burn any cameras stationed inside the ground. It was always fun having Bob around the place; there was never a dull moment. He demanded £2,000 compensation for the 10,000 fans he argued had stayed away thinking that the game would be shown on TV. In a calmer moment when he had put his box of matches back in the drawer he argued that he had no grumbles with the match being shown but his complaints were about the size of the BBC fees, the BBC's contract with the FA having been negotiated by people who didn't have a clue about football. Burnley were offered a paltry fee of £10 for that game and this was classed as a "disturbance fee". You have to say that sometimes Bob Lord was right.

A home defeat against Chelsea was a sickener, and with me going through a bad spell the goals would not come. One more did come against Manchester United, but it was only in another defeat, this time by 4-2. Liverpool were well ahead, all thoughts of the title coming to Turf Moor well and truly gone. We scraped two miserly points in the two draws against Arsenal and then Everton. The forwards looked as if they wouldn't score in a month of Sundays.

The miserable run continued right into March with a defeat at Nottingham Forest. It would be March 12th before our luck changed at last.

To cap it all, this was the depressing run during which I scored a hat-trick in a cup tie at Tottenham and yet we still lost 4-3. Within ten minutes we had scored twice and we all leapt ecstatically when the second went in. The first had gone in after just 40 seconds. This was *Boy's Own* stuff. Hundreds of supporters had come down, but by the end of the game they were just numb with disbelief. Spurs levelled it at 2-2 but even then we went 3-2 up with my third. Then came the two Spurs goals that won them the game. Their last and winning goal came just two minutes from the end. Emotion and feelings just drained from us. Our bodies were empty of any remaining strength and our heads were just blank. Nobody but a footballer can even begin to understand the depth of despair you feel when you lose to a last-minute goal. We were criticised greatly after the game for not shutting up shop after we had gone 2-0 up but the truth is it was just not in our nature and certainly not in Harry Potts' or Jimmy Adamson's.

For the fourth successive year we felt that fate and luck rather than any superior team had knocked us out. On the Sunday morning you read the newspapers. You read them with a sense of disbelief. The press reported that this must surely have been one of the great games of all time – but that meant little to us. They praised us for being attack-minded instead of aping Leeds and bringing nine men back into defence. They said it was a giant of a match and how we deserved admiration not censure. And one key incident was pointed out. With Alan Gilzean on the floor, seemingly injured, Burnley swept upfield sweetly and there was Andy Lochhead, unmarked 15 yards from goal with the net at his mercy. At this point the referee blew his whistle so that Gilzean could get attention. But before he blew it Gilzean had risen to his feet and was jogging back upfield, perfectly OK. Ninety seconds later Gilzean hammered in the twenty-yard winner. On such decisions are footballers' lives and the fate of a season decided. *The Observer* made one telling comment. *"As the crowd filed out of the ground, dazedly jubilant or unbelievingly despondent, according to their affections, a Burnley supporter, presumably remembering some of the more lurid fouls, commented bitterly: 'Nice guys finish last'."*

Where did we go from here, we all asked as we reported for training on the Tuesday. Monday we'd been given off as a gesture; we had given our all, no one could say we had given less. It was Bob Lord who told us that in a rare meeting after calling us to the boardroom. He told us how proud he was, how the defeat was undeserved. He gave us a real pep talk. He told us to go all out and bridge the eight-point gap between ourselves and Liverpool with our two games in hand, not forgetting we had to play them at Turf Moor. He told us to forget about Tottenham, it was water under the bridge. He reminded us there was a place in Europe to fight for and he was sure all of us would enjoy flights to the capitals of Europe and the best hotels. Just every now and then you felt proud to play for Lord and this was one of those times. We left that room talking loudly; if Liverpool thought we had given up, then they could think again.

But our woes continued. Everton equalised in the 86th minute and deprived us of a 1-0 win. The mud was knee-deep and made it a day for musclemen and dray horses. One paper described it as worse than playing on an unmade bed. O'Neil, thanks to the whacks he took at Bournemouth, was a shadow of what he had been. The critics all said the same thing: where one pass would do, we used two; where two passes would do, we used three.

At last, on March 12th we scraped a win. To be blunt, January and February had been abysmal, but Harry Potts remained upbeat, saying that surely the club fortunes would change with 12 games still to play and that there was still the incentive of the Fairs Cup. Dear Harry; if there had been an earthquake in Burnley he would have told us not to worry and that things would eventually look up. And so, it came to pass, in a home game against Newcastle, things did indeed look up. There was a 1-0 win with a Willie Morgan goal. We played like robots, stiff, wooden, uninspired, lacking in any kind of sparkle, but we won; the curse was lifted. There was no joy though; it was a scraped win in a miserable game against a nine-man defence. The fans weren't happy but Harry Potts answered the critics. "We play well and lose games. We play badly and win a game. I know which I prefer," he said.

Goals seemed to have dried up for me and since the Tottenham hat-trick there had been just one to add to my list. Thoughts of equalling or bettering Ray Pointer's post-war record were fading. Faint doubts that I had lost my touch became more worrying. Harry Potts put the proverbial arm round my shoulder and said all the right things. George Beel's all-time record of 35 in a season was unattainable. Bert Freeman, before the 1920s, had scored more than 30 goals in a season twice. George Beel did it twice in the 1920s. Any dream of scoring 30 or more myself looked remote and even in a second consecutive win – 2-1 at West Brom – I didn't score. It's funny how some grounds are good grounds. West Brom was certainly one; in the last eight visits Burnley had won five and drawn three.

But then – bingo – a hat-trick against Nottingham Forest in a 4-1 home win. But only just over 10,000 people were there to see it. There are worries today about the poor crowds at Turf Moor but even in the 1960s, with winning teams and great players on show, there were days when the Burnley public stayed away in droves for the smaller games. It was the same then as now; come the big teams, Liverpool, Leeds, Manchester United, then over 30,000 crowded in. For other games it was often a struggle. The hat-trick rejuvenated me, got the target back on track again; 27 to equal the record, 28 to beat it. In just one game, the race was back on again.

Goals came in the next five games as well which meant at the end of the run I was home and dry. Tom Jones put in an appearance at the Casino Club, heavy snow fell and caused havoc, the local coal mines increased their production even though they had fewer men – a sort of last defiant gesture as if to say "keep us open" – and on April 11th against Sheffield Wednesday I equalled the 27 goals scored by Ray Pointer. At Villa in the next game I passed it. Some grounds are good, some grounds are bad and Villa belonged to the latter group. No one could remember when Burnley last won there but at least I got the one goal we scored that day in the traditional defeat. Elation, joy, jubilation, euphoria, exhilaration: how many more words do you want? Are there any more? If I knew any more, I'd keep on going.

The remaining question was in what position we would finish the season. Second place was definitely possible but Leeds had games in hand. Liverpool were way ahead. We heard stories from other players about Liverpool at that time, how poorly paid they were, how they were sent out to play with feet and ankles and legs strapped and bandaged to keep them upright when common sense said they should not be playing with some of the injuries they were carrying. Our physio was quick to point out that their dressing room after a game was buried in yards of tape and bandage. If you were out injured Shankly didn't want to know you. He only had time for the fit and the strong and the ones able to play. Once out through injury you struggled to get your place back, so nobody at Liverpool wanted to be out injured. Some of them played when they could hardly walk. Their players were not paid well. Footballers talk and we heard on the grapevine that any player out injured might as well not exist; Shankly just blanked them as if they'd personally let him down.

The Easter holiday games were crucial; a good Easter and we would be sure of a place in Europe as long as the powers that be didn't say or do anything stupid like deciding that Burnley were not eligible as they were not a city. That worry was there for quite a while. To finish runners-up would have been a marvellous achievement, to have finished as champions nothing short of sensational and it was only the poor January and February that had ruined that chance... If only...

"Irvine's flair crowned fine team performance" was the headline after the 2-1 win against Sheffield Wednesday. Two goals and the record equalled, the second from the narrowest of angles after one of their defenders made a hash of passing the ball back in the mud. The ability to read and anticipate a situation got me this goal. Yet having said that, the amount of thought that goes through your mind happens so quickly and so instinctively it's as if it doesn't happen at all. The cheers rang out as we left the ground and I can remember them to this day. The pundits and experts who plied their trade in the newspapers were saying I was the new Greaves. Seven goals had come in just four games; I was labelled the "prince of goal-getters". At the beginning of the season the name Irvine was unheard of outside Lancashire and Belfast, and now it was well known. I was 23; felt ten feet tall, the world at my feet. Ten years ahead of me. Life doesn't feel or get any better. I made some daft remark, if I remember rightly, afterwards to the press. "I could have run through a brick wall if necessary," I said.

Five games remained. Surely I could reach the magic 30. Liverpool had 56 points with four games left, Burnley 49 points; surely too much to catch up. Leeds were breathing down our necks. Liverpool and Leeds had both to play at Turf Moor. We thought of games we had squandered, draws that should have been wins, all the "ifs" and "buts" that are part of football and its cruelty. In the Easter game against Sunderland I had come up against the legendary Eire international Charlie Hurley. He was a colossus but didn't stop me scoring on a pitch that was like glue. Alex Elder had something thrown at him and was furious until he looked down and saw it was an Easter Egg. We ate it in the dressing room afterwards. Doubt still remained as to whether we would qualify for Europe even if we were second. Officials at the FA said we didn't qualify because we were not a city and didn't have any kind of Trade Fair. Burnley Saturday Market and the tripe and black pudding stalls clearly didn't count. But the Football League supported Burnley and said the opposite, saying that we should qualify on merit. If Burnley were turned down after finishing in the top four we should be furious, said the Football League. If rejected, Burnley planned to appeal to Sir Stanley Rous; known for his fair play, they said. A few seasons earlier Burnley had already been turned down when they had "qualified".

Trouble was also brewing in the Bob Lord camp after Everton fielded 11 reserves in a game against Leeds United because they had a cup game coming up. Leeds had won and gained two points on Burnley. Lord, indeed all of us, were fuming. In their European Championship season Burnley had been heavily fined for playing ten reserves in a game against Chelsea because of two big games following it, one against

Hamburg and the other a cup game. It ended 4-4 and no one could have accused Burnley of gifting the points to Chelsea. Actually, while this storm brewed Bob Lord was somewhere on a cruise liner.

When Lord returned he had a job to do first though before he blew his top with the Football League. One of the club directors, Dr Iven, had already given me one of his trilbies as a gift to commemorate the hat-trick at Tottenham. When Bob Lord heard of this he was quick to promise me one of his and said, "if you break Ray Pointer's record you can have mine". I came back from Birmingham after the Villa game with the match ball. I got the inevitable questions. Which was the best goal? "The second against Nottingham Forest when we won 4-1," I replied. Which was the luckiest? "The one that went through Gary Sprake's legs at Leeds." And the most satisfying? "The 28th."

When Bob Lord did return from his cruise he didn't quite hit the roof regarding Everton's reserves as people expected him to, saying that he actually understood their position. There had been suggestions that Everton should be made to play the game again. What a furore it caused though. Compare that to today when the big teams field their reserves as a matter of policy in the Carling Cup and even the FA Cup in its early stages. Consider a team like Chelsea who today can field a "reserve" team that is anything but, when they have two world-class players for every position. How things change. When Burnley did this just over 40 years ago, and were honest enough to say they were "resting" five of their players, it caused uproar and condemnation. Today, nobody bats an eyelid.

What a game it was against Liverpool at Turf Moor; 36,530 people squeezed in; half must have been from Liverpool. While there was no chance of catching them we beat them 2-0, and what a coup that was. My goal was simple. Alex Elder floated over a free kick and to my amazement I was left unmarked. "Thank you very much," I muttered and sweetly headed it in. Goal number 29 in the League and number 41 altogether including internationals. It was a goal that illustrated perfectly what a great decoy Andy Lochhead was.

Liverpool were watching him and not me. Hadn't anyone told them it was me who was the dangerman? The pace was frenetic on a surface that was again almost unplayable. There should have been a penalty when I was tripped, there was the usual fisticuffs and rough stuff; such an integral part of the '60s game, hard man Gordon Harris versus hard man Tommy Smith. The unbreakable versus the immovable. They were both booked, and to be booked in the '60s meant you really had to do something above and beyond the realms of normal violence. Ralph Coates' goal is sometimes said to have been the best of the season. He made a fifty-yard run, shrugging off challenges, riding tackles, rounding defenders as if they weren't there and then a superb shot from 20 yards. It brought the house down. Adam Blacklaw made some memorable saves.

Bill Shankly was thunderous afterwards. Neither he nor Liverpool could stand to lose. "If we can keep this team together they can keep the club at the top for years," wrote Keith McNee. Its days were already numbered though; it would not stay together for years to come. The words "if only" spring to mind again.

The good times were back and we beat Tottenham 1-0 in a heatwave in London. Revenge for the cup game we lost 4-3? Almost but not quite: I can still feel the dejection of that day. Spurs were shoddy, niggly, petulant, Blacklaw back to his brilliant best; Coates was devastating. He later signed for Spurs in the early '70s and displays like this at Tottenham let the crowd know in no uncertain terms just how brilliant he could be. He was unplayable. Lochhead scored the goal.

And then there was Leeds. Oh dear, how do you describe them? There was rough play, gamesmanship, confrontation and provocation, even brutality. There were certainly players who set out to hurt you and Leeds look this to a new depth.

In the penultimate game, on May 7th, 1966, second place in Division One was at stake. Even with nothing to play for Leeds were always ugly. In this game they were just appalling. The game was watched by Field Marshal Viscount Montgomery (of El Alamein, to give him his full moniker). He chose well and the game became known as the Battle of Turf Moor. Montgomery was one of Bob Lord's heroes; Edward Heath in later years was another. Their strange relationship had begun at Wembley in 1962 when Monty and Lord met. Then they had met again in Bournemouth when Monty asked Bob Lord how was it possible that a small club like Burnley, on such limited resources, could keep up with the big clubs. "Come and see for yourself," replied Mr Lord. He had then invited him to Turf Moor to see how a good club was so well run. In truth, at that time, it was well run. No one can take that away from the man.

It was another big crowd of 33,000 who came to see the game, but what they saw wasn't football, it was just a war, settled by the most bizarre goal you could ever wish to see. The press described this game as spoiling, bitter, nasty and downright disgraceful. Manchester United versus Arsenal, November 2004 was just a picnic, a stroll in the park compared to this X-certificate stuff. Modern football is just a breeze; the Roy Keanes, Patrick Vieiras, Kevin Muscats, Dennis Wises of this present world, they're just pussycats compared to the real hard men who plied their trade as footballers in the '60s.

The *Daily Express* was just amazed that spectators didn't witness at least six broken legs resulting from the dangerously vicious lunges which masqueraded as tackles by three Leeds players in particular – Norman Hunter, Billy Bremner and Jim Storrie. The *Express* went on to say that it could not fathom the behaviour of professional players whose sole aim seemed to be to maim each other. *The Guardian* described the players constantly pushing, tripping and squaring up to each other. *The Sun's* description was almost identical. Leeds and Revie's plan was simply to contain Burnley with a nine-man defence and to do this by any means possible. It worked. And then to cap it all Alex Elder scored the most freakish own goal ever seen at the Turf. Johnny Giles booted the ball downfield. Elder reached it but, hassled and kicked by Storrie, seemed to panic and from near the corner flag just whacked it high across his own Burnley penalty area – and was then horrified to see it swerve into the Burnley goal with Blacklaw stranded. A simple back pass would have sufficed. This is one event in Alex's life that he will remember forever; the other is the penalty that

never was that he gave away in a cup game against Blackburn
Rovers when Burnley were leading 3-0. Inspired by that goal,
Rovers went on to draw the game 3-3 and win the replay.
Poor Alex, he was distraught after the game. The foul tally
was 15-15 but the press generally agreed that this should be
ignored because it was such a gross distortion of what actually
happened and that Leeds were the guilty ones.

Following incidents where Bremner laid me out in the
centre circle, Storrie flattened Willie Morgan, and Paul Reaney
scythed down Ralph Coates, the referee called all 22 players
together to give them all a dressing down. How interesting it
became to count the number of times that in games involving
Leeds, other referees in other games had to call all 22 players
together. In truth Andy Lochhead and I in this game were well
and truly snuffed out by Hunter and Charlton. Hunter versus
Lochhead – truly a confrontation for the history books.

In the inquest afterwards everyone was blamed: players,
club officials, referee, trouble on the terraces which flared
up; but after the game the players came off smiling, hugging,
chatting, and shaking hands as if nothing had happened, said
the *Daily Mirror*.

"Football, bloody hell," said Alex Ferguson years later.

You have to wonder what Monty made of all this? Perhaps
he thought all football was like this if this was one of the
few games he ever attended. In the boardroom afterwards
he commented on how sorry he felt for Alex Elder. Prior to
the game he had been given a tour of the club and training
ground. His car stopped several times between Gawthorpe
and Turf Moor so that he could chat to people in the street.
There was a civic luncheon in the town hall. Amazingly, one
of the people he met was one of his former batmen. Before
the game he was escorted onto the pitch to meet the players,
the crowd gave him a terrific reception. Bands from the 4th
Battalion East Lancs Regiment and 5th Battalion Lancashire
Fusiliers entertained the crowd with some stirring music.
Brass Bands were commonplace before a game in those days.

And then he watched the game. I use the word "game"
loosely. He must have gone back to his HQ at the Keirby
Hotel shell-shocked.

Harry Potts and Bob Lord were livid afterwards, saying it was a shocker of a game and that from the pitchside Potts could see things going on and heard players saying things he would never care to repeat. Along with the Newcastle game it was the most horrific he had ever seen. Burnley didn't start the rough stuff he said, but would always look after themselves in such circumstances. Brian O'Neil had a knee injury so bad his leg was twice its normal size.

Battered and bruised, nevertheless we won the final game of the season just two days later at Sheffield Wednesday. O'Neil didn't play; his knee was still the size of a balloon. Of the final seven games we had won five and were safely in third position. We had won 24 games and lost 11, scoring 79 goals along the way. Fifty-five points was six behind Liverpool and the same as Leeds, who had a better goal difference. The win Leeds had over that Everton reserve team was crucial, as was their brutal victory at Turf Moor.

There was no 30th league goal for me, and I have always regretted it. After I scored against Liverpool game we had three more games and I didn't score again. I sit here now and think how the chance of ever repeating the golden season of '65/66 was taken away from me just a few months later. Those 29 goals represent the pinnacle of my career and with cup goals as well I scored 37 that season. These goals are what the people of Burnley remember me for, why they still talk to me and ask me to their social functions. It is a record that should remain for a while if not forever. One part of me would love someone to exceed it, for that would mean Burnley were enjoying success. The other part of me wants it to stay forever. It is the mark I have made on the world into which I was born. I look at the record books and feel such pride to see my name there and so do my sons. My grandchildren will feel that pride when they are older, I hope. Of course my career went on for several more years but it was never the same, and at the age of 23 I had already reached the level that I could and should so easily have surpassed. Forgive me if I have spent such a long time in these two chapters about season '65/66, but what I achieved that season is my lasting legacy and my pride and joy. I had a God-given gift but, on a night at Goodison Park it was taken away.

CHAPTER ELEVEN

EUROPEAN FLINGS AND A NIGHT AT EVERTON

There have been more phone calls with Joan in Carrickfergus. She can remember that my mother Agnes and her first husband Willie Black lived in the Shankill Road area of Belfast, but not how many children they had, although two of them were Billy and Lily. On the death of her first husband she then married Herbert Hamilton sometime around 1927 and it was Herbert who was Joan's father. There were no other children, said Joan. I was puzzled again because Jean had told me that she too was a Hamilton. What happened to that marriage she couldn't say, other than they separated and that she only met him once more after that and she, Joan, was forbidden to speak to her father. As far as Joan was concerned she only had one real father whom she loved, and that was Alex Irvine, who was as good and loving a father as anyone could hope for and treated her as his very own. Alex and Agnes never married and went on to have seven children of their own – Sandra, George, Peggy, Jean, Joey, Bobby and myself.

They had met at school many years previously and had never forgotten each other. Alex worked so hard and was good to all of us, and while he was alive they were such happy times. Agnes, a good cook, was a good mother, knitting woollen jumpers and stockings for us as she sat by the fireside. Alex had joined the army in World War One but returned home wounded with a plate in his arm. He always used to joke that his arm got an inch shorter every year.

"During World War Two; yes, he was injured in one of the raids on the dockyards, but not too badly. Then it was on Halloween night during the blackout that he was badly hurt when a friend was giving

141

him a lift back to the station after their shift. Corporation Street in Belfast, that was, but though he recovered he had terrible pains in his head ever afterwards. Three years after this accident, or was it four, he was taken so ill at work he was sent home. That was the Friday. We called for the doctor but he never came. We've always had a mind that it was because he was drunk that night. On the Saturday he did come and all he could say was, 'there's not a lot I can do so just give him plenty of fluid.' The doctor came again on Sunday and all I can remember is that he said it would be better if he died. Everyone who heard him was shocked at what seemed such a callous and insensitive thing to say but I suppose in hindsight he was saying that even if he recovered he would just be a helpless invalid.

"So Mum prayed that he would die and he passed away early on the Sunday evening. At that time there was only me working so mum had to find a job, which she did in Jeremiah Ambler's factory. Later, when I joined the ATS and was posted to England, I used to send 12 shillings a week back to her.

"Do you remember the apples you used to 'borrow' from the orchard next door?" Joan asked. "We never went short of apple pie, did we? And the vegetables you used to dig up from the farmer's field? Yes, he did catch you once or twice but you used your charm and cheek to explain to him that you were only taking enough to help out your poor mum and her hungry family. Ah, Billy, they were happy days. And then I always laughed at one memory of you playing football when you were small. You were playing at Greenisland and the changing room was an old railway carriage. Up and down you went with a bag over your shoulder shouting 'tickets please, tickets please.' I still laugh now when I think about it. And in Sunnylands School there used to be a picture of you with your international cap hanging in the hall. Whether it's still there I don't know but they were very proud of you."

Small talk and chitchat about my boys and their families took over the conversation until it ended. But afterwards one thing bothered me. My mother and father never married and this is something I never knew till now. I was, to put it mildly, just a little bit stunned to learn this. Today, nobody would be at all concerned but then, in those days in the '40s and '50s, with their stricter attitudes and when society's rules were so different to those of today, were the "Irvines" looked at with any aversion? Were we seen as being different from other families? Does that now explain why the headmaster of Eden School seemed to have such a down on any member of the Irvine family? We were children "born out of wedlock" as the saying used to go in those days. And that's what we were. Does it explain why the Irvines always got the blame for any trouble in the village? It takes quite a while to stop thinking about it.

I was now engaged to Rita Berry whether Mother disapproved or not, and no matter how much she wanted me to marry a Carrickfergus girl my mind was set. Out of respect for my Mother, and torn between what she wanted and what I wanted, I had left Rita in the summer. But I realised when I left her just how much I missed her and that it would not have worked out my giving her up to marry a Carrick girl. Mother made her disapproval known from the very start but my life and career was in Burnley, not Carrick. I made the decision that I could not base my life on what Mother wanted. She was hurt, angry, and disappointed and it left me feeling dreadful. She had given me every encouragement to grab the chance to play football for a living and I was grateful for that. Now she must back me in my choice of Rita, I thought, and if she couldn't, then so be it. It marked the end of any close relationship. I returned to Burnley and Rita.

How disappointed we were not to be taking part in the World Cup in the summer of '66. It was the game against Albania in Tirana that cost us. We let people down with the awful display we put on. Even though the game had been months earlier I squirmed just to think about it, and still do to this day. With just 15 minutes to go and me having put us one up, we just gave it away. How could we? Albania were no better than a Third Division side, just hoofing it as far as they could and chasing it, but we were just as bad. Truth is we were a shambles, and if only we had won we would have played Switzerland in a play-off for the World Cup Finals. George Best, Derek Dougan and I all missed easy chances. We couldn't blame the rain that poured down or the bewildering referee; we were like novices towards the end. The Swiss manager who was there to watch couldn't believe his luck;

he had assumed we would win at a canter. The gloom in the hotel afterwards was like nothing I had known before. We just sat there silent, sad-faced and depressed. We were shocking, and never again were to come so close to the chance of an appearance in the finals.

In June I'd had a huge row with Bob Lord. We had a friendly in Belfast against Mexico and I returned to Burnley a couple of days late. When I got back there was a telegram waiting for me from Bob Lord telling me to go and see him at his factory in Burnley. Apparently I was supposed to go and explain to him why I was late. So I went up to see him, got to his meat factory and just wandered round a bit lost at first, couldn't find his office. So I went into one of the doors and ended up where they were chopping up great carcasses. I asked one of the blokes there, where did I find Bob Lord. Next thing I know he was standing behind me with a face like thunder and he very rudely told me to follow him to his office. When we got there he shut the door and proceeded to tell me off for talking to one of his workers. Hang on, I told him, all I was doing was asking the bloke where to find you. By then I was as mad as he was, and sarcastically told him that when I was a little boy, Mum used to tell us if we were lost to ask a policeman. I couldn't find a policeman, I told him, so I asked the bloke I found chopping up meat. Anyway, we had the mother of all rows for the next hour with him actually telling me how to be a better centre forward, even though I'd just broken the scoring record and scored 29 goals in the League.

Eventually I was in a fury so I thought, in for a penny in for a pound, and told him if he was going to tell me about scoring goals I'd tell him how to be a better butcher and that his meat was awful and he should start selling decent meat. Good grief; it seemed to shut him up and then I went on to tell him that while I was at it I wanted more money because I was the best goalscorer this club had and I didn't see why I should be on less money than anybody else. By then he was coming to his senses and we both began to calm down and he announced that yes, all right, he would give me another £20 a week and there and then I got £20 to put in my back pocket. After that I never saw an extra penny.

European Flings and a Night at Everton

We all thought we'd do well in 1966/67. We had some great players, Andy Lochhead and I were a great partnership and we had lots of young players in that team. Jimmy Adamson was a great coach even though I didn't like him as a man. If only he hadn't been so superior. Harry was always the same: a friendly greeting, an encouraging word, a smile, a quick question about how's the family, or the girlfriend, or the digs.

We were certainly all looking forward to some foreign travel now that we were in the Fairs Cup. My old landlady, the one who was a clairvoyant and used to tell me that one day I would travel, was absolutely spot on.

By Christmas, 1966, midway through season 1966/67, Burnley were in the top six, had scored a bucketful of goals, and lacked only one thing: consistency. There had been a great beginning to the season with three consecutive wins and it wasn't until the ninth game that there was a defeat. In October there was another string of three consecutive wins and by the end of the year I had another 13 goals, well on the way to the magic 20. Ask any striker; if he has scored 20 by the end of the season he is well pleased. The Turf Moor set-up from boardroom to boot room remained second to none and on top of all that there was European football to look forward to. It seemed miraculous then, and still does today, that this small club in such a small town could still compete with the big boys – Everton, for example, had just paid £110,000 for Alan Ball. You lost count of what Manchester United spent. With a management team of Potts and Adamson, particularly with the coaching of the latter, we often had a tactical know-how far in advance of anything from the so-called bigger teams. Free kick routines, sweepers, wing backs, target men, moving comfortably from 4-2-4 to 4-3-3; all these things we saw at Burnley in the 1960s. If there was just one small problem, maybe it was that people looked to me to repeat the 29 goals of the previous season. A spell of seven games without scoring following the first two games certainly had me worried, but from then until Christmas they came at fairly regular intervals. Defenders now knew all about Willie Irvine and the ratio of bruises to goals increased.

The bruises certainly doubled in what was by now recognised as the annual battle and kicking match against Leeds United. If last season's had been deemed horrific, the repeat was even worse, if that was possible. The law of the jungle seemed to prevail; all normal rules went out of the window. This was the Leeds team that had been taken off the field by the referee for a cooling down period in the game at Everton. At Turf Moor it wasn't soccer; it was just a shambles, the word "brutality" an understatement. The game was an insult to any spectator. It was described as guerrilla warfare, and it was suggested by one reporter that it should be expunged from the records and replayed behind locked doors. A disgusting, disgraceful and deplorable debacle were other words. The result, by the way, was 1-1. Why Leeds came in the first place is a mystery. I remember one Leeds player telling a pitchside cameraman to hang on to the ball when it went out of play, to waste some more time. On top of all this there were crowd scenes and violence and there were times when the game should have been abandoned because of the missile-throwing. On the Friday night before the game we thought that it could not possibly be as bad as the one in May. Wrong.

Harry Potts was incensed and challenged Don Revie to a TV debate to discuss the game. Dear old Harry, he was so wound up after the game he tossed out the challenge in the post-match interviews. Revie was dismissive and told us to put our own house in order, going on to say he couldn't think of anything more useless, and that he would not take part in anything which dragged the game down further still; words that had us all open-mouthed in disbelief on Monday morning. Several thousand fans had come over from Leeds, 1,500 of those in three special trains. Central Station was no place to be at 5pm after the game with the stationmaster describing them all tactfully as being rather rough and ready. A bit like the team they followed, then.

Stuttgart, however, on September 20th, was a welcome interlude to the hurly-burly of League football. The hotel was in the centre of a city with tree-lined streets and the giant Mercedes-Benz factory. Glorious sunshine met us when we arrived and there was almost a holiday atmosphere.

It wouldn't have been a surprise to see some of the directors with their pet cat or budgie. Let's be honest; little Burnley in Europe again, it was a great achievement. On the plane there were rumours that Tommy Docherty would be at the game to watch Willie Morgan. Morgan had a copy of the paper, and said nothing, simply smiling and folding the paper away. Bob Lord's comment was pure Bob Lord: "Rubbish, just rubbish". How interesting, though, that simultaneously there was a bid of £40,000 to bring John Connelly back to Turf Moor. It was Connelly himself who decided not to return, choosing instead Blackburn Rovers on the grounds that it would be a mistake to return "home". He was still only 28 and in his prime. Blackburn also paid him a handsome signing-on fee, while Burnley were not prepared to do so. In similar circumstances I don't think I would have returned home either.

For the game itself the stadium was not even a quarter full. There was an eerie, practice match atmosphere and we proceeded to outplay them from start to finish. Somehow we contrived to score just one goal, scored by me from a Brian O'Neil cross, and then somehow contrived to give away a penalty. We were furious though at the sending off of O'Neil for what was nothing more than a 50-50 challenge. If this referee had been at the Leeds game he would have sent off half the Leeds team. It was our first experience of the German diving technique. This bloke was a master, going down like a bullet had shot him.

I recall the evening dinner was a rather subdued affair. We were miffed that Brian had been sent off and equally miffed that a dubious penalty had been awarded to Stuttgart. We were miffed at the supper on offer. We had heard so much about the sumptuous banquets served up on these glittering European occasions and waited with bated breath for the first course of the feast fit for a king. When potato pie arrived we felt a tad disappointed.

Stuttgart were poor at Turf Moor in the return game and Blacklaw didn't have a shot to save. Lochhead and Coates scored in a 2-0 win and with better luck and finishing we could have had five. In all fairness it was an anticlimax of a game without atmosphere or that little bit of "edge" that brings a game to life. The high spot was the six-course banquet laid on with style and panache afterwards at the Simonstone Hotel. We tucked in heartily after a job well done. Not for one minute would Lord Bob of Burnley have ever contemplated providing potato pie even if it was filled with prime Bob Lord steak. Not only did they sample a Burnley feast, but every member of the Stuttgart party was presented with a stainless steel breakfast set. In his after-dinner speech the Stuttgart president said they had travelled hundreds of miles in football and were always proud to make new friends. It must have been tempting for blunt Bob to tell him, "well, next time you have visitors give them something better than potato pie."

In October, on Monday 3rd, I got married, tied the knot, plighted my troth and said my vows. Rita won't believe me but I remember it as if it were yesterday. I can tell her the name of the church – St Peter's. I can tell her what she wore – an empire line satin dress with a lace coat and train. I can tell her what she carried – a bouquet of pink roses. Brother Bobby was best man, Andy Lochhead was groomsman, and afterwards we wined and dined at the Sparrowhawk Hotel in Burnley. When I'd asked Rita to marry me it had been via a phone call from Germany. "Yes," she said, as long as I asked her father first, which I duly did in their front parlour on my return. It was at the same time that we learned we'd play Lausanne next in the Fairs Cup. Adamson declared this would be the team he would have chosen to play because they were footballers and not strong-arm men. Nevertheless some of us rather fancied a trip to Barcelona but hey, never mind – Lausanne, the Swiss Alps, chocolate and cuckoo clocks and Lake Geneva would do very nicely for us simple Burnley lads.

After the wedding, which was on a Monday, I was back into training the next day. I've heard a story since then that physio Jimmy Holland was supposed to pass on the message that I could have Tuesday off but he forgot. But in the next game I gave myself a nice little present; the winning goal against Blackpool. It was the fourth game in eight days and we thought nothing of it. Today our pampered footballers and managers would be moaning and groaning about too many fixtures. I remember the goal, blasting in a shot from a narrow angle after Gordon Harris had done all the hard work. It broke a dry spell in League matches for me as well... Get married... Score a goal... I should get married more often, I thought.

Winning goal in one game and then in the next Adamson showed his tactical skill when Chelsea, a formidable side, were easily disposed of at Stamford Bridge. I honestly can't remember whether I was "rested" or injured, but without me Adamson pulled a masterstroke by playing a sweeper at the back, something certainly unusual in those days in English football. I found an old cutting a while back and, though yet again you have to say Adamson often lacked personal skills, as a coach and tactician he was supreme. If I say he lacked personal skills, maybe mine were none too good either on occasions.

The Times (well, where else would you read reporting like this) said, *"Here is a side that looks fully capable of having some sort of say in the continental game; a side bearing all the studious stamp of Adamson the Burnley captain of four or five years ago. The swallows have come and gone since those days but the faithful nightingale, which is Adamson, remains on the same bough. He is now the club coach and the fact is amply proclaimed in the style and cut of the Burnley of today. They looked a team without a weakness, perfectly slotted, tongued and grooved in all their fluid work, a team that always moved intelligently off the ball to change the point of attack."*

Adamson came back from Lausanne, a club with a lovely stadium, beautifully situated in William Tell country between the blue Lake Geneva and the Jura Mountains, confident that he had seen nothing to trouble us, even though they had been Swiss champions seven times and won the cup six times. Their Stade Olympique was the most modern in the country and was a true community sports ground hosting half a dozen other sports as well.

As a gentle warm-up we thrashed Leicester City 5-2 in a brilliant display where we fired on all cylinders. By now Ralph Coates was known as the "exclusive (*sic*) pimpernel" in the *News of the World*. The most exciting prospect for years, said the *Daily Mail*. They could have had twelve said *The Sun*. They should march through the streets of Burnley with bass drums and 76 trombones, said the *Daily Express*. And then we lost the next three League games on the trot – so much for drums, trombones and champagne football. Those blokes knew nothing.

But three days after Leicester, Lausanne were disposed of quite easily. With the tactical introduction of the sweeper system again it was me who lost out. No footballer likes being left out and I was not best pleased and sat watching the game from the stands in Lausanne. I saw chances going begging and thought it could have been my night for a hat-trick. The brilliant Leicester display had been just a matter of days earlier, What do they say? Never change a winning team? At least that's what they said in the 1960s, unlike today when the top teams can field two sets of players to suit any occasion. Well, Adamson changed it all right and did his usual job of telling me with his poor bedside manner. I was furious, but the 3-1 win justified the decision as far as he was concerned. After the game I refrained from telling him that if I'd played we'd have won 6-1. I was too interested in the good news for Andy Lochhead. Prior to the game he received the news that his wife had given birth to their first child, a daughter. He went on to assist with both of the first two goals and then scored the third himself. The celebrations after the game were long and thirst-quenching. Andy will not thank me for revealing to the world that he was paralytic that night and that it was yours truly who had the unenviable job of getting him back to the hotel and getting him into bed.

In the return game at Turf Moor, Lausanne put up little resistance in a 5–0 defeat, one of them scored by me on my return to the side, and in addition to that, Burnley hit the woodwork four times. Only 16 teams remained now and there was a firm feeling that Burnley could go all the way, especially with people like Joe Mercer saying that Burnley were one of the best teams in the country. He was ecstatic about Lochhead and Morgan, unable to believe that Scotland could ignore Andy. He would later try to sign him for Manchester City and even got as far as agreeing a wage with him. Andy went to meet him and took a payslip. "Put that away," said Mercer, "we'll pay you twice as much." Dear old Bob Lord vetoed the move, or was it Adamson who saw in Andy a possible centre half when his days up front were over? Andy's dream move never materialised. Footballers tend to be philosophical but it has maybe niggled him ever since. City signed Francis Lee instead and Andy was shifted to Leicester City.

With the league season becoming more and more patchy – though the goals total mounted up nicely thanks to Andy, who scored all four in the home game against Villa, and several games where we scored fours and threes – it was the European games that became the main focus and when the draw was made in November for us to play against Napoli the whole town was united in its excitement. For a town where people took their Wakes Week holidays in Blackpool or Morecambe a place like Naples was an unattainable million miles away. They were the wealthiest and most fanatically supported club in Europe. They had a team that cost the best part of a million pounds, their president was a multimillionaire shipping tycoon, their average attendance was 72,000 and their 80,000 capacity stadium even had its own hospital. Sophia Loren was their star supporter. "What a wonderful attraction they will be," said Bob Lord beaming. "We have never played an Italian team before." If only he had known what was in store he might have asked for the draw to be done again. "The crowds out there are fanatical," said Adam Blacklaw, which must go down as the understatement of all time. If only he had known what was coming his way. "There is a ten yard wide moat round the pitch," he added, with a degree of irony he couldn't have realised at the time, seeing as he would be thrown into it.

With players like Omar Sivori and Altafini they really were a glamour side from a city of just over a million people who lived in the shadow of Mount Vesuvius. It was the stock joke of the city that no one knew what was the most volatile, the people or the volcano. We would eventually find out. Naples, from the south of Italy, only had one aim: and that was to topple the northern giants like Inter and Milan and Juventus from their perch. Bob Lord must have wept into his cash register when he heard things like they had £600,000 worth of season ticket holders and even for an away game 30,000 supporters went with them to Rome.

Anyway, while Andy was slamming four goals against Aston Villa, Bob Lord was having his own little contretemps with a man named Bates. Yes, that one; Mr Ken Bates, of Chelsea and now Leeds fame. Smarting from a rejected bid to buy shares and join the board at Turf Moor a year earlier, seen off without much effort by Bob Lord, the youthful Ken Bates had then set his sights on Oldham Athletic. Having successfully achieved his aim and become chairman, he had the novel idea of writing in his programme notes about all the players Oldham had tried to sign thus far. Lord described as a lousy breach of the soccer code the listing of 25 players with Bates' comments beside their name. He was particularly annoyed that a Burnley player had been named – Mick Buxton – and beside his name was the comment "refused to part". Lord denied any enquiry had ever been made and firmly announced that should Bates ever telephone the club about any matter he would without hesitation slam down the phone. It may seem a trivial matter by today's standards but then it was considered an "inducement" to name a player in this way and was viewed very seriously. Smarting from Bob Lord's chastisement Bates retaliated in the next club programme when he inserted a two page spread outlining all the ways Bob Lord had breached soccer etiquette under various headings. Lord was furious, of course, and answered back by saying that Bates was only piqued because he had failed in his bid to infiltrate the Burnley board, prevented from doing so only "due to the inexperienced stooges" he used. It's funny to think that Ken Bates and Bob Lord could so easily have ended up on the same Burnley board in the same room – for how long, one wonders? A confrontation between those two would have put any meeting between Andy Lochhead and Ron Harris into the shade.

The goals tally tells its own story as to how season '66/67 progressed. By December 31st Burnley had scored 51 goals in League games; from then until the end of the season the tally was just 15. In the penultimate game at Sheffield Wednesday the season finally fell apart with a 7-0 defeat. If you add to that a total of five broken legs at the club, a third-round exit from the FA Cup at the hands of Everton, in truth it became a dismal season by the end, with a final home crowd of just over 11,000.

By Christmas there were just two more highlights to come: the 5-1 defeat of West Brom on the final day of the year; and then the disposal of Naples in the Fairs Cup. The two goals I scored against West Brom were the final ones for me that season in the League, the second one being a classic Lochhead-Irvine combination goal with Andy heading down and me putting it into the net. A month later, on the final day of January, the season for me would be over.

But when Napoli flew into London airport they were confident of a straightforward win. Such was their knowledge of Burnley they thought Turf Moor was the name of one of the players. Sophia Loren didn't travel with them and few of their 52,000 season ticket holders came either. Who can blame them? Drab, gloomy, Burnley on a damp, foggy January night is not for the faint-hearted. Sivori, their world-class inside left, might have known everything about what to do with a football but his geography was less impressive when he announced that Burnley was up near the Scottish Borders. Condescendingly he proclaimed that Burnley would find it difficult to score against the tight-covering Naples defence and counter-punching raids. He was right about the punching bit. Among his soccer souvenirs was a medal given to him by Sophia Loren with the inscription "Conqueror of Rome". She would not be giving him one inscribed "Conqueror of Burnley". It was announced that "he doesn't like flying, it makes him very nervous". Several Burnley players actually flew during the game when they were kicked several feet into the air.

By the time of the Naples game in late January, Jimmy Adamson had decided, or at least it seemed to me, that Willie Irvine was the scapegoat and reason behind Burnley's faltering performances around the turn of the year and the two defeats against Leeds and Newcastle. But maybe there was another reason. The squad spent some preparation time in Southport and after the coach journey back to Burnley I slipped into a local club and had a shandy. I enjoyed a drink or two, and still do, but on that day, after the coach journey home and with a mouth like the bottom of a budgie's cage, it was one shandy and nothing more. Jack Butterfield, the club's commercial manager, was also in there and reported that I had been drinking. Was that the reason I was dropped for the Naples game at Turf Moor? Relations with Jimmy Adamson were already poor and I fumed silently as I watched the game from the Bob Lord Stand. Maybe he had decided to drop me anyway. I shall never know. It was Harry Potts who gave me the news that I wasn't playing and told me it was nothing to do with him. "But you're the bloody manager, Harry," I thought. "What do you mean it's nothing to do with you. Who's picking the team now, you or Adamson?" Mind you, with the tackles that were flying around that night, maybe I was better sitting watching. No, the truth is I was dejected and angry. I learned years later that Jimmy didn't think I was a team player; maybe that too affected his thinking.

What I watched was a game that was as brutal and bad-tempered an exhibition of football as I have ever seen or taken part in. Crude tackles, trips, elbows, deliberate fouls, body-checks, constant provocation, constant retaliation and endless infringements did nothing to convince people that Italian football was anything other than totally wretched and inept. The Italian national team had already been humiliated in the '66 World Cup and now this exhibition in Burnley took football violence to a new platform. And that's not forgetting Argentina or Don Revie's Leeds.

Even in a game of constant hostility one incident stood out, when Andy Lochhead was floored in the penalty area and while he lay motionless on the floor, Naples defender Juliano Panzanato stamped on his head. He had to be sent off and indeed he was. Andy's head recovered in time to hear Panzanato saying that in the return leg he would "keel" him. Andy looked at Panzanato and with that deep, masculine voice of his had the last word. "Oh no you won't; you won't be playing, you'll be bloody suspended."

Burnley won 3-0 with goals from Lochhead, Latcham and Coates. Napoli were stunned and swore vengeance in the return game. Their supporters back in Volcano City could not believe the news and within hours were stirring up hatred and making their threats that no Burnley player would escape alive from their cauldron of a stadium. Cool Jimmy Adamson added insult to injury when he said we could have had six or seven and that now we could go and win over there. At the after-match meal the two sets of players sat face to face on separate tables and simply glowered at each other. The Burnley boys ate heartily while, according to Keith McNee, the Italians sat like a bunch of naughty boys who had just had their bottoms smacked good and proper. After the meal they returned to the Keirby Hotel still scowling. Interviews were in short supply, although one of them is alleged to have said, "If you thought that was rough wait till we get back to Naples." Letters flooded in to the local newspapers expressing outrage at the Naples tactics and congratulating Burnley on their restraint. Nevertheless, even in restrained mode, somehow Burnley had 35 out of the 59 free kicks awarded against them. I've often wondered since if 59 free kicks is a record.

The return game in Naples took place on February 8th, by which time the players had time to stoke up their tactics, and the fans had time to stock up on fruit and vegetables to hurl at the Burnley team as they came out. Quite a few boots and shoes came down as well, which either means that these were wealthy people who had shoes to spare or that several dozen of them walked home barefoot. It was a game I missed and with a leg in plaster it was just as well I wasn't there to slow down the escape from the ground after the game. The great escape was aided by an armoured lorry, nine jeeps full of militia, and a dozen police motorcyclists as the club made the journey to Capodichina Airport five miles from the ground, immediately after the game. And all this because Naples could only manage a 0-0 draw.

The game itself, where every Naples tackle came under the heading of "atrocity", was a one-way procession of Naples attacks against do-or-die Burnley defending. Harry Thomson in goal was simply stunning, making so many world-class saves that he must have used up the remainder of his lifetime's supply. The Burnley players were hacked, body-checked, tripped, elbowed, thumped and spat at for 90 minutes as well as (it must be said) being given a soccer lesson. But still Napoli couldn't score. The crowd reaction was predictable as southern volatility exploded and raged at the Burnley party. Yet it was the after-match scenes which made the headlines. As the final whistle went, Thomson held out the hand of friendship to a Naples player and was promptly spat at. As the two of them grappled and snarled, Adam Blacklaw jumped up from the bench to intervene. As the rest of the team vanished a dozen members of the stadium staff set on Blacklaw. He and several of them disappeared over and into the moat as Blacklaw, never a shrinking violet, decided that if he was going to meet his maker, so would half of his assailants.

However, Blacklaw somehow broke free and dashed to the dressing room with his attackers in hot pursuit. With Adam half in and half out the dressing room door, somehow a gun appeared from beneath an overcoat and a hand grabbed him to pull him back into the corridor. There then followed a huge tug of war with Blacklaw saved by the Burnley team holding onto his legs trying to pull him into the dressing room, and the other half of him being held by stadium staff trying to drag him into the corridor. Presumably it was at this point that all thoughts of an after-match drink in the players' lounge evaporated. In the mélée the glass door was shattered and Blacklaw was arrested and taken away. Half a dozen policemen in uniform holding guns can be very persuasive. He was released, however, quite quickly with an apology from the Naples president who only the day before had been reassuring the English press that, "This is not the Congo, we are not barbarians, you will see what good sportsmen we are tomorrow." It later transpired that Harry Potts received the award for the most reckless bravery. Knowing that all the English journalists were being penned in the press box by angry fans, Harry set off on a lone journey to find them to get them to the coach. Poor Harry. No one had told him the pressmen had already managed to scarper with another police escort and were well on their way to the airport.

As for Adam, he dined out and drank copious pints in his local for years on the strength of the story he had to tell of the day he took on the might of the Napoli stadium staff single-handed, his proudest moment being when he threw one of them down the stone stairs and heard a very satisfying crack as the poor sod's head hit the bottom.

And as for Harry Thomson, described by one hack as "a god in a green jersey", he came out of it with one of the greatest sporting replies of all time. Asked by an Italian journalist, still thrilled and awed by the series of stupendous saves Harry had made in breaking the hearts of all those thousands of Naples fans, whether he considered this to be the greatest game of his life, Thomson managed to look suitably cool, unflustered, and a little surprised at the question. He thought for a careful moment and then replied in a casual Scottish drawl, "Not at all, I always play like this."

As the plane took off from the airport no one is quite sure who it was who shouted down the length of the cabin, "Hey Bob, isn't there supposed to be a banquet?"

The fact that Burnley players suffered five broken legs during the season is a sad commentary on the state of the game in the '60s. You went into many games during a season knowing that there were players on the other side who would deliberately and coldly set out to hurt the opposition. Some of us were just bad tackles waiting to happen. The tackle waiting for me was not far off.

Is there such a thing as fate? Does it really exist, or is it just something that exists in our own minds as a ready excuse for things that happen in our lives that we are too lazy or uninterested to do anything about? Is there really an unseen power that predetermines all the events in our existence? Do we manage our own lives or are we at the mercy of chance happenings or other people's decisions? Do we make all our own choices or are our choices made for us by the actions of people outside of our control? How do two paths cross? What is it that makes two chains of events coincide one day and which then means that two people will meet by chance?

If I felt that my own life was in my own hands, and that it was me who was managing it, that feeling ended on Tuesday evening, January 31st, 1967. Today, in retrospect, it's as if all the events in my life prior to that were leading up to the one incident that was such a watershed.

If there was a decision made by others that had such an effect on me, then maybe it was the decision by Liverpool Football Club to sell Johnny Morrissey to Everton. I'm told they paid £10,000 for him and he had made only a handful of appearances for Liverpool. They deemed him expendable and from that moment our lives were predetermined to come into contact with far-reaching consequences for me. Johnny Morrissey was small, strong, worked hard, and had a lethal shot. He was a winger-cum-midfield player with the ability to run up and down tirelessly, and get crosses over. His lack of pace he made up for with energy and competitive aggression. At Everton he spent his first years in and out of the team, never really claiming a permanent place until later. He was in the Everton team on the night of January 31st. That one moment in time when his leg came into contact with mine still has its effects today.

The third round FA Cup tie against Everton began with a 0-0 draw at Turf Moor. Adamson brought me back for this game: there's that word "destiny" again. At the time, "Yes," I thought, "no way should you be leaving me out." Nearly 40 years later I curse the day he brought me back. The first game was poor, with Everton setting out their stall to defend, defend and defend. It was nothing like the awful game against Naples, but nevertheless all the underhand niggles, bad tackles and trips were there. It was a stop-start scrappy game where Burnley should have put away at least one of the five clear chances that came our way. Twice in the last few minutes Ray Wilson threw himself in the way of shots and certain goals from me. Football is a swine of a game sometimes. The difference between a goal and a miss or chance gone is sometimes so fine, and yet the centre forward is blamed time and time again for the missed opportunity. I was, allegedly, having a poor spell, but a poor spell hinges on so many things and the shots miraculously blocked by Wilson were perfect examples of that fine borderline that exists between success and failure. In the minds of Burnley fans it wasn't Ray Wilson to be praised for his astonishing agility; it was Willie Irvine who was blamed for his misses. Such is football. For Everton fans Ray Wilson was the right man in the right place at the right time. For me he was the opposite; and there's that word "fate" again. Why did it have to be Wilson, who was at the peak of his game, in that place at that time? Tell me that. A goal would have won the game. My leg would have been safe. Ralphie Coates, too, finished the game wondering how on earth he had missed a gilt-edged chance. As far as I can remember Everton, the cup holders, had just one shot in the game. The replay was just three days later.

Alex Elder, who didn't play, commented in his newspaper column on what a rough brawl the replay was. One Everton player had actually physically grabbed the referee, pushed him several feet and nearly knocked him over when a free kick was awarded against him. He got away totally unpunished. Another Everton player slapped a Burnley player in full view of the referee and received just a gentle word in his ear and a pat on the back. Some Everton players played it hard, said Elder, with tactful understatement. Then he referred to the Everton fans who booed and jeered as I was carried off. "Rabble", he called them, and made the not unsubtle comment that some of their players who prefer to kick the opposition should themselves suffer a bad injury and then they might change their ideas. Everton had taken the lead but I had equalised. At half-time I can remember going back into the dressing room fearing that this was a game where one of us would get hurt and I can clearly remember saying how careful we needed to be because they were out to hurt us. How right I was.

In this niggly, physical game I knew the leg was broken the minute he made contact with me. In his report Keith McNee described it as a crash tackle, adding that many spectators from this area believed it to be a foul and over-vigorous. The *Liverpool Daily Post* described Morrissey as going into every challenge like a bulldozer. The referee in his infinite wisdom awarded a bounce-up. Did he even see it properly? As I was carried off, crying with pain, I could hear the jeers and catcalls of the Everton supporters. I remember thinking what bastards they were and I stuck up my fist and waved it in defiance, not so much as a gesture at them but more of a rallying call to my own team. Years later one Burnley supporter, Tony Scholes, still remembered being at the game and seeing his father turn to a friend in horror at the sight of the tackle. Alan Bailey, another fan, was there and heard the break. It was sickening, he said. Dave Wynne was 19 years old and close up to the touchline in one of the enclosures. He, too, still has the memory of me running down one of the wings and being brought down by the tackle. I was his favourite player, he told me and he cried when he heard and saw it. After the game he remembers the coach in which he was travelling being bricked by Everton supporters. The coach window was shattered and he was hit by the glass and one of the bricks. Most sickening of all, though, he added, were the sounds of Everton supporters mocking and jeering as I was carried off.

Another supporter from Barrowford recently sent me this letter. He wrote it after I did a local radio show and commented on the game at Everton.

Dear Willie,

Just a few lines to say how much I enjoyed your interview on Radio Lancashire. I was at Goodison that night you broke your leg. I was in the stand and I heard the crack. I know you would not name the player who did it but I will, Johnny Morrissey. I think I am right. In fact the left back for Everton that night was Ray Wilson and as I was working in a weaving shed at that time I could lip-read. And Ray Wilson went up to Johnny Morrissey and said what did you do that for and gave him a right telling off. I think I am right with this match. I think Alan Ball was playing for Everton and the referee was Kevin Howley. Hope you don't mind me dropping you these few lines. There was no one happier than me when you were knocking them in and not forgetting Andy Lochhead.

No one was more upset or horrified than Carole Lochhead and my wife Rita sitting up at the back of one of the stands. Carole certainly heard the break and turned to Rita immediately to say it didn't sound at all good. Rita was five months pregnant with Darren and was brought down to the medical room after the game in tears. By then the leg had been put into an inflatable splint. All of the Burnley team were shaken and distressed by the injury and maybe the "fight" went out of them, if that's the right word to use. It was as if a mood settled over them. Alex Young, Everton's "golden boy", scored his second and the winning goal.

A dreadful and distasteful scene occurred afterwards in the medical room where I was still lying on the table, when Harry Catterick, the Everton manager, came in. There has always been the story floating around that he came in to apologise for the tackle. Not so. He came in; looked at me lying on the table and told me that it had served me right, that I'd got what I'd been asking for. Catterick and Harry Potts had once been playing colleagues at Goodison Park but that didn't stop Potts being absolutely livid. The Everton coach, who clearly had more sensitivity about him than Catterick, took him away. Gentleman Harry Potts had a peach of a temper on occasions. In his programme notes in the next game at Turf Moor he made no mention of this. How could he? You don't put this kind of thing in programme notes. I refused to go to a Liverpool hospital, saying I preferred to be taken to Burnley where I knew I would be among friends.

Bob Lord was livid. In the Everton boardroom after the game he gave full vent to his feelings and told the Everton directors in no uncertain terms what he thought of their team and supporters. He fumed about the treatment given to me as I was carried off. He pointed out to them how angry he was at the rough play and that on two occasions he had seen Everton players deliberately kick a Burnley player with the ball nowhere near. It became so heated that eventually one Everton director asked him to leave the room. Without further ado Bob Lord did just that and vowed never to set foot in there again.

Not long ago I was in touch with an Everton supporter who was at both games, and the Everton view, of course, is different. He recalled that the Everton fans at Turf Moor for the first game were incensed by the Burnley rough play and they actually wondered if we were Leeds in disguise. It was a blood and thunder affair, he said, with Burnley kicking everything that moved. Derek Temple, normally a winger, was playing at centre forward in place of Alex Young and in particular came in for some rough treatment. At Everton the fans called Temple "Shirley"; he was gifted but never a "hard" player and on occasions Morrissey would act as his unofficial bodyguard. Temple eventually had to go off after the rough treatment he received. In the replay, said the Evertonian, there was an air of revenge around Goodison Park, not in the physical sense but in the fact that the Everton fans wanted to beat these upstarts from Burnley with skill and flair, not the boot. Johnny Morrissey was a hard man he said; he held no fear and never held back but Jack Charlton in his "little black book", allegedly says that he is one player he will never forgive.

It's funny how different sets of fans have such different perspectives. Another Evertonian revealed that he remembered it like yesterday.

Burnley were definitely no shrinking violets; you may recall the dirty Burnley chant to the tune of Alouette. It was in my opinion on a par with Leeds at Goodison in '65. Do you recall Andy Lochhead's "accidental" clash of heads with Brian Labone. Labby was forced to leave the field with blood gushing from his head, this resulted in Jimmy Gabriel switching to centre half and absolutely relishing the physical battle with Lochhead. My outstanding memory of the game was the magnificent header Alex Young planted into the Street End from a Morrissey corner. The Burnley keeper was Young's cousin, he rushed from his line both fists raised above his head but still couldn't reach the height of Alex's leap. I've never seen anybody leap so high...

As I've written, it was a hard game in the '60s: there's that word "hard" again. Time and time again you'll hear players from that time say that it was a man's game with no quarter given and none asked. Every team had its share of tough, uncompromising players, never afraid to get hurt, never afraid to dish things out, and Burnley were no different. The protection from referees then was nothing like what it is today. Some games were just a battle and a battle is what the two games against Everton were. It was a night when somebody was going to be badly hurt and sod's law put its marker on me.

I saw a cutting from the report of the game recently and Keith McNee's final paragraph, I confess, left me in silence, thinking of what might have been. *"Irvine will have bittersweet memories of this one of course. It was the night he gave us a nostalgic reminder of his deadly finishing ability: it was the night when his bright career died a temporary death and with the passing, also died our cup hopes."*

As far as I am concerned it was more than a temporary death; neither my career nor I was ever the same again. Something was taken away from me that night and it was never regained. Sometime just before the World Cup in 1966 Alf Ramsey is reported to have said he wished I had been born an Englishman. That's how good I was.

CHAPTER TWELVE

GOODBYE BURNLEY

One of my sons has been trying to uncover a little of the early family history. He knows I am trying to find out more about the family and my past, especially the bit about my mother's brothers and World War One. There isn't much to go on but he's found four Quinns who were in the Royal Inniskilling Fusiliers and killed in World War One in 1916 and all are buried at the Thiepval Memorial Cemetery, at the site of the Somme. Two were killed on the same day, on the 6th of September, and there is no mention of their parents, whereas for the other two it gives the parents' names and these are not relatives of ours. Joseph and Patrick are the names of the two killed on the 6th. They could well be the ones related to us and could be two of the four. Maybe there were only two, not four, and the story has become exaggerated over the years, but Joan seemed so sure there were four. Maybe two of them were not in the Inniskillings, but that seems unlikely because if there were four of them they would have all joined up in the same regiment.

If they were killed on September 6th it's likely that they were killed in the Ginchy area. The whole campaign gained a few yards one day and then lost them the next as thousands of lives were wasted in utter futility. Temperatures were in the '70s that day and it was muggy and overcast. The Inniskillings had been involved in digging the forward trenches, an activity which often came under heavy enemy shelling and machine-gun fire. What a waste, the trenches they dug were eventually abandoned as the Germans counter-attacked.

Can you picture them? The uncles I never even knew huddled in a half-dug trench along with dozens of other terrified boys, frightened out of their wits, desperate for protection and shelter as those bullets and bombs scared the daylights out of them and killed them. I get a lump in my throat just thinking about them in that

place of utter desolation and without a chance of escape. You wonder
what they were thinking, what their last thoughts were, what was
the last thing they saw? Did they hear the skylarks singing overhead
in moments of respite from the artillery? Did they think of Antrim
and home, their sister Agnes and the rest of their family? Did they
wonder just what in God's name they were doing there in that
living hell? Or were they just obliterated in an instant without ever
knowing what hit them? Were there two of them or four? Maybe I'll
never know for sure.

There are over 72,000 identified graves in the Thiepval Cemetery.
Ninety per cent of their occupants were killed between July and
November 1916. So the mystery remains. Possibly there are two more
Quinns buried in unknown graves. My sister Sandra in Scotland
might know more; my mother spent her last years with her before she
died and it's reasonable to assume they talked. Maybe brother Bobby
has answers, but I haven't seen or spoken to him for years.

1966/67 ended with everyone at the club wondering how
things had gone so terribly wrong. Fingers pointed at injuries,
loss of form, defensive lapses, bad luck and inconsistency. The
simple truth is that with my leg broken the goals just dried up.

The Willie Morgan Supateek opened in March with its
array of designer labels and was attended by a galaxy of
star players and guests. Of course I was there, along with
the crowds and all the girls in short skimpy dresses. As a
teammate and part of the Burnley family we had grown up
with, we liked Willie but he revelled in the limelight and his
Georgie Best image. Willie could play football like an angel
can sing, but like the promise of the team of '66 the shop
didn't last long either.

There are some who will say that the Turf Moor lean years
began when John Morrissey's tackle snapped my leg in that
heated FA Cup tie. I won't quite go along with that but I
would say that my broken leg was certainly one of many
turning points in Burnley history. Though the leg healed, a
part of me didn't. Football is all about "what ifs" and "buts"
and "if only". What if Morrissey and I had not been destined
to meet so sickeningly at that one moment in time, during

that one particular game? Would I have gone on to score over 20 goals a season for several more seasons? Would the story of Burnley Football Club have taken a different course? Would I ever have joined Preston or Brighton and become part of their history?

It would be several years and a never to be contemplated relegation to Division Two before another group of Burnley players would come along in the early '70s, a group which would make one last failed attempt at clinging to the big time with style and panache. Ironically I would play against them at a time when I was enjoying a final flourish and an Indian summer, miles away in the warmth and friendliness of cosmopolitan Brighton. It was something I couldn't possibly have considered when I was carried off the Goodison Park pitch in agony with my leg shattered, while my wife sat in the stand horrified, and while Bob Lord fumed and Ray Wilson berated Johnny Morrissey.

Adamson was confident we would do well in '67/68. They look "slick" in training, he told the press, and the playing staff was one of the strongest in the division if not *the* strongest. In theory he was right; in practice it wouldn't turn out that way during the season. The previous season had been marred by constant injury to several players and in my own mind my broken leg had been a major reason why Burnley faded so badly. Now it was healed and I was raring to go. I had worked so hard in the close season to get fit and no one helped me more than Len Kinsella, another player who'd had a broken leg that season. We worked together and I owe him a lot for training with me through the summer.

Funnily enough, during the time when the leg had still been in a pot there had nearly been a disaster. To give Rita a break from looking after me and our new son, I actually went to stay with Tom and Nan Whalley for a short spell and during this time was taken out for a drink by Matt Walker, owner of Hindle and Walker, a Volvo garage. I was still on painkillers and having a bad time with the leg but nevertheless we managed to get out for a drink... or two. Matt gave me a piggyback lift up the stairs back to my bedroom afterwards at Tom's house but somehow I lost my grip on Matt's back, fell off, and slowly slid all the way back down the stairs to the bottom. It could have been a disaster but somehow wasn't and oddly enough after that I had no more pain.

In truth, the time I spent with my leg in plaster, and then the period of recuperation, recovery and training was a bleak time. It's the same for all footballers with a bad injury who have to spend such a long time on the fringes of things. Suddenly you are no longer one of the chosen few, no longer in the centre of things, no longer involved in the team talks or the matchday build-up. You're out on the edge, not excluded, but at the same time not included either, and while all this is going on you wonder night and day about whether you will fully recover.

Will you get that first team place back? And when you recover will you still be wanted? You're out of things; the word "redundant" would not go amiss; there's a sense of isolation and no longer belonging. It almost feels like it's a crime to have been injured and that, now, you're just useless and a nuisance. Kind words can only go so far. As a result of this it was a time when I was difficult to live with and it was my family who bore the brunt because of the boredom and the arguments and the confrontations.

Meanwhile, Adamson was really confident and thought that we would have a first-class season, that with the reasonable degree of luck that all clubs need, Burnley had nothing to fear and we would hold our own with the best. Bob Lord was typically bullish, saying that with average luck and minimal injuries we could go places. Playing staff, backroom boys, training ground were second to none, he announced and emphasised that this small town club could retain its premier position. Sadly his mention of the previous season's leaky defence was to be repeated in the coming months.

He was right about going places. We went to lowly Stockport County for the first friendly and lost 1-0. Admittedly they were the Fourth Division champions but we came off the field thinking, how on earth did we lose to that lot, even if it was just a friendly. For me, it felt good though just to be back, especially after one storming fifty-yard run from the centre circle and a rasping shot just over the bar.

The game marked the debut of new boy Frank Casper. All eyes were on him for one simple reason: he had been bought from Rotherham and this marked a complete new turn in the running of Burnley Football Club. Both Andy and I wondered which of us would make way for him. As it turned out all three of us played and it was clear that the Lochhead-Irvine partnership was still deemed to be one of the strengths of the team. It was Ralphie's place he took, but Ralph was unavailable anyway because of an appendix operation. But the question remained; if Casper had been bought, who was to make way for him when we were all fit and available?

In addition to being just slightly unsettled by this there was also the sale of Alex Elder to Stoke City. It made you think. Who's next? In a matter of months three players had gone and two of them, Elder and goalkeeper Adam Blacklaw, had been bedrocks of the side. Emlyn Hughes was the only full-back in Britain more expensive than Alex. The conveyor belt continued with the new talent at one end which was then despatched elsewhere at the other end when it reached its sell-by date. You knew your turn would one day come. Bob Lord always used to argue that any player sold was past his sell-by date but that wasn't always true. Maybe his injuries the previous season and his disputes with the club added to the willingness to sell Alex Elder. But he was only 26 and in his prime and everyone at the club, including Alex, thought he wouldn't go just yet. But if your time was up, then your time was up and he signed for Tony Waddington without hesitation for an alleged £50,000.

In the first league game of the season against Coventry it was Casper and I who scored. I was up against a big, tough, uncompromising defender called George Curtis. Even without a suntan I thought he was the nearest thing to a gorilla you could find but with the suntan he'd gained during the summer I really did think I was playing against one. Curtis took no prisoners in any game he played and I came off delighted to be in one piece and without another broken leg. As we came off there was a confidence and an optimism. "Back to normal" I thought with a smile, but it was misplaced for this would be a season of toil, inconsistency, being dropped, put back; an in-and-out kind of season eventually ending with a transfer request and then the actual transfer itself as it all became unacceptable and on some occasions just downright infuriating.

It affected my home life and domestic relationships and became the classic football story of frustration and discontent, which you then take out on other people, in particular those closest to you and who mean the most. I must have become almost impossible to live with as relationships were stretched to the limit and almost broke down. I used to sit back and wonder how things could have changed so much since just a dozen months previously when I had set a new scoring record. I looked at Jimmy Greaves banging in the goals with monotonous regularity as if it would take an earthquake to stop him. That should be me, I would think. Why am I not still doing that? And then again I would remember the night at Everton and that tackle.

Something was wrong. There was no pain, I felt fit, but for some reason, though I was fine for the first half hour of any game, the training staff noticed that the longer the game went on, I was running with the slightest of limps. To the spectator it might have been unnoticeable but when the staff spotted it there was some concern and it contributed to the decision to use me as a substitute, coming on for the last half hour of a game. I can't say I was pleased but there was always a funny side to things, like the day I came on as sub against Cardiff and who should be playing but Brian Harris, an ex-Everton player, who as far as I remember also played in the game at Everton when my leg was broken. So Adamson brought me on and Harris came up to me and announced, "Good, now I'm going to break your other leg." As I jogged away from him I couldn't help but think, "And for this I get paid the princely sum of £60 a week." Sense of humour essential, I suppose.

Even as early as September I was in the reserve team as Casper was preferred and two young lads called Colin Blant and Martin Dobson were emerging. We called Colin "Muffin the Mule". I'll let you, dear reader, figure out why. He loved the greyhounds and there was one night he really did lose the shirt off his back when he bet that as well. Martin

Dobson went on to become an England player and one of Burnley's finest. Not bad for a lad who was rejected by Bolton. There are plenty of Burnley folk who wonder why he never eventually became manager of Burnley. Almost out of spite and cussedness I slammed two goals in for the reserves. But then it was back in the first team and I only mention this occasion in particular because it was against our favourite opponents Leeds United at Elland Road and Gary Sprake gave me his usual gift. He really was a gifted 'keeper but sadly will always be remembered for the gaffes he made like the one in this game. Casper shot, Sprake fumbled and the ball ran loose. With uncanny instinct I just happened to be there and almost felt sorry for the bloke as I poked it over the line. His face was a picture as if to say, "Why is it that when I make a cock-up it's always you who's there to make the most of it?" Sadly, Leeds scored two and we lost. If there were goalkeepers like him in every team I'd have scored in every game I played. Though we were the league's leading scorers the defence was still as leaky as a sieve and the old problems remained. They remained for me too. I had only played at Leeds because Ralph Coates was injured again and the resentment just grew and grew.

There were now demands for the club to buy a defender and Colin Waldron would be the chosen one. When he signed he was not to know, and neither were the rest of us, that humiliation was waiting for us at West Bromwich Albion in the shape of an 8-1 defeat. It was an unthinkable scoreline in the town of Burnley. Was this not the club that for several seasons had been up there with the best, won a championship, played in Europe and had so many great players? At half-time we were losing, 4-0 maybe, I can't remember exactly, so Harry Potts, ever the optimist and encourager, says to us, "Well OK lads, just go out and you win the second half 5-0." It was a sound, flawless plan and would have worked a treat except for just one slight hiccup; it was West Brom who scored four more, not us. After the game a young lad went up to goalkeeper Harry Thomson and gave him his autograph book to sign. Harry, who'd had a nightmare game, dropped that as well. Harry sat with his head in his hands in the dressing room afterwards. "For fuck's sake don't drop that as well, Harry," someone shouted. Footballers are nothing if not resilient.

I'd been blessed with a proper run in the side for a few weeks, but towards the end of that run the West Brom date, November 11th, is still imprinted in my mind. When you walk off a field having lost 8-1 words can't express how you feel. Knowing as well that they could have doubled their score, we were so bad.

I was to play only seven more games in Burnley colours. If there was a low point maybe that day was it, and by now I had it in my head that I was one of the regular scapegoats for any defeat that came our way. I found Jimmy Adamson more and more difficult to relate to and our relationship just plummeted although it might not have been obvious to others. He became my scapegoat and in the time-honoured way these things happen, when things are not going well you look for someone other than yourself on whom to heap the blame. It was a vicious circle; I played poorly, I became frustrated, my home life suffered. The more my home life suffered, the poorer my game became. You begin to think one thing: that you must get away and make a break, make a clean fresh start and thereby, as if by magic, end the cycle of decline.

In January, Gordon Harris was sold. Another linchpin of the side gone, and he had jumped at the chance to join Sunderland for £70,000. He was possibly as unhappy as I was. He, too, had once been in digs with Tom Whalley and would often confide in him. Gordon would visit Tom for his sound, quiet, fatherly advice. "Time to leave, I think," Tom suggested to him. The deal was all kept very quiet and done in the space of just a few hours, and as Sunderland's manager Ian McColl was leaving the building having concluded the deal, Coventry's Noel Cantwell was walking in ready to make his offer. Possibly nobody was more delighted than Gordon's wife, who was as outspoken and vociferous as Gordon. For ninety-nine per cent of the time she was a quiet lass, but like many of us could and would let fly when she was upset, and she was certainly upset at what she saw was the unfair treatment being dished out to Gordon. The difference was, there was no gag on her as there was on Gordon and so she let rip at the club via the local paper. She accused the club of making him a scapegoat, she was angry he had been dropped for disciplinary reasons. When Bob Lord had said he wouldn't tolerate thugs in the team even if it meant relegation, it was a reference to Gordon. Then he was fined £150. His wife was livid and the rift between the Harris family and the club became impossible to heal. He had to go and with that deal concluded I wasn't to know that I would be the next. But what I did know was that I had a sneaky admiration for Gordon's wife and her public blasting of all things BFC and Bob Lord.

The private rift between Jimmy Adamson and myself grew ever wider in contrast to the steady relationship with Harry Potts. By then he had been at the club for ten years and at that time only Matt Busby had been a First Division manager longer. To have kept little Burnley in the top flight for so long was an enormous achievement and his ideals of fair play and playing to enjoy the game were still the same as they had been when he began. He was the classic nice man, yet if there was injustice against the club he could blow his top when the occasion demanded. His encroachment onto the field of play and angry repositioning of the ball in Paris against Reims, when their players were stealing up to ten yards as they took their free kicks, has become the stuff of legend.

It had been Harry Potts who calmed me down after a dressing room row with Jimmy Adamson in '64/65. Adamson hadn't been coach for long and I hadn't been in the first team that long. Maybe I was just brash and cocky but it was a game against Chelsea and as we changed into our kit he made some comment that left me incensed. I had a bad elbow and it had been giving me terrific pain. "I hope you won't use that as an excuse for a poor game," said Adamson as he walked by. I was all for getting dressed again and walking out until Harry talked me round.

It is possible Jimmy still remembers a boot room incident when he gave me a dressing down for something I had or had not done, I can't remember which. I stood and looked at him and said, "I don't like you." So Jimmy replied with elegant calmness, which is the way he was as a player, "And Willie, I don't like you either." Years later I look back and think it wasn't all Jimmy's fault. If he gave me reasons to dislike him, then I'm pretty sure I gave him reasons to feel the same about me. It's an inevitable fact of life in a football dressing room that not every personality will get on perfectly.

Mind you, talking of anger and confrontation, there was still the graveyard that was Halifax to come, but that's a story for later.

In February the inevitable happened: my transfer request was granted as the need to get away grew and grew. An old cutting from the time sums things up:

Willie Irvine transfer listed as a potentially £60,000 player showed just why he cannot command a regular place in the Burnley side with whom he was once so effective. The heading ability, which was once his strength, seems to have deserted him... Irvine just wasn't with it in the penalty area.

There's a sort of touching sadness to this short paragraph when I read it now. It followed a defeat in a game against Nottingham Forest on February 24th, 1968 when we lost 1-0 in a dreadful game. Was it only just two seasons earlier that I had been the toast of Burnley and the new glamour boy, the Irish international, the lad who couldn't miss, who could do no wrong? But now, at the age of only 24, everything was undoubtedly going wrong, including my private life, and there seemed only one way to get things back on track and that was to turn over a new leaf, to get away and make a fresh start.

Jimmy Adamson took me on one side and said to me that he didn't want me to go. "You are the reason I am going," I told him. Looking back, was I unfair on him? Did he merit the anger I displayed towards him? Was I right to have harboured this resentment for so long? Should I have looked at and into myself for the reasons behind this apparent decline? Was I lacking in focus and distracted by off the field events? Unhappiness with myself on the field meant I came home and took things out on my wife Rita. They were dark days and a brooding Irish temperament didn't help matters.

Hindsight is a wonderful thing. It can never solve the problems as they occur, but at least years later you can sometimes see why things happened in a different light. They say time heals but in this case it didn't.

"Willie Irvine's request for a transfer has been granted by our board of directors," announced Harry Potts and there was an immediate thought that Coventry City and Noel Cantwell would again move in, having been pipped at the post for Gordon Harris. My immediate reply was that I would be delighted to be going. With brother Bobby living in the Midlands and my other brother George, who was at that time an RSM in the Irish Guards, saying that he would retire to the Midlands, I would have been quite happy to move to Coventry. There was speculation that Tommy Cummings, the former Burnley player, now manager at Aston Villa, might also have been interested. Three weeks prior to all this conjecture Burnley had allegedly turned away an enquiry from Blackburn Rovers.

The granting of the request took a huge weight off my shoulders since it was clear that my career at Burnley was at best uncertain, at worst finished. Another factor had been the lack of reserve games to play in, thereby giving me no chance to regain form and make any kind of improved impression. Harry Potts had been sympathetic, telling me to keep fit and that things always had a habit of turning out for the best. When I'd threatened to quit and walk out if I didn't get a transfer he was there again with his patience and counselling. With another club I was certain I could rekindle enthusiasm, rediscover the old spark and hit regular good form. I sat back and waited for the offers to pour in. They didn't, until Preston North End and Bobby Seith made contact.

But the anger about the way this transfer came about still rankles today. A reporter called Len Noad used to ring me nearly every day to ask for any news. By the same token he'd give me any news he had and it was from him I heard that just about every Division One team was interested in signing me – and this included Manchester United, Arsenal, Wolves and Everton. I was a known, proven goalscorer and I was wanted. But nothing came of them and the whisper was that Bob Lord was blocking any possible move to a big club. No club official ever told me of their interest. Jimmy Hill, acting for Coventry City, twice phoned me, and given the chance would have signed both me and Andy Lochhead. Nothing came of it.

Goodbye Burnley

I'd been putting transfer requests in every day for eight weeks. I'd hand in a letter every day to Harry Potts. "You know what this is," I'd say. He'd take it off me, nod and smile his gentlemanly smile and either put it in his bottom drawer or in the bin; I never found out which.

In all honesty I was not best pleased to find that Preston were the only club with which I could talk. Their decline had been steady and relentless and the old glory days of Tom Finney in the First Division were long gone. Whereas Burnley under Bob Lord and Harry Potts had successfully retained their position of being a top club, Preston had been one of the many small town clubs who simply could not compete both in terms of finances and production of players. In 1960/61 they had been relegated, finishing bottom of Division One. But I had to get away. Adamson just gnawed away at me in the back of my head where, rightly or wrongly, I saw him as the reason for my stuttering form and season. I couldn't play for him and you have to want to play for the man in charge. It's from him you get your inspiration. In fairness there were many players who had no problems with him. His coaching was excellent, studious, thoughtful and creative. As a tactician he was outstanding. Players later came along like Colin Waldron and Paul Fletcher, who were devoted to him. Martin Dobson wrote glowingly about him in his newspaper column. But I just couldn't relate to him. I wanted to be the best, to improve, to score; but in my head I was telling myself that it wasn't going to happen at Burnley any more. Jimmy Adamson rightly takes his place in the long list of all-time Burnley "greats", but we were two blokes just destined to go our separate ways.

When Bobby Seith took over as Preston team manager from Gordon Milne in 1967/68, he had a sinking ship to rescue in a very short space of time. It was a dispirited club which had just had a run of six successive defeats; new players couldn't be tempted to join and critics pointed anyway to the waste of money on previous purchases. Seith didn't do a bad salvage job and made an immediate difference. This was the same Bobby Seith who had been a member of the 1959/60 Burnley Championship team. As a young lad I have half a memory of cleaning his boots when I was in charge of first team kit and his Burnley connections gave us a common ground which naturally interested me. But then so did a generous signing-on fee. It was Bob Lord and Burnley policy not to pay signing-on fees but other clubs did. That, plus a better wage, I cannot deny made me willing to sign in spite of Preston's vulnerable position. Seith persuaded me with simple and direct honesty. If I scored the goals, Preston would not go down. The truth is I didn't know, and didn't even check, just how near the bottom they were. It seemed a simple enough situation to me; just go there and score goals. That, plus the age-old fact that people respond to being wanted, was enough. Seith made me feel that I was needed and I could relate to him quite comfortably.

It also occurred to me that there was a certain irony that he, too, had left Turf Moor in circumstances that were far from cordial. He played 27 times in that championship-winning season, but interestingly it was only in 1999 that he received a belated championship medal from the club, having been denied one by Bob Lord. There's an interesting story that when he returned to Burnley to receive the medal he stayed, by coincidence, in what had once been Bob Lord's old house. He must have slept with a broad smile on his face that night.

They were hectic days leading up to the signing in March 1968. Rita was a Burnley girl through and through, and close to her family, and although ready and willing to be uprooted was dreadfully unhappy. She thought going to Australia couldn't be worse than moving the 21 miles to Preston. It is not easy being a football wife. Forget the guff you see on those glossy TV soap dramas about football and footballers' wives. The reality then, and even now for the legions of bread and butter footballers, was far different. Yes, there are temptations offered to footballers by female hangers-on and admirers, and God forbid I had my temptations as well, but the real life situation for most football wives is one of absent husbands, looking after the house, bringing up the kids, getting them back and forth to school, making ends meet, keeping things going and retaining some semblance of normality; in fact all those normal things any housewife does. But then there's the one that sets them apart: uprooting and moving house and children more often than they would wish, and doing it with precious little help from their moody, ritual-obsessed, footballer husbands, by and large far too preoccupied with concentrating on football or having a drink with the lads. I had to laugh recently when one manager banned his players from even helping their wives with the Christmas shopping.

Once we actually got to Preston, Rita would sometimes make the journey back to Burnley by the bus for the day. Once there she'd burst into tears with her mother as soon as she saw her, and then again at the end of the day when they stood at the bus stop waiting for the return bus. The word "lonely" doesn't do her justice, and there was little Darren and baby Stephen, born in 1970, for her to look after very much on her own.

When I put the pen to paper there was a strange mixture of feelings. There was no regret at leaving but there was a tinge of sadness that Burnley had been the place where I had spent eight years of my life and had come to regard as home. I thought about the good times I'd had as a teenager when I'd arrived and then progressed through the ranks, plus all the help and advice I had received from coaches and trainers. I thought of goals scored, the record I had set, the good people I had met like Tom and Nan Whalley who had become my second parents. There had been European trips, great games at places like White Hart Lane, Old Trafford and Highbury. Now it would be Carlisle, Rotherham and Hull. And if I failed it would be places like Barrow, Shrewsbury and Southport the following season. But it also meant a signing-on fee of £5,000 and a wage of £75 a week plus appearance money, which was £15 more than I was getting at Burnley. One of the Preston directors helped me in the purchase of a nice house at Fulwood.

Let's do it; go where you're wanted, I thought, and put my name on the line. The truth is I'd have gone anywhere to get away, even Morecambe for £20 a week. My turn had come, the conveyor belt had spewed me out and I wouldn't be the last: some other poor unsuspecting sod would certainly be next. He didn't know it in March 1968, but Willie Morgan's time was almost up as well. And when Willie went in the summer of '68, I doubt Andy Lochhead knew he would be the next to go in October. That year was a vintage one for the Turf Moor cash register. Bob Lord no doubt slept and dined well. But how did supporters feel, I wonder, as one by one, Elder, then Harris, then me, then Morgan and then Lochhead were all sold in just about the space of 12 months? We formed half of the team that had once been described as better than the Championship side of 1959/60. Just where did it go wrong?

CHAPTER THIRTEEN

PRESTON AND ON TO BRIGHTON

At the last minute it seemed though that the Preston deal was off as discussions then began to include a possible part-exchange deal including full-back John Ritchie joining Burnley. There was a game at Ipswich on the Saturday and the aim was to get me signed up in time for that. On Thursday evening nothing had been settled but then on Friday morning, after further last-minute talks, a straight cash deal of £45,000 was accepted. By the time the deal was concluded the Preston team coach had left for Ipswich so Bobby Seith packed me into his car, got us to the station and from there we headed for Ipswich via London. I had previously scored in nine "debut" games in various competitions at Burnley. I changed in the Ipswich away dressing room after a blur of a journey; surrounded by teammates I had never set eyes on before. I didn't score and we lost 4-0, which is more than a defeat; it's a thumping. After the game I sat with my new colleagues around the table and cheerfully announced, "Well, not to worry, lads; we can win the game next week and get back near the top." Typical me. They looked at me aghast and amazed. I can still hear today one reply. "What?" he said. "We're near the bloody bottom." My heart sank. For some reason I had it in my head we were in the top half.

"Bloody hell," I thought. "What am I doing here, what have I done?"

In the home debut game, though, it all came good as I scored in the win against Aston Villa. Villa took the lead after just a few minutes but the game ended 2-1 to Preston. My goal was lucky. I was probably offside but strikers need luck and it came my way that day. I wasn't going to grumble. The crowd seemed to take to me straight away. Maybe they were just grateful that here was an Irish international with a good scoring record who had come to join them. There was a run of eight unbeaten games and relegation, so close just weeks earlier, was avoided. In eleven games I scored six times. There was a hat-trick against Huddersfield Town. "Magnificent display by Willie Irvine," said Preston reporter Norman Shakeshaft. I felt ten feet tall. That is what strikers need – praise. Because from that the confidence grows and you can't wait for the next game. "Neither the wind, rain nor mud in atrocious conditions could stop the irrepressible Irvine," he went on to say. In truth the whole team played better as Seith's influence, man management, coaching and tactics paid off, but fans see things much more simply. Irvine had arrived, Irvine had scored goals, and Irvine had kept them up. I didn't grumble and lapped up the praise and the plaudits, as any good striker would do, basking in the glory of being the saviour. It felt damned good after all the frustrations at Turf Moor.

Preston were not relegated but the final table near the end of the season made interesting reading. Preston, Rotherham and Plymouth were all at the bottom end with just a handful of games to go. Bristol City were also near the bottom and they, too, avoided relegation over the course of the last four games. On April 27th, 1968, City were 20th in Division Two with 32 points. Preston were a place higher with 33 points. But Rotherham, who were 21st, could still manage 35 points if they won their last three games. Plymouth were already bottom and relegated. We were one of the remaining games City had to play and I well remember being in the hotel at Bristol on the morning of the game, and in walked one of the City players. I sat stunned as he offered us £2,500 to share if we would throw the game. Disgusted, I walked out, followed by Derek Temple. "I'm a professional," I stormed. "I want no part of this."

I've no idea if any of the others followed us out or if they stayed. If there was one game in my whole career in which I was desperate to score it was this one and, yes, I scored our one goal, but we lost that game 4-1. I've no idea if they took the money or not; I had left the room and don't have a clue what was said or done after I left, but what I will say is that I saw things happening in that game that you would normally only see in a Sunday morning parks game. After 18 minutes we had given two goals away. By the end of the game we had conceded as many goals as we had done in the entire previous eight matches. The points gained in that unbeaten eight game run showed promotion form. I know the City player's name but for legal reasons it won't be mentioned here. After the game I felt dirty and tainted and, when returning to the dressing room, saw the tray of teacups filled up with tea, and furiously kicked them all over the dressing room.

Norman Shakeshaft could not have known about the attempted bribe but commented in his *Lancashire Evening Post* match report: "...a strange match...with defenders conceding corners they would surely have never done in earlier matches... The marking has been tight since the defeat at Ipswich but on Saturday Bristol's lively forward line were allowed vital yards in which to move. Preston's strong rearguard collapsed for two vital periods (one in each half) and let in two goals on each occasion. For these brief periods the whole defence looked shaky..."

Would even hardened, cynical professionals throw a match, having just gone eight games undefeated? Who knows? As it happened Rotherham also lost that day, making us both safe.

Being at once-great Preston was interesting though: just like Burnley they had to sell to survive, but unlike Burnley there was no seemingly endless line of youth team talent coming through. They had clear money problems and being there gave me the chance to step back and see just how well organised Burnley FC was in terms of all its teams and coaching with the Turf Moor factory still in full production. At Preston there were high hopes of Bobby Seith whose knowledge of the game was first class, and who was much respected and very popular with the players. I felt at home, settled, satisfied and was scoring goals. The Kop had a song based on the *Mighty Quin*, a Manfred Mann hit of the time,

"Come on without, come on within, you'll not see nothing like Willie Irvine."

I have to say when I heard the roar of that song for the first time, sung by the Kop end in unison, it made my hair stand on end. Then I did something in one game that people still talk about today. It was the game when an opposing defender hoofed the ball upfield with a mighty swipe. The referee, quite close by, in anticipation of it sailing over his head turned his back. Big mistake. The ball hit him with an almighty thwack in the middle of his back and laid him out in a heap on the floor. I couldn't resist walking over and standing over him, arms folded, posing like a hunter stands over his "kill." It brought the house down. Who says Mike Summerbee was the first great crowd entertainer? Today I'd probably be booked for doing such a thing; wasn't Paul Gascoigne booked for playfully yellow carding a referee in Scotland after he picked up the card the ref had dropped? Is there much humour at all in the game today?

In a game against Norwich I scored after just 15 seconds and for all I know that might be the record for the fastest Preston goal ever scored. Sadly we lost but the headlines were for the speed of the goal.

On another occasion in a home match I missed an absolute sitter and my follow through took me onto the surrounding track on my backside. One bloke in the crowd told me in no uncertain terms what he thought of me, so I turned to him, half took off my shirt, made as if to hand it over to him and then said loudly so everyone could hear, "Well you have a go then, I don't feel too good today." The crowd at that end just fell about laughing, including the bloke who had been ranting at me.

But to score the one solitary winning goal against local rivals Blackburn Rovers was another goal that gave great satisfaction. It came during the run of eight unbeaten games, which began just after I arrived. Derby games between Rovers and Preston have never been quite as intense as those between Rovers and Burnley. But for me, with memories of all the games I'd played against them for Burnley, it was an extra special game. One goal. A penalty. My old colleague Adam Blacklaw was in goal for Blackburn and I grinned at him as I put the ball on the spot. He dived the right way but the ball was past him before he could blink. I could hear him fuming and cursing, "You lucky bastard". The decider. Hallelujah.

Then there was the time that Tom Finney, later to be Sir Tom, congratulated me and told me how well I'd done. It was nothing to do with football though. After some games we'd go round to the Supporters' Club at the back of one of the stands for a drink. Most times it was a nice unwind, with maybe a few backslaps and congratulations and handshakes with the supporters if we'd done well. Just occasionally, of course, there'd be the supporter who'd had a few too many, and of course one came over when Rita and I were sitting with Tom Finney and his wife after the game. Lovely man, Tom Finney, a real gentleman and always a pleasure to talk to; a man I looked up to and had the greatest respect for. Of course this chap weaved his way over and had clearly decided that anything Irish was only fit to be insulted. He rudely lobbed an Irish coin on the table and said, "Here, you have it, it's no good to me, I can't spend it here, take it back to bloody Ireland with you and you spend it."

We all looked at each other and groaned silently. I had a quick think: I could either give him a few rude words and a smack or do something smart. There was a cigarette machine over in the corner so over I went, put the coin in, and out came a packet of ten cigarettes. Suddenly he looked quite nervous as I walked over to him and looked at him with narrowed eyes. Casually I lit a cigarette, winked at him, then offered him one and, with a big smile, said politely, "Thanks, do have one, you've just paid for them." The oaf wandered off. "Well done, Willie," said Sir Tom, "you handled that brilliantly."

For the first few months of the 1968/69 season I could do no wrong. Success breeds success, as they say, and an old cutting announces that it was a happy place to be and that I was enjoying my football more than at any other time. There was a nice incentive from director Bob Bolton who was a keen gardener. Every time I scored he presented me with a rose bush for the garden and if there was a hat-trick there would be two. It was a lovely gesture but I began to get backache digging them in, I was playing and scoring so well. I'm told I was the biggest crowd favourite since Tom Finney – high praise indeed – and just shows the value of a goalscorer. You can miss plenty but as long as you put some of them away regularly you become a hero. As a goalkeeper you can make one blinding save after another, but just make one mistake, and all that good work is undone and it is remembered for a long, long time.

I worked well with Bobby Seith and in his and my first full season there was never any thought or danger of relegation. There were clean sheets on 18 occasions. Of all the goals scored it was me who scored 19 of them. 13 of them came in the first 16 games. That's some scoring rate and the old Manfred Mann number became a regular chant. But all the time the underlying factor was the lack of money and pressure from the bank, which meant that players were sold rather than bought. There was no youth policy and it all boiled down to just being a survival game. While the defence was miserly, more than satisfactory, the team scored only 38 league goals that season. That's a total that will take you nowhere and by the following season, '69/70, the place was as dispirited as ever and supporter morale was as low as it could get when good players were sold for poor prices, like Ken Knighton for £45,000, a price which was allegedly forced by the bank because Preston were no longer allowed to make cheque payments.

It doesn't take long in football for things to go wrong. The previous season, I had taken a whack that was to have serious effects. It was a cup game at Stamford Bridge which we drew 0-0. The name David Webb springs to mind but then he was one of a complete posse of Chelsea hard men. He caught me with a scissors tackle and the tackle gripped my left leg. As I turned one way my left knee stayed where it was: game over for me. It was diagnosed as ligament trouble and I carried on playing, which is what we used to do in those days without the benefit of state-of-the-art medical technology. But I struggled, scored less and less with a yard of speed missing. In the games I played at the beginning of the new season, the second full season for me, I was only half fit and it was clear that an operation would be needed. Form suffered and there was heckling and barracking on some occasions with few fans knowing what problems I had. The knee continued to give me pain to such an extent that I collared the club doctor one morning and told him how bad it was. He gave me a note and instructions to get to the hospital for X-rays. Several X-rays later and after a consultation with a specialist the news was not good. There was a chipped bone and calcium had got into the joint between the fibula and tibia. The consultant, by the way, was Graeme Garden's father, yes he of *The Goodies* fame. Didn't make my leg get better any quicker though.

Bobby Seith and I discussed when to have the operation. Immediately, and be OK for the end of the season games, or later in the season and hope that by then Preston would be safe from relegation. I chose to get it done straight away so in I went, the job was done, and I came out on Christmas Eve. The funny part was when I was coming round from the anaesthetic after the operation. You know how it goes; you don't really know where you are for the first few minutes and in the background I could hear heavenly singing and angels' voices. In this confused, drugged state and with this chorus line of divine voices wafting by my bedside I truly thought I had passed away and was about to meet the great goalkeeper in the sky who saves us all. When I came round fully, the singing was still there and I looked down the ward. It was just a motley band of carol singers going round the wards.

The effects of this injury were just as significant as the leg break at Everton although that thought didn't occur to me at the time. The leg break may have changed me in ways that I have never been able to properly analyse but the Chelsea injury was just as long-lasting in its effect. I got back to some semblance of fitness but there was still a degree of pain that shouldn't have been there and every so often I just buckled under with the intensity of it. Back in I went for more examinations and it was discovered that the surgeon had cut through a nerve and that this hadn't healed properly. All I could do was stop training and rest until it healed. I played only 16 games in '69/70 and scored just five goals. Not once in the games I played was I fully fit and in the meantime Preston North End slid ever closer to relegation

Seith, as all managers do, but with some justification, was quick to say that the club's lowly position was no reflection of their general play, but more a result of not being able to score goals, a result of my absence. "On this score we have sadly missed Willie Irvine's striking power. He has never been fully fit at any time during this current term. He lost the sharpness which means so much in front of goal and naturally the whole side suffered because of this."

Preston were relegated and descended into the murky depths of the Third Division. Their old nickname "The Invincibles" hadn't been applicable for a long time. A 4-1 win over Charlton had raised supporters' hopes but there was no follow-up so North End finished bottom, five points from safety. It was Blackpool who came to Deepdale and put the boot in when they won 3-0 to seal promotion.

Seith was sacked, just weeks after being given the dreaded vote of confidence by the board. The chairman announced a determination to drastically reorganise the club. It was Alan Spavin and Alan Kelly who selected the team and they asked me to play though they knew I wasn't fit, and though I knew I'd struggle I agreed. It was a gamble that I might just nick a goal and then they could keep Blackpool from scoring. Good plan, bad ending. There was a huge crowd, over 34,000, unsegregated, and it spilled over onto the touchlines but there was no trouble; the Preston fans were too resigned and sombre for that. For the Blackpool fans and their manager Les Shannon, a former Burnley player, it was a memorable day. Fred Pickering scored a hat-trick for them, Preston created not one decent chance, and it was a team full of weaknesses. A lad called Micky Burns starred for Blackpool and it was typical that he had been previously unwanted at Preston and dismissed as an amateur. In Blackpool's goal was my old Burnley colleague Harry Thomson. He played to the crowd wonderfully going down on one knee to the massed ranks behind him and bowing. "Arise, Sir Harry," they called out in unison, which he duly did – several times. At the end of the season some of the Preston fans then symbolically laid a Preston coffin a level deeper in the cellar of the Old Original pub at Bamber Bridge near Preston. At one of the final games *The Carnival is Over* by the Seekers was played over the tannoy. It was a fitting end if you were a Preston supporter or

Tom Finney, who must have despaired. This was also the era just before the cynical and violent rivalry of the '70s and '80s began. I know that many Blackpool fans and officials were saddened by Preston's relegation.

Of course there was rivalry, in just the same way that there was rivalry between Burnley and Blackburn, but prior to the rise of soccer hooliganism there was a camaraderie and friendliness between all the smaller clubs of north-east Lancashire. Supporters from Preston, Burnley, Blackpool, Bolton and Blackburn all recognised the similarities between our small clubs and small homely towns; all of these clubs struggling to compete with the city clubs from Liverpool, Manchester and London. The writing was already on the wall for these clubs and they would all go through bleak times in the '70s and '80s.

If Bobby Seith in his managership did two things; firstly he put off the inevitability of relegation for just a little longer, and he also saw the emergence of the superb talent of Archie "Go Go" Gemmill who eventually went to join Brian Clough at Derby County and scored a memorable World Cup goal against Holland in 1978. I played alongside him several times and he was a gem of a player. Archie responded to one thing and that was criticism, which enraged him, then made him play all the better. We met again in an international game when he played for Scotland and he had a blinder. As we came off he said to me, "Not bad for someone you were always criticising, eh?"

With a change of manager there are uncertain times for all existing players, who wonder if they will be part of the new man's plans, whether they will fit in or not. The comfort zone for anyone who has descended into it disappears overnight. For those with a mortgage to pay, the worries double. It was a new situation for me to be at a club where the manager was dismissed. There were chilling words in the local press and from the chairman. There were suggestions that Seith should have been sacked sooner, that a hatchet job was needed, with both playing and coaching staff pruning and even directors themselves. There was the suggestion that some directors were just not up to the job and were not ruthless enough and that those who clung to the notion of "the good old days" should be the first to go. Directors were needed who would put their hands in their pockets. The kind of manager needed would himself need to be ruthless in his selections and tactics, decisive and firm: someone who accepted the standards of the '70s. When they talked about the standards of the '70s did the irony not escape them that the '70s was a period when real soccer violence emerged? It was a time when the "good old days" were well and truly laid to rest. The word was that there was no particular manager in mind. After Seith went, my turn too would come eventually.

CHAPTER FOURTEEN

INDIAN SUMMER

While writing this book I heard of the death of my sister Jean in Canada. I knew she was dying and had been waiting for the inevitable to happen, and when the news came I sat and thought and relived all the times in our youth when she had been one of the mainstays of my life. I just felt so far away and helpless and useless. It was Jean who had been so encouraging and supportive, had slipped me bus fares when I needed them, had often taken the place of a mother I rarely saw, gave me treats, presents at Christmas and a shoulder to lean on when things went wrong. Nobody could have been more proud when I was signed on at Burnley. Although you know that someone is going to pass away, that it is only a matter of time, and that death will bring a merciful release from the pain and ravages of cancer, it doesn't make it any easier to bear when it happens.

Her husband Donald wrote to us from Ontario to say they were pouring the morphine into her at the finish and that in her final days, more than halfway between life and death, in one of her moments when she could speak, she had told him that she'd had visits from me, Bobby and Sandy. She had even told him that the nurses would only let us in one by one and that she had been delighted to see us one last time. Morphine does strange things to a person's mind; it makes us hallucinate and dream. I know that, but did she dream of our visits or by some strange process did she really see us, even though we were all thousands of miles away? I'd like to think it's the latter but we'll only find out when one day we meet again. Donald went on to tell us that she loved us with a pride and a fierceness that was second to none. "She taught me how to enjoy life and how to die with dignity," he added, "but I miss her so much." Donald enclosed a newspaper cutting about her, and her picture stared at me from the page. It described her wonderful singing voice, the quick smile and her great sense of humour. She was a great one for giving out hugs and kisses to adults and children alike. Everyone loved Mamma Jane.

Something has left my own life now that she has died; you take stock of your own existence and it made me think again about my own life and achievements and where I am now. It won't be the last time I ask my family, or myself for that matter: "Have I done all right?"

And then we got some more news about our family, this time from Bobby, and some more of the questions for which we wanted answers emerged. It was Dave who tracked him down, contacted him, wrote to him and to the delight of both of us Bobby responded and talked with a willing readiness. He, too, remembered the length to which our mother went to feed and clothe us, working and cleaning in "the big houses", as he called them, for the grand sea captains who used to live in them. There was one occasion when in one house she told the story of how a penny had been left under a vase as a test of her honesty. Bobby said she had found the penny but had replaced it with two halfpennies, as if to say to the lady of the house, "How dare you do this to me? Yes, I found the penny, and though it's now in the shape of two smaller coins that I have left there deliberately, it's still there."

He had nothing to tell us about my father but knew that he and Agnes weren't married, and he assumed that though she was separated from her second husband sometime in the '30s they were not divorced, something that was a taboo thing and you just didn't do in those days. If a woman was unhappy she was just expected to grin and bear it, carry on having the man's children, have his dinner ready on the table when he got home from work and be in his bed for his pleasure after he'd been out for a few drinks. But my mother Agnes was a woman with a fierce pride and would never have submitted to this from anyone. She had a mind of her own and the mother that I knew was proudly independent and resilient. She would never have allowed herself to submit to mistreatment or abuse, but none of us know why she and Herbert Hamilton separated.

Bobby had no recollection of any untoward attitudes or problems in the village caused by the fact that Alec and Agnes were not married. Perhaps the villagers sympathised, and if they had known each other from childhood then people might just have thought, well this was one of those things destined to happen and didn't she now deserve a good man to live with?

But two things he did know. Over Christmas he had visited Sandra in Scotland and they had talked about all these things. Agnes was born on December 1st, 1896, and Sandra said she had two, not four, brothers killed in World War One. She was quite sure about that, and that in Agnes' first marriage to Willie Black there had been nine children and most of them were either stillborn or died in early childhood. There must have been so much tragedy in her life. We knew about the twins Lily and Billy but three of the others were called Elsie, Sadie and Albert.

Bobby certainly remembered the two occasions we played together for Ireland, the first against Wales when Mother came to watch Mike England kicking me black and blue and being very upset by it. And then he remembered a game when I scored against him, a shot from 18 yards at Turf Moor, and how I grinned at him afterwards. And then there was the time we played against each other at Stoke when we were both made captains for the occasion.

I know I should get in touch with him myself. One day I will, but it's been so long and it's as if there's a bridge to cross, and it's just taking that first step after all these years that becomes so difficult. It's up to me now I know where he is. Maybe I can say sorry for something I did when we were still at Sunnylands. There was one night when he brought his girlfriend home and he left his new record on the chair while he slipped upstairs for something. "Why Must I be a Teenager In Love?" By the time he came down it was no longer brand new. I had sat on it and it shattered into a dozen pieces.

"I'm always very proud of Billy's achievements," he told Dave, and reminisced about our boyhood days in Eden and at Sunnylands, playing football together. It brought a lump to my throat to hear that, from a brother who I haven't seen for so long, the last time being on the occasion of my son Jonathan's wedding: August 12th, 1995, to be precise.

Not surprisingly, when I take a group around Turf Moor it isn't often I am asked about Preston or Brighton. Yet the funny thing is, the time I spent at those two clubs isn't that much less than the time I was at Burnley; just a couple of years less. Maybe it's because I returned to Burnley, live there now, had a business there and, given the chance, always sing

the town's praises. People are often so surprised when I say
I had four seasons at Deepdale, although one of them was
only for a matter of weeks. If asked, I would readily say that
the first full season at Preston was a happy one. It was a club
I had come to like enormously because of its homeliness and
the grand old architecture of the stands. It had stained glass
windows in one part and not even Highbury had anything
like that. One stand was clothed with ivy growing up the
walls. There were fascinating things about its history that
intrigued me. At the turn of the century sheep grazed on the
pitch and ladies were admitted free. In World War Two the
army had commandeered the whole place and prisoners of
war were kept there. Proud Preston, it is known as, and I can
appreciate why.

And then Brighton. I would certainly say that the promotion
season at Brighton where I played such an integral part, was
perhaps the happiest of all. Ask me about Halifax and I'll just
grimace.

Bobby Seith and the players were shocked when he was
dismissed by Preston, and other than Bobby nobody was more
disappointed than me, since it was his persuasive tongue that
had taken me there in the first place. The *Lancashire Evening
Post* had been agitating for his dismissal as soon as relegation
became a certainty. Two days later he was sacked.

We now lived in Preston and had a family to worry about.
More than once I wondered what would happen next.

What happened next was simple enough. Alan Ball was
appointed as manager. Bearing in mind that the other
candidates mentioned were Ian St John, Jimmy Armfield
and Billy Bingham, all illustrious names, Ball did well to
be chosen. I suppose the reasons were obvious enough – he
had a fantastic knowledge of the lower divisions which is
where we now were. He was known as the "James Cagney"
of football on account of his abrasive style and small stature
and he had done a good job at Halifax Town for three
seasons. The experts considered that he would have them in
Division Two before long. He was also the father of World
Cup star Alan Ball junior. His brief was to sort out the club,
get promotion, and to get straight on with it. This he duly did

and announced that eight of the playing staff could be got rid of. The bank tightened its grip and reduced the overdraft limit so his next announcement was that he was quite prepared to sell anybody. Off went star man Archie Gemmill to Derby for £59,000. In came Bobby Ham for a paltry £7,500. Kevin Keegan did not arrive, even for a fee as high as £18,000. Not too many people realise that Ball was within a whisker of signing him from Scunthorpe before Bill Shankly took him to Liverpool. The bid of £18,000 was on the verge of success but the whisper was that the bank would not release funds unless it was guaranteed personally by a backer or from the board of directors. Keegan slipped through his fingers. Imagine that: Keegan at Preston. Had he signed, the history of the club might have been transformed. Imagine that: a partnership of Kevin Keegan and me. Mouthwatering. It's the story of football though, isn't it? The occasions something "nearly" happens, and football is the story of one little word – "if" – and is the more fascinating for it.

I wasn't an immediate cast-off in '70/71. In fact I played 13 games and scored five times, not exactly disastrous, but it was clear I wasn't quite Alan Ball's chosen one. As soon as he found out the knee injury still troubled me his attitude seemed to change. In pre-season training I was doing my absolute best but recall being shouted at when I slowed up on one occasion. I mentioned the knee. "Knee... Injury... What bloody injury?" he replied, turning almost white with surprise. Ironically, the first game was against Halifax, his old club, a 1-1 draw. The second against Stockport we won 1-0 with a goal from me. The third game at Torquay we lost 3-1 and Ball went apoplectic with me after the game in the dressing room. I seem to remember hitting the woodwork at least three times; it could even have been four. He came into the dressing room and shouted at me that he "could have put them in with his dick". I let him know in no uncertain terms what I thought of his post-match analysis and asked him what he had ever done in football, what medals had he ever won, what European games had he ever played in? "What's your claim to fame?" I yelled at him, the air turning blue. Let's just say I wasn't on his Christmas card list after that.

Then there was the occasion that his son Alan came into our dressing room after a game and began to bollock us for our performance. Of course he was a great player and had won a World Cup winners' medal but again I was furious and turned on him, telling him in no uncertain terms to get out; we were nothing to do with him and who was he to bring his unwanted opinions into our dressing room, which he had no business coming into. I fell short of actually manhandling him but could happily have done so. He left.

My last game for Preston was against Tranmere on December 26th, 1970 in a 3-3 draw at Deepdale. The attendance was a poor one of just over 7,000, which for a Christmas game was pretty bad. Since October I had been dumped into the reserves and when manager Alan Ball commented on the poor gate I sarcastically suggested to him that if I had been a regular, scoring, the gate would have been doubled. That for him was finally it. The James Cagney of football had no more time for me, nor I for him to be honest. The one advantage of being out of his plans was that at least I didn't get the cigarette smoke in my face any more. During a team talk he would have his fag packet in his hand and the sessions more often than not depended on how many cigarettes were left in the packet. "This will be a 12 cigarettes session," he would announce if that's what he had left in the packet. Given the opportunity I'd have taken half of them out and thrown them away if I'd ever have been able to get my hands on them.

By the end of the season Ball had done two things: he had won promotion back to the Second Division at the first attempt (at Torquay I had told him his football knowledge was nil so I guess on that score I was a bit off the mark); and he had shipped me off to Brighton on loan for the last three months of the season. The season had begun badly but bit by bit, Preston came closer to the top places and by the end of the season, with me gone, a 1-0 win at Fulham won promotion. In fairness promotion in his first season was a great achievement. When Preston won at Fulham, who themselves were hoping to clinch the championship with a victory, it's said that their chairman Tommy Trinder was speechless. Top spot for Preston came with a home win over

Rotherham in front of more than 28,000 spectators. The truth is I could have opted to have stayed at Preston, and from the fringes and with a role as a bit-part player, might have been a part of this success. Ironically, the team Ball had created at Halifax were third.

But Ball didn't want me, hadn't exactly taken a shine to me, nor I to him. The offer of a three-month loan to Brighton was made and Rita and I looked at each other. Against it was the fact that a move from Preston to Brighton would be 200 miles or thereabouts further than a move from Burnley to Preston. It seemed a huge distance for Burnley girl Rita, who would be leaving the closeness of family and relatives. The four of us – by now we'd had our second son – would be well and truly on our own. There'd be no bus rides home for the day like she could do from Preston to Burnley.

Pat Saward was manager. I'd never even heard of him but we thought, what the hell, what have we got to lose; three months in Brighton sounds nice. If nothing comes of it, at least we'll have had a holiday by the sea. Pat sold me the place with his charm and persuasive ways, embroidered with little tales such as that sheep once used to graze on the pitch, in World War One the army used to practise shooting there, aiming at crows flying overhead, and the Goldstone Ground was so named because once upon a time, on land there, an ancient Druid stone had been found with reputed magic powers. He didn't tell me that he'd tried to sign Ian St John from Liverpool before me and that I was second choice. Or maybe he wanted to sign both of us. Funny how things work out; the following season would turn out to be memorable.

Ah well, I'd done a bit of geography and knew that Brighton was down on the south coast. We looked it up; it looked a good place to go: "London-by-the-sea" as it were, full of attractions; The Royal Pavilion, Regency architecture, terraces and gleaming white crescents, old fishermen's cottages, cinemas, theatres, nightspots, plus three miles of sea-front, shingle beaches, swimming pools, and children's boating pools and amusements. Let's face it, we thought, this couldn't be worse than the greyness of drab, industrial Preston.

I remember 1971 for something else as well – old money

was replaced by new. Decimalisation, they called it, and out went shillings, half-crowns, and threepenny bits. For a while it took some getting used to. The swinging sixties were on the way to being replaced by the savageness of the seventies. The early seventies might have been emerging as a golden age for football but outside of that, unemployment was rising. Edward Heath was Prime Minister and relationships between government and unions were about to plummet into chaos. The miners began to flex their muscles as the government sought to diminish union power and curb unofficial strikes. There were massive demonstrations, which were not always peaceful. At the beginning of the year 66 people had been killed in a surge of fans at a game between Rangers and Celtic. All of us were stunned. Princess Anne was named Sportswoman of the Year for riding a horse.

Violence in Northern Ireland was about to mushroom with murders and bombings, imprisonment without trial and the killings of soldiers. I watched it all from afar and felt horrified. This was my birthplace that was being torn apart and I still had family there. I used to visit my mother back in Ireland every now and then and one occasion is still imprinted in my mind. I was waiting in the railway station for the train down to Carrick. There was a bar there and with about half an hour to wait I chatted to an old schoolfriend who happened to be in there. "What the hell is going on over here?" I asked him and talked quite a lot about the whole situation, the politics of the thing and some of the terrible events. Another bloke was standing near to us and it was clear he was listening in on the conversation with great interest. Did he think I was police? Did he think I was an undercover soldier? God knows, but I could see him reaching into his inside pocket and my friend realised straight away he's about to pull out a gun. "For God's sake, put that away," he ordered him and the hand released the gun. "There's your train, get on it now while you can," he told me, taking me outside and shoving me onto it. Happy to do so, I got on shaking like a leaf.

And so, with all this as the background and new decimal money in our pockets to confuse things, all Rita and I wanted to do was to find somewhere in Brighton to live.

The club had promised to organise a rented property for us, a lovely flat in Shoreham-by-Sea. We kept the house in Preston for when we went back. The problems of being a football wife hit Rita hard. Strange place, strange flat, me away frequently. In the first week one of the boys took very ill while I was away for three days. All Rita could do, young, panic-stricken and frightened, was knock on the flat below and ask for help. She knew no one but the woman she begged for help, a total stranger, turned out to be a real saviour and called her own doctor who came every day for the next week. They became the best of friends and bit by bit we got to know other players and their wives. Only a footballer knows what his wife goes through at times like this. They are a special breed. Some of them are strong and can handle it. Others don't. Rita might have had floods of tears on several occasions and suffered from my moods, but she coped, stuck it out and adapted every time we moved.

Saward was good at this point. He had replaced Freddie Goodwin, a good manager who found relaxation from the problems of management by heading over to the stables at Worthing and riding over the Downs for a few hours. Birmingham City had noted his success and appointed him even though he still had 18 months of his contract to run. Controversy followed, though, when Birmingham were fined £5,000 for "poaching" members of the backroom staff. The Brighton directors, however, had noted the success of Pat Saward, assistant manager at Coventry City. He was a former Aston Villa and Republic of Ireland international with a reputation as one of the best coaches in the country. There had been something like 50 applications for the job but the directors wasted little time in appointing Saward. Where Goodwin had been quiet and serious, Saward was the opposite; extrovert, infectious and bubbly, he had even been a male model, and it was getting towards the end of his first season there that he took me on loan in March 1971. There couldn't have been a greater contrast to Alan Ball.

Pat Saward was a gem of a manager and a pleasure to play for. He said what he thought, but never offensively; in a matter-of-fact, plain-speaking kind of way, rather than aggressively. There was a story that when he first arrived he had told the players, "I couldn't care less about the length of your hair. As long as you do well on the field you can wear knickers if you like." But the truth is he did care and we respected him for it. He had us kitted out with jackets and smart trousers and hated scruffiness. From a good-looking ex-male model like him, that was not surprising.

Money was tight at Brighton, so he built up his attack-minded team with loan signings and bargain buys. He went round supporters' groups campaigning for money. Directors and players accompanied him on sponsored walks – no mean feat to persuade them to do that – and he set up what he called a "Buy a Player Fund". That's exactly how he came to sign Bert Murray, who was known as "The People's Player". Bert and I became the best of friends and remain so to this day. Somehow Pat Saward had the knack of making people feel important. He instilled pride and a sense of identity. He was just about the first manager to be dubbed "the loan arranger" and had a slogan he took round with him: "This is your club as much as mine. Help make it great."

Pat loved attacking, entertaining football and worked tirelessly for the club. There was one occasion when he had to be given oxygen after collapsing through exhaustion. He had this ability to lift people and I would have run through that proverbial brick wall for him.

Just like at Preston, I came into the team when they were in the bottom half of the table and had been close to the relegation zone at one stage. Fourteen games and six goals later relegation was avoided. One of them came in my debut game against Fulham. I had a good game and the knee was fine. Afterwards Saward and the team were delighted for me. "Bloody hell, why aren't you in Preston's team?" one of them asked. "How come they have let you go?" The effect was much the same as at Preston. It's a team game and a team effort but it's the man who comes in and scores the goals who becomes the hero.

My move was made permanent with a £7,000 deal in July. Saward must have liked what he saw. But there was a worrying wait in between the loan spell and finding out that it would be made permanent. We went back to Preston and waited… and waited… and waited… The worries began that Saward had either forgotten or changed his mind, or that Ball was being awkward. He must have noticed I'd scored six times down there. But at last the deal was done and, realising that Brighton might do surprisingly well during the forthcoming season, I told a good Preston friend to bet on us for promotion. The odds were ridiculous, something like 100- 1 and I know he put a tidy sum on. I didn't. To this day I have never found out exactly how much he won.

I chose a house for us to move into so that Rita, the boys and furniture would follow. Not such a good choice, these things are best left to wives. It seemed OK to me but when the furniture van arrived and the removal men began to unload all the furniture it was absolutely obvious I had chosen one that was useless and far too small and within minutes we realised that the new neighbours were going to be anything but sociable. It was chaos, with furniture cluttering the street and furniture half in and half out of the house. The furniture went back on the van and an irate Rita, far from happy with good old Willie, was all set to take herself and the boys all the way back to Burnley there and then. Sense prevailed and we went to see Saward who put us into a hotel for a week and showed Rita all the other available houses.

The permanent deal meant I was on £85 a week, plus appearance money, plus £60 for every point won. This was good money, so finances were secure, the knee was fine, everything looked rosy. We had a fine house and Brighton was a great place to live. Ronnie Corbett lived just round the corner and had this enormous Rolls-Royce or Bentley, can't remember which, but anyway the first time I saw this car coming round the corner I was convinced there was no one driving it. There was no sign of a face, until, as the car got closer, I could just see this pair of eyes looking over the steering wheel. I recognised the driver straight away but clearly he didn't know who I was. Maybe he was a Chelsea supporter.

In the following season, to everyone's surprise with an amazing 12 away wins, Brighton won promotion, coming second behind Aston Villa and Andy Lochhead.

Willie Irvine

At the beginning of what was a marvellous season for all of us, Saward had sat down with his staff and decided that tactics for the coming season should be based on me and Kit Napier having the skill and experience to get through defences and to be in the right place at the right time. It sounds easy but it needs the right players, and Saward, by hook and by crook, had assembled his squad carefully, and cheaply too. It was away from home where we were so surprisingly good and it was often due to an attack-at-all-costs policy with sometimes as many as five front-runners. At Bristol it paid off with me snatching an equaliser in the dying seconds and the elation was enormous from all of us. Another late goal flurry saw us win 3-1 at Torquay after they had led 1-0 until the last ten minutes. At one point I was actually known as "late-goal Willie" because of a last-minute goal at Wrexham, another at home to Halifax, one at home to Walsall in the FA Cup, and then the goal at Bristol Rovers.

There had been some stuttering and stumbling in the first few games but then came a run of six straight wins. At no time were we lower than 11th and a turning point was beating Aston Villa, the leaders, when they came to Brighton. Once we were in the top four we felt sure that promotion was ours. Saward, with a joke or a smile, an arm round the shoulder or a bit of geeing up, knew just how to keep a dressing room happy or dispel any tension or nerves.

One game, away at Halifax, sticks in the memory – irony of ironies since Halifax would eventually be my final club. Our coach never arrived to pick us up from our Manchester hotel where we were staying on March 5th. We crammed into four taxis for the drive over the Pennines. It was a pig of a journey. For some of the southern lads who had no idea of life north of Watford it was like a journey to the end of the world. We went up hills and down dales – the southern boys thought they were mountains; even the sheep looked evil and stared at us as if they'd never seen humans before – we traversed the grim moorland roads, we drove past dark mills and huge factories and terraced rows on a journey that was like going back in time. Of course I was familiar with all this and happily chuckled and wound up the lads in my taxi, saying things like "Just wait till we get over the next hill: the road stops and becomes a dirt track, then we have to walk to the bus stop." The drivers lost their way more than once as the little convoy huffed and puffed across the wilderness and then through gloomy narrow valleys full of drab little houses.

When we arrived at The Shay, Saward jumped out and handed in the team sheet, just avoiding the fine for late arrival. Not only had we had this journey of a lifetime but we had also somehow managed to change into our kits in the taxis, no mean feat when we were squashed in four to a car. I saw bits of Bert Murray's anatomy that not even he knew he had. More than one other motorist looked in horror on seeing a footballer's bare backside squashed up against the rear window. Football is a funny game and we saw the funny side of the journey, even the Halifax ground called The Shay. Did you ever see The Shay in the '70s? A more depressing sight you couldn't wish to see, and one day I'd end up playing there. But we ran out and thrashed them 5-0 and one of the goals was mine. That win got us into third place and promotion was in sight. We scored five goals in another away win at Shrewsbury and by the end of the season had scored a phenomenal 43 goals away from home. The supporters chose my good friend Bert Murray as player of the season but in truth it was a team effort. Bert was versatile though, and had switched to full-back during the season without a grumble. 34,766 people saw the final home game when a point against Rochdale, who were in danger of relegation, saw us home. We'd played this game at 100 miles an hour until the score became 1-1. At this point I'd noticed Saward and the Rochdale manager talking on the touchline. Somehow the game seemed to slow down dramatically except for me putting in one almighty challenge on their centre half and almost scoring. "Bloody hell," he said, "don't yer know we're playing for t'draw now?" No I didn't, nobody had bloody told me. Marvellous, and the celebrations were long and loud, especially from a certain Norman Wisdom who was a Brighton fanatic and was once a director. I met him briefly at a party the actress Thora Hird threw for the team. We drank champagne in the dressing room that was one of the

Willie Irvine

most ramshackle and dilapidated in the division. It even had woodworm, but we didn't care. They say fortune favours the brave and it certainly favoured the "attack away from home" policy of Pat Saward.

Among my few bits and pieces of memorabilia is a torn, battered, moth-eaten copy of a little programme-size souvenir booklet produced by Chris Bale, who was sports editor of the *Brighton and Hove Gazette*. It's the story in pictures of that memorable season, one of the happiest and most rewarding I spent. The cover is falling off, it looks like it has been put through a mangle, the corners are dog-eared, but I look at it now and all the best memories come back as if the 30 years and more that have passed by since that year have melted away. It says in the blurb it was the most exciting season since Albion had won promotion from the Third Division 14 years earlier.

I flick through the pages and am reminded of the chairman Tom Whiting, Pat Saward's right-hand man Mike Yaxley, Ray Crawford the coach, and a bloke called Joe Wilson who had been at the club in one capacity or another since Noah's Ark first hit the waves. Every club has a bloke like this working behind the scenes. The groundsman was called Frankie Howard – we pulled his leg mercilessly with a name like that – but his green, grassy pitch was regarded as one of the best in the country. I'd go in of a morning and greet him with, "Ooooh er, now then Mrs... lissen."

I used to love to listen to Frankie and his tales. He'd been a winger at Brighton and, by all accounts, a good one. He was quick and he said the secret was that when he was heading towards the sea on the left wing he used the ground's slope. There was a six-foot drop from one end to the other so that fans at the north end could only see his top half by the time he reached the other end. It put 20mph on his speed, he said, but it made it difficult to stop and he often ran out of the ground! And the tricks they used to play on each other in the '50s had me in stitches. Once they stripped down a player's new bike and pulled all the bits and pieces to the top of one of the flagpoles at the ground.

The funniest story he told, though, was when they nailed the boots of a player called Bert Addinall to the wooden floor

202

and then fell about in stitches when he tried to walk away in them.

Ray Crawford had been at Ipswich and played for England and knew all about the hassle and sometimes pain of being a centre forward. You listen to someone like that. As a young lad I'd watched him when he had been in his prime, banging in the goals with a partner called Ted Phillips.

The pages of the booklet aren't even numbered but there I am on the first page that hits you, scoring against Bradford City, soaring like an eagle, eyes on the ball, shirt flapping, hair flying. Bang, back of the net, bloody magic. Next page, scoring the winning goal against Halifax on our home ground, seizing on a faulty back pass and going round their keeper to make sure it goes in. "Willie's coolness in these situations shows his international class.". Chris Bales' words, not mine. Next page: two pictures of me, one back to the camera, slim, muscular, striped shirt, number 9 big and bold on the back. Bertie Lutton is slamming the ball home. Under that one is me taking a pot shot, great picture, almost horizontal above the ground; damn, missed.

Next page, after 17 games, seventh in the table, five points behind Bournemouth at the top. Albion's most unusual goal comes next and I'm responsible for it; a goalmouth scramble, me in the middle of it, the Chesterfield goalkeeper thinks I have fouled him and stops playing and puts the ball down for a free kick. He walks back a couple of yards to take the kick and everyone bar just one player walks back to take up new positions. But there's just one problem. The referee hasn't blown for any foul so Kit Napier, cool as you like, puts the ball in the back of the net. Mayhem, stunned Chesterfield players. Stunned Brighton players for that matter: Albion 2 Chesterfield 1. Who gets the other? Me.

Kit Napier was a cornerstone of our success,. He was brave, with pace, bursts of acceleration, and two-footed. He was another one to eventually fall out with Pat Saward after promotion and went to Blackburn.

Nearly halfway through the booklet: 22 games played, Brighton fifth, five points behind Notts County, Brian Bromley scores; me, arms raised in joy, and a dejected Mansfield number 5. Brian was one of Pat Saward's bargain buys and this was one of the last-minute goals that became our trademark. Twenty games played, slipped down to sixth place but now only four points behind Notts County. Aston Villa are third now. A phenomenal 30,538 watched us beat Bournemouth 2-0 in what for us was the big derby game. They had Ted MacDougall, one of the most prolific scorers of all time. Twenty-five games played and by now Andy Lochhead and Villa have taken over at the top. We were only three points behind.

The middle pages of the souvenir have all of us smiling and holding champagne glasses. I've wangled myself a position in the centre of the picture, hair all over my face. Pat Saward, just to my left, looking cool and calm as if this kind of thing happens every day, but as a former male model this could be his photograph face. Good-looking fella.

Page whatever it is – it's a bugger they're not numbered – and we go second: Albion 3 Wrexham 2, one from me. And then, the big one, the promotion crunch game, at home to Villa. Chris Nicholl was playing. He was another former Burnley player and a giant of a centre half, a fellow Northern Ireland international. But he didn't stop me scoring. Nicholl always looked a great prospect at Turf Moor; even as a 17-year-old he looked outstanding, and we were amazed to see him go to Halifax. After a Nicholl tackle I finished up on the floor and, landing on my fingers, ended up with two of them dislocated and one broken. Clutching my hand to my chest in agony I limped off to the trainer, holding out my hand like a dog holds out its paw, much to the amusement of both sets of players. "It's your fingers," said one of them. "What the fuck are you limping for?"

It was a win that really made us think and believe that we could do it: win promotion and get our names into the Brighton history books. There were a few drinks that night. The BBC cameras were there for that game and there, next to the Villa page, there's the picture of me scoring and this goal was voted by BBC viewers into Goal of the Season runner-up. Thanks. Eddie Spearritt slipped a short ball to Brian "the General" Bromley. Bromley gave the ball to John Templeman who went on a tremendous run before giving me a slide-rule pass and then the *coup de grâce*; a cracking, rasping, bullet shot into the roof of the net. A lovely classic move you couldn't have bettered on the training field. Sometimes these shots go anywhere; this one whistled straight in. During the game Andy Lochhead and I didn't speak except when he stood in the centre circle for the kick-off after I had scored. "How did you score that?" he asked. "God guides them in," I answered, grinning. I have a DVD copy of the goal with Barry Davies commentating in his inimitable style. His words are simple but his voice slowly rises to the final crescendo.

"Bromley... Templeman... Beamish back again to Templeman... this is Irvine... WHAT A BEAUTIFULLY HIT SHOT... "

And then Davies stays silent to let the roar of the crowd take over.

The move starts deep in the Villa half with a Bromley jink and a little side pass to Templeman. His legs are like a giraffe's and he covers the ground with his huge, long, bounding strides. He flicks a long pass forward to Beamish who returns it to him as he strides forward. He's covering half the pitch in seconds and sees me in the corner of the box. I take it with my left foot; one touch to my right and then the third touch dispatches it like a missile. And afterwards our coach Ray Crawford asked me: "Willie, why didn't you hit it first time?"

Next page, Ken Beamish is pictured with a flying header. He was a £35,000 bargain and demonstrated that the saying "the early bird catches the worm" is absolutely true. Pat Saward left Brighton at 5am one morning to sign him. I've half an idea he signed him from Tranmere, who we played the same day.

Albion 3 Blackburn 0 and I scored. I always seemed to score against Blackburn so that when I see their old centre half Derek Fazakerley, I always say, "You won't recognise me now, will you?" He always asks why. "Because all you ever saw was my back and you could never keep up," I reply.

Forty-one games played and we are just one point ahead of Notts County who are third behind us. It's tight and nerves begin to fray but this is where Saward is so good with his calming influence. Then it was Albion 2 Rotherham 1.

Willie Irvine

I thought Rotherham must be the end of the earth when we played in that gloomy, depressed town but I changed my mind when I got to Halifax. I remember the goal I scored at home to Rotherham because Swift, their centre half, had the shirt off my back, he was pulling it so hard while I was in the act of scoring. It was the first goal of the game but the winner after they had equalised came in the fourth minute of injury time. The ground erupted but I also remember it for their goalkeeper McDonagh having the game of a lifetime. Without him we could have had ten.

Now here's the back end of the booklet. Did we by some quirk play Rochdale twice in the final two games? The final table reads: Aston Villa top with 70 points and then us in second place with 65 points, just three ahead of Bournemouth. Absolute jubilation. Rita seems to remember we partied for ten nights solid. This was a first for me. To actually win something; although there was one month when I won best-trainer award. God, the memory of the prize: Saward had a men's shop in town, a trendy Carnaby Street type shop, and the prize was always £100 worth of flash gear. Now in those days you could kit yourself out in some style for £100. I came out of that shop looking like a ponce with garish multicoloured rainbow trousers and a flowered shirt with one of those big Peter Wyngarde collars (1970s cultural reference: Wyngarde played Jason King in a popular TV show). There was more gear under my arms in carrier bags. I met Rita in the street and she collapsed in howls of laughter. She shouldn't have laughed though; I had hysterics at the sight of her in almost identical gear. Today we'd call it fancy dress; in the '70s you actually wore the stuff. I was lovingly nicknamed Omar Sharif in those far-off days on account of my swarthy good looks and moustache. Rubbish, I was far better-looking.

The team picture on the back cover is spoiled by the creases of age, the fading of the edges and bits of Sellotape. Never mind, it's a priceless memento – in spite of my ridiculous Mexican bandit moustache, plus the obligatory '70s hairstyle. Eat your heart out, Omar. We all had those big hairstyles then. I just wish I had some left today and didn't look quite so old.

Indian Summer

At the end of the season there was a holiday in Majorca for the team, but poor old Willie missed it because I had to stay behind to train for the forthcoming international games. A good season and a few goals, especially the one on BBC *Match Of The Day*, had reminded the selectors I was still alive. So the lads went to Majorca for a knees-up without me and the wives and children were packed off to the Isle of Wight to a Warrens Holiday Camp. They must have been thrilled at that. No men/women gender equality at the Albion, thank you very much, in those days. The women and children went to grey skies and cold damp chalets. Can you imagine Posh and Becks putting up with that? I think not. The boys had a great time with beers by the pool under a warm hot sun and blue skies. The wives came home early, it was so awful.

If there was a climax to this marvellous season it came at Wembley in May with an improbable, fantasy scoreline of England 0 Northern Ireland 1. Forgive me if I dwell on it but it was a night all Irishmen from the North will cherish forever. Promotion and recall to the Northern Ireland team; what more could a man ask? I will not forget the band of Brighton fans who travelled up to Wembley, not so much to watch England but to cheer me on. When I went over to applaud them I felt ten feet tall. I still read the words that Malcolm Brodie wrote after the game. For any Irishman reading this book, here they are. I make no apology for including them all.

The cold light of dawn is breaking. More than seven hours have passed since that glorious chapter in this British International Championship fixture at Wembley last night. Yet I still cannot forget the scene.

An occasion to savour, to place alongside the 1957 Danny Blanchflower led triumph on that same pitch. An occasion which will be recalled with nostalgia and pride as well as those feats in Sweden in 1958.

The blood tingles yet at the thought of it. Here was an Irish side, some of them only half fit, playing defensively through necessity, hitting a goal and then containing an England team which Sir Alf Ramsey had selected, not on an experimental basis, but to win.

A fairytale goal, for it was scored by player-manager Terry

Neill, making his 50th appearance – only his second goal in a superb international career.

Look back then on that 33rd minute as rain fell heavily. Wolves' midfield player Danny Hegan took a corner on the left – a planned set piece. He put a short one to the near post. Neill whispered to centre-forward Derek Dougan "leave it to me". The Doog went to the far post and so did several England players. Over came Hegan's ball, perfectly flighted, perfectly placed, Willie Irvine jumped, missed, and it struck Terry Neill on the head.

"Immediately I noticed it bounced between the 'keeper and myself. I pivoted and hit it into the net," explained Neill who has had many wonderful moments in his football life. None will ever match that one.

And when I entered the dressing room my thoughts went back to that November day in 1957 when the first Wembley victory was achieved. As if by magic Blanchflower appeared to congratulate the team. Then Bertie Peacock came in. One only wished that Peter Doherty and the others could have joined in those celebrations.

Neill was surrounded by newspapermen. Impatiently the television crews waited for him to give his verdict to the nation. Eventually he did so wearing only the top half of a tracksuit with a huge towel covering the rest of his body. The rain and chill of the night didn't affect him.

What a team performance. We had eleven players who gave everything. The rain and perspiration saturated their shirts. Every sinew, every muscle was strained. They had pride in playing for their country and oh how they wanted to win and help in their own way to provide a talking point back home other than the bullet and the bomb.

Eleven heroes all of them. There have been much better internationals – the standard never attained great heights but for Northern Ireland this was a memorable victory. And that is all that counts.

The defence was magnificent and the same goes for the middle four, while up front Dougan strove gallantly and a vicious Norman Hunter tackle near the end almost brought a fisticuff retaliation. Fortunately the referee didn't bother and nothing marred the show.

Indian Summer

Man of the match? There is no difficulty in naming him. Spurs goalkeeper Pat Jennings who was described by Neill as "the best in the world" gets the unanimous vote. And I would certainly go along with the Neill reasoning. Jennings brought off some remarkable saves with a one-handed effort from a Mike Summerbee cross among the greatest ever seen at Wembley.

Adjectives fail to describe his brilliance, yet it was all done so calmly, coolly, competently.

Neill too had his finest hour, Not only did he score that goal, but he masterminded the tactical plan which frustrated a disappointing England who became so desperate in the second half they introduced substitutes Martin Chivers and Martin Peters.

Hegan, as I anticipated, was the key figure. Once he got the ball, an Irish breakthrough was initiated. And he was ably aided and abetted by the always buzzing Eric McMordie, who again suffered from a touch of cramp, but not nearly as much as referee Bill Gow who had to be treated by both trainers on the whistle after collapsing. Yes, the game had everything.

Pat Rice, Sammy Nelson, Dave Clements, Alan Hunter, Tommy Jackson, McMordie, Hegan, Dougan, they were all out of this world as they coordinated perfectly, kept possession of the ball and rarely sent a pass astray.

It was a night when some played better than others, but this will always be for them a team performance. That is the way Neill wants to see it. That is the way every one of those green shirted players wants to see it too.

England's new boys disappointed. When their attack formation was announced I feared the worst. Would this be a massacre? Even Neill admitted similar thoughts crossed his mind. But the defence, which held out against Scotland until the last five minutes at Hampden Park, Glasgow, on Saturday, again proved its worth and in the process ruined many reputations. This was no fluke Irish win. There were no lucky off the line saves. No lucky breaks, although England pressurised for most of the second half. They played it tight, snatched that goal and then decided to hold out, come what may.

The tension at the finish was almost unbearable. The hands of the stop-watch would not go round fast enough. Then there was that referee cramp episode. The final whistle seemed an eternity in coming. Slowly, ever so slowly, the end did arrive.

Colin Bell, the England skipper for the night, was the last to touch the ball. Irish players hugged each other in exhausted jubilation. As the band of The Royal Army Medical and Ordnance Corps walked onto the pitch for the National Anthem, everyone looked at the happy Irish, the dejected English.

The teams lined up in the centre. Standing out like the husband whose wife only uses a certain washing powder, was McMordie, the only Irishman in a white jersey. He had exchanged it with a member of the opposition.

Someone asked Hegan for his. "Not on your life. I want to keep this as a souvenir for my grandchildren," he said in a thick Glasgow accent.

Players will cherish those jerseys. They will always think of the result sign on the huge electric scoreboard – "England 0, Northern Ireland 1." It illuminated the dark of the night.

I won't forget it either. It has been a difficult season, probably the most difficult in the history of the Irish game at international and domestic level. Yet the displays have been wonderful. First the British amateur championship was won and now comes this triumph over England at Wembley, which keeps Northern Ireland in with a chance, admittedly an outside one, of winning the Home Countries series.

And, remember, not a match could be played in Belfast. Let's hope the return won't be long delayed. For those heroes of Wembley deserve a welcome which only a Windsor Park crowd can provide.

Wembley – Tuesday, May 23rd, 1972. It is an occasion for the soccer history books.

England. Shilton, Todd, Hughes, Storey, Lloyd, Hunter, Summerbee, Bell, Macdonald, Marsh, Currie.

N Ireland. Jennings, Rice, Nelson, Neill, Hunter, Clements, Hegan, McMordie, Dougan, Irvine, Jackson.

What a night, etched into my memory forever, but now I'll tell you my version of the Northern Ireland goal. Yes, the ball came across from the Danny Hegan corner and Derek Dougan went over to the far post, taking defenders away with him. Yes, it left Terry Neill and me with some room and I did go up for the ball. I was about six yards out and Peter Shilton came out to get it, but he was never going to make successful contact. I did head it, he stuck out a weak hand, and I landed on the floor with the ball dropping between us. I got up ready to hit it home but was off-balance and that was when Neill nipped in and scored himself. Thanks, Terry. At the time it didn't matter and in the glory of the win it didn't matter who scored, did it? But then all these years later you think a bit. It's Terry who gets his name immortalised on the score sheet. Such is football. It could so easily have been me carrying that matchball home.

CHAPTER FIFTEEN

HALIFAX AND BEYOND

Oh God, why did I choose to go to Halifax? If there are some events in our lives over which we have no control, like Goodison Park and the broken leg, and then the meeting with Webb at Chelsea and the twisted knee, there are for sure other events in our lives over which we do have total control when it is we who make the choices. After 11 league games and five goals at the beginning of the '72/73 season, which you can hardly describe as poor, I was then discarded; yesterday's man. I had the choice of joining Torquay, West Ham or Halifax. And also, unknown to me, I could have gone to Hearts, where Bobby Seith had gone after leaving Preston. It wasn't till years later that I discovered this, when he told me he had enquired about me while at Brighton. "You'd have been a riot up here in Scotland," he told me. Like we say, sometimes your destiny is in the hands of others. But in choosing Halifax and joining them in December 1972 I well and truly ended my own career.

The euphoria of promotion hadn't lasted long. Pat Saward changed. He seemed to become unapproachable, or at least he did to me, and where once I could see him whenever I wanted, now I seemed to have to book an appointment two or three days in advance. We all had to. Brighton, now a Second Division club with a new office and dressing rooms, and with new players coming in, went on the slide and results were dreadful. The hammerings were frequent and regular. Saward for some reason had decided Barry Bridges was the player he wanted to bring in. He would bring them success in the higher division and the team, when he arrived, would be fashioned around him. The old maxim; if it ain't broke, don't fix it; was sadly ignored. Saward, during the summer, took me on one side and told me of his plans to bring someone else in, he didn't say who, and replace me, but that "he'd see me all right".

Kit Napier, with whom I had such a good partnership, went. Other players went as well, supporters became disgruntled and in November a losing streak of 12 games began. Bridges didn't arrive anyway until after the season started and by the end of the season was mostly on the bench having scored just four goals. I have nothing against him, this is how football operates; but if Bridges was not the answer, then nobody could quite fathom out what the question had been in the first place. After eight games I was up among the top scorers, if not the division's leading scorer in all competitions. But Saward had his new man he was determined to bring in and from early October I was the old model. By the time that disastrous 12 match losing run had ended, Brighton were well and truly at the bottom of the division and I had gone to Halifax. Saward was sacked before the end of the season when he made a memorable remark: "I have no more answers, I am in a fog." So, by just a few months, I missed the next manager who was brought in. In a move that shook the soccer world Brighton appointed the legendary Brian Clough and Peter Taylor. And under them I don't think Bridges started a game. Instead of George Mulhall at Halifax, I could have been playing for Brian Clough who had scored 250 goals in 271 games at Sunderland.

With supreme irony, almost the last game I had for Brighton was against Burnley. It was November 1972 and Saward decided that a partnership of the speedy Bridges and the wily poacher old Irvine might make a good combination. Old? I was only 28. Burnley and Adamson were on their way up that season and back into Division One. They had lost the previous week at home to Leyton Orient and so we thought this could be two home points for us. We had a few early flurries but then their passing football took over and Martin Dobson scored from a corner. It was a typical Burnley rehearsed move but they had quite a number of them and you never knew which one they would use next. Adamson preached the virtue of the "team" and it showed that day. He was never one for individuals or free spirits. Perhaps that was why we never got on. There might be room for just the one – such as Leighton James, but eventually he, too, would be sold.

"If" – there's that word again. Only two letters long but for me the biggest word in the football vocabulary. I look back now and ask who in their right mind would turn down West Ham, but neither Rita nor I wanted to live in London. Torquay – what a delightful place to live and a wonderful place to bring up the boys, but too far away from the North. Don't forget there were no fast motorways in those days to make it a comfortable six-hour journey back to Rita's family in Burnley. Plus they were a Division Four side and struggling to boot. And so we chose Third Division Halifax *and* a big drop in wages. The drop in wages was tempered by the comfortable nest-egg I had built up, and I loved Lancashire folk and their warmth.

Some of the decisions we make haunt us for a lifetime. Halifax was mine. And if only Saward had told me about Bobby Seith and Hearts, my life history would have taken another course and been so different. I'd learn later why I was never told. From being a man for whom I would have once run through walls, I can only think of Saward now as the man who caused me to miss out on a possible move to a top Scottish club at a time when there were some great Scottish players and Rangers and Celtic didn't quite go around dominating the game to the extent they do now.

And so to Halifax. Just writing the word makes me shudder. There's a story that goes round football that any manager who ever wanted to sign a player for Halifax would always do it in the station bar as soon as the lad got off the train. If a player clapped eyes on the ground, nobody with a ha'p'orth of sense would ever have signed. I signed with my eyes open. I had seen the ground, having played there after Brighton's hysterical drive over the Pennines from Manchester. I had seen the town of Halifax with its Victorian gloom, the now closed giant carpet factory, the palls of smoke, the rows of tiny houses, and the woollen mills, or at least what was left of them. The Queen went to Halifax in 1974 to open the headquarters of the Halifax Building Society and left immediately afterwards – wise woman. There's also an enormous chimney called the Wainhouse Tower, which in 1875 was intended to be a chimney but was never used so it became a folly with spiral steps up to the top. I only put that in here because so many people drive through Halifax and wonder what it is. Now you know. Today Halifax has smartened itself up, has restored a number of its old buildings and isn't quite the end of the world it once was. Once upon a time it was one of three places that nobody in their right mind would visit, Hell and Hull being the other two. That I chose to play there is still a decision that I rue today but it had just one thing in its favour. It was but a short drive to Burnley where we knew we could look for a house. It was the only consideration.

The ground is called The Shay and is built on the site of an old rubbish tip. How apt. In 1972, to say it was primitive was an understatement. Players ran out from what was called The Patrons' Stand. It was just terracing with seats added on top of the cinders. Opposite this stand was the Main Stand, which had bench seats underneath the leaky roof. In between the pitch and the stands was a speedway track, more cinders, and sometimes those cinders found their way onto the pitch after a particularly spectacular cycle meeting when they were spewed up by the back wheels of a skidding bike or a manically accelerating rider. Landing on a little pile of cinders during a game brought tears to your eyes, I can tell you. Fortunately football matches and speedway meetings took place on different days. Mind you, on the other hand, maybe it would have been more exciting if they'd been at the same time and the bikes came onto the field.

The floodlights were erected in 1961 and Real Madrid were invited to mark their inauguration. Wisely they declined. Behind one goal was the Tramshed End: yes, there used to be tramsheds up at the top behind the wall. This end was just a shallow curved bank of cinders and ash. Opposite this, behind the other goal, was another bank of ash and cinder but the central area might just have been terraced when I was there. From this end there were splendid views not so much of the football on offer, but of the tramsheds at the other end and Beacon Hill and the Pennines to the left. During its short and undistinguished history two things are worthy of mention. In the winter of '62/63, when the great freeze gripped the land, the club opened up the pitch as a skating rink and earned a few welcome pounds. And then in 1966 Jack Charlton opened one end as a golf driving range. But this was soon stopped as too many balls hit the stand roof and there were worries that the thing might collapse.

It was here in this splendid arena that I came to practise my trade and hone my skills, but instead I saw the ghost of my career finally fading into nothing. Where once I had been an Irish international, George Best's bosom buddy, the glamour boy of Burnley Football Club and banged in a record 29 League goals in that glorious season not so long before, I now performed in front of bus sheds, stray dogs, pigeons, people sitting on rickety wooden benches, and a few spectators dotted around on the cinders. If there was a worse venue in the whole of the Football League I had yet to see it. Though Alan Ball was not my favourite person in the world, I have to say that his creation of a winning team in this stadium before he arrived at Preston was little short of a miracle.

We rented a house in Luddenden (pronounced Luddnun by the locals, or at least that's what it sounded like to me). George Mulhall had said he would arrange for us to have a decent house, "a lovely house" was I think the expression he used. His idea of "lovely" and mine turned out to be rather different. It meant another move for the family, another change of schools for the boys, more upheaval for Rita. There were similarities with *Last of the Summer Wine* country except it wasn't pretty. It was another place of pubs, Co-op shops, Methodist and Baptist chapels, mills and terraced houses, with the canal, road, railway and river running side by side along the rain-sodden valley bottom three or four miles from Halifax.

Even in the early '70s you could still find plenty of cobbled streets there and even old gas lamps. When the smoke didn't fill the air, it was filled with fog. Mind you, the smoke was always there, I suppose, you just couldn't see it for the fog. In truth it was like stepping 100 years back in time. In Luddenden, up the hill from, and not quite the same place as Luddenden Foot, the Brontë sisters' brother Branwell had whiled away the day many years before quietly getting drunk. You could hardly blame him; there was nothing else to do. Today the old mills have either been demolished or they have been converted into smart apartments. The industrial landscape has been softened; the last gas lamp quietly removed, probably standing in some architectural salvage yard ready to be transplanted into a trendily converted hilltop barn.

And the house: it was cold, damp and miserable. It turned out to be a council house and was opposite a graveyard and it was there waiting for us while Rita stayed in Brighton to sell the house down there and I stayed with a family in Mytholmroyd, a couple of miles up the valley, and which is a name they can never pronounce properly on the news on TV. My absence knocked little Stephen for six. Suddenly at a very insecure age he found his father had gone missing and was too young to understand why. "Don't leave yer milk on the doorstep, luv," said the neighbour, "it'll get pinched round 'ere." And there the rot set in almost immediately with George Mulhall, who made it difficult if not impossible to get back to Brighton to visit them after the first few weeks – and the forever-disappearing milk drove me mad. When the Brighton house was sold they all moved up north again. Another move for the two young boys meant that yet again they didn't know if they were coming or going. We slept in this wretched place in one downstairs room with the electric fire on all night when the coal fire went out. The minute Rita moved north she got tonsillitis and slept on a camp bed in front of the fire with the kids running round like wild things until her parents managed to get over.

The streets were steep and cobbled and in February, when the snow and ice came, they struggled up the hill to the tiny school. It was three steps forward and two slides back with little Stephen, just two years old, hanging on to Rita's coat so he wouldn't slide back down to the valley bottom. Things were so bad at the school (don't ever make the mistake we made and tell the teachers you won't be there long) that Rita took Darren out and kept him at home until we moved back to Burnley, which became a huge priority so we could get away from this awful place and the "lovely" house with its charming views of the local cemetery. In sub-zero temperatures and huddling round the fire it was then that we thought of the offers I'd had to go to Denver, Tampa Bay, San Diego, Dallas and even South Africa. Rita had followed me to Preston, to Brighton, and now to "Luddnun", but crossing an ocean was a no. We had a visit in Brighton from one American who arrived wearing a Stetson and cowboy boots. We waited for him to say "Howdy pardner." He couldn't persuade us.

So as we shivered by the fire in Luddenden, with the windows icing up, the draught coming under the door, and the snow falling outside, we thought back to him and the offer he had made: a car that was 30 feet long, a house with a pool and a permanent blue sky overhead, plus great money.

I turned that down in favour of Halifax. Least said soonest mended I suppose. But when I landed there I could never have known that at the ripe old age of just 29 my career had just months left instead of another five or six years. It's clear now after all these years why Saward kept quiet about the Hearts deal, because if I'd gone to Hearts it would have screwed up his plan to take Lammie Robertson from Halifax in part exchange for me. Football managers – A Level Machiavellis the lot of 'em. For many of us, our lives and futures were determined by behind-the-scenes deals, negotiations that were kept from us, and in my case sheer bloody dishonesty. When deals were made like this one we were just stooges shuffled around like pawns and it was 20 years before I ever found out.

I joined Halifax when they were near the bottom of the division; they'd only won one of 12 home matches. Crowds were down to maybe 3,000 on a good day, and the pigeons that landed on the pitch during a quiet spell. Only 12 months earlier 20,000 had seen them beat Manchester United in the Watney Cup. By the end of the season Halifax avoided relegation to Division Four only on goal difference. Four teams finished with 41 points. Rotherham was the unlucky one. At least my one solitary goal counted for something. It's about all I remember and the manner of my final league goal was quite fitting. I don't even know who the game was against, I really was past caring. Whatever, a ball came across into a crowded six-yard box. It was like Poundstretcher on half-price day. The goalkeeper and centre half collided and fell in a heap on the floor cursing each other. The ground was so empty you could hear what they said to each other at the other end. The ball ricocheted off them and landed with a plop at my feet; it just sat there inviting me to kick it. Ever deadly from three feet I lashed in the ball. My one and only Halifax goal, the climax of my career and most of the crowd fell about laughing at this comedy of errors. I'd like to say it was a stunning twenty-five yarder, or a bullet header from a pinpoint cross – but no, it was pathetic.

By this time George Mulhall had finished me off. Did you ever see that Richard Harris film *This Sporting Life* in which he takes the part of a Rugby League player? At the end of his time he's weary, battered, racked with pain, spent, finished, disillusioned, had enough. Well, that was me except I played football. There'd been a game at York when he accused me of not trying and not earning my money. I flew at him and told him I'd come up here to play for him at half the money I was once on, could have earned huge money in the States in the sunshine and where was this "lovely" house he'd promised me instead of the shabby dump by the burial ground? It only needed a couple of hooting owls, a bit of mist and a full moon and you could well imagine Vincent Price or Christopher Lee coming across the road in long black capes. I let fly at Mulhall and there and then ended my career. I played for a team without spirit, without heart, without class. In a team like that Pele would have struggled to find life. There was no motivation, no inspiration, and no desire to play for this man.

He dropped me and that was that, until the John Angus testimonal game at Burnley near the end of the season. Of course I was invited to play and told him I was accepting the invitation and *was* playing, that it was an honour to be asked and this was the place where I had started my career. No I wasn't, he said. I was on the bench for the game at Walsall. "But will I be playing?" I asked. "No," he said. Fuck him, I thought, he can go and whistle. I didn't go to Walsall. I went to Burnley instead to play in John's game and Christ did the fun and games start then. I was fined two weeks' wages and he had me in every day for extra training which he personally supervised, running round and round that bloody pitch, till I was dizzy. It went from *This Sporting Life* to *The Hill*, the film in which that bastard sergeant Harry Andrews tries to break Sean Connery. Apart from the fact there was no hill it was a bit like that. I just ran, and ran, and ran till I was nearly on my knees. But God, I refused to buckle or complain, and this was morning and afternoon with one break in between. The end came when I suggested one midday break with mock chirpiness that I treat him to lunch. Took him to lunch; back we came, cracked a joke, me trying to look fresh as a daisy. And it was Mulhall who gave in. "Get off home, go away," he growled, or words to that effect. And that was it, goodbye Halifax.

"The trouble with you is," he'd once said, and it might have been in the slanging match at York, "you've too much money," meaning of course I'd no hunger for the game any more. Too true; but the irony escaped him, that it was he who had destroyed what hunger I still had, the enthusiasm, the love of the game; and even before I'd turned 30 I'd approached that jaundiced, cynical stage all ageing pros get to, of hating training, the rain and the drizzle, not wanting to leave the house in the morning. You perform like a robot, just going through the motions, all feeling gone. After a game your whole body aches and everything that was once a joy is just a chore. You can't wait for the end of the season and then what really kills you off is the thought of the next batch of pre-season training when a summer of inactivity has to be worked out of you with drills, gruelling runs, hill work, endless exercises, training till it hurts and the occasions when it makes you physically sick.

The only bright spot was the drive to Halifax in a morning, or back home on a spring evening, once we'd left Luddenden behind and found a house in Worsthorne on the edge of Burnley. Goodbye, council house with damp running down the walls and overgrown graveyard over the road. From Worsthorne you take the road over the hills and drive across the moorland. I'd sometimes stop the car just to drink it in. I'd watch the curlews and lapwings, and the skylarks wheeling and singing overhead. Lambs would frisk and play in the fields and I lost count of the foxes I'd see running across the fields between the farms. On a blue-sky day with not a cloud to be seen in the sky I felt how good it was to be back home in this tremendous landscape with views that stretched for miles. Then I'd turn down the spectacular tree lined Mytholm Steeps with its incredible gradients and twists and turns into Hebden Bridge. Not for nothing is this area sometimes called Little Switzerland. But then, once in the industrial valley bottom, the spell was broken. Halifax and Mulhall beckoned.

I left Halifax Town with no regrets; save for thinking, why did I choose this club? Too late though, clocks can't be turned back. I knew why I had done it; to go back to Burnley, to find somewhere to settle, for Rita to come back to her roots, and so that our boys would no longer be pulled round from pillar to post, from town to town, and school to school. It hadn't worked out, I accepted that part of it, but not the manner of it. Mulhall and I just didn't get on and we came to a mutual agreement that I should leave. There was some interest from Rochdale but it came to nothing and along came a little homely semi-professional club from the Northern Premier League called Great Harwood. It's near Accrington, which in turn is between Blackburn and Burnley. It was a club where a lot of old pros went in their twilight years; there had been the great Ronnie Clayton, Roy Vernon and Bryan Douglas, all wonderful international players. While I was there, I played alongside old colleagues like goalkeeper Adam Blacklaw and Les Latcham with whom I had once been in digs. Training was a couple of nights a week, in my case if I felt like it, and on occasions there were crowds of nearly 5,000. But whereas the other players' twilight years were well into their 30s and even 40s, I was still at an age where I should have been in my prime, banging in goals like Jimmy Greaves went on doing for donkeys' years. I didn't stay long, only a matter of months if I remember rightly.

Willie Irvine

So what does a footballer do when he hangs up his boots and joins the real world? And by real world I mean the place where I had to organise my own life, instead of allowing a football club to do it. It's a massive change and not always easy to adjust. For me it was easier in the sense that any remaining deep love for professional football had been squeezed out of me at Halifax. I was ready to finish. There had been offers to go to Ireland to play but what I wanted to do was not acceptable to the clubs who were interested.

For me it would have been ideal to live in Burnley and fly over to play but no club wanted to pay the airfares on a regular basis. If I had been desperate to stay in the game, yes, we would have moved to Ireland; more change, more disruption, another move for Rita and the boys. But there was another consideration, having had one close-up experience of a man with a gun in Northern Ireland, who I was damned sure was going to shove it right in my face: the thought of returning to a place being torn apart by sectarianism and violence appealed to none of us. Who in their right mind would have wanted to take three young boys to live in that environment? Fly in, play a game, pop a few goals in for Glentoran or Linfield, fly out again, fine. Live there, no. Ironically, in later years, Stephen would serve there in the army.

The setting-in of the rot at Halifax coincided with the opportunity to start a business in Burnley. So Willie Irvine, footballer, became Willie Irvine, businessman. There weren't many of us around in Burnley with a Beatle haircut and a Mexican moustache and I must have looked like a backstreet dodgy car salesman, but it was full steam ahead to get a DIY business off the ground, especially once the Halifax fiasco was over. A friend had a warehouse available for rent on Clifton Street near the town centre. David Doney had the premises; I had the "name" and some capital.

As a footballer I never knew my adze from my elbow, I never knew there were so many different sorts of screws and nails. Do you realise how many different kinds of saws and hammers there are? I had to learn a whole new vocabulary; I thought a soil system was an old-fashioned outdoor Irish loo down the bottom of the garden.

I thought louvre doors were what you went through to get into that famous museum in Paris. I'd get mail about Osma rainwater systems; what on earth was an Osma rainwater system, I'd mutter; and there was Easyfit doubleglazing. Easyfit... rubbish... anything I'd ever fitted in my life before had been anything but easy. I had to learn about chipboard, hardboard, pinboard, contiboard, contiplas, blockboard, wallboard, plasterboard, mouldings, beading, and 101 different kinds of wood: plywood, softwood, hardwood, whitewood, stripwoods, even now I've no idea what stripwood is; plus laths and laminates and melamine and grains and fascias and veneers, which I'd always thought was something nasty you didn't talk about in polite society...

Then there was tongue and groove cladding; what the hell was tongue and groove cladding? The roller blinds were something else.

"Ah good morning, do you stock roller blinds, Mr Irvine?"

"But of course, sir; I have satinite, linen, washable, grainy, embossed, grainy embossed, washable grainy embossed, PVC, plain, floral... would you prefer them to roll up, or roll down?"

"Willie, I need a hammer."

"No problem, would you like a big one or a small one, a lump hammer or a claw hammer, a hammer that hits the thumb or misses?"

"Na then, dust tha 'ave any saws?"

"Follow me... why yes here they are, we have tenon saws, fretsaws, bow saws, coping saws, handsaws, mitre saws, tension saws ... but sorry... no jigsaws."

A bloke once came in and asked if I stocked musical saws. He must have noticed me staring at him as if he was not quite the sharpest tool in the box.

"Ha ha, I see you're puzzled," he announced, and then explained it was part of his club act and spent the next hour testing every saw in the shop to find the one that was just right. I must have heard *Danny Boy* a dozen times before he switched to *Some Enchanted Evening*. It was the day I realised I didn't sell earplugs, and the day I had a migraine for the first time.

My head was spinning in ever decreasing circles with all this stuff. But at the same time I was happy. Where once I had been a football name on TV, the only time I got on the box now was on the warehouse security system.

We opened from 8.30am till 5.30pm but I was in there at all hours. I should have called it "Arkwright's". Every town had its half-day closing and half-day closing was Tuesday, the day that all of Burnley was shut. If you were out of bread, milk or fags: tough. But you'd find me in there somewhere in my little office buried in paperwork and accounts and figures and stocktaking and orders and delivery notes. Once upon a time the only papers I looked at were the sports pages.

And I had something else. I had a *briefcase*. I was a businessman so a briefcase was a must. It was shiny and new when I bought it and I took it home and looked at it as it leaned against the chair where I had put it so I could admire it and even polish it. It was a beauty. I had never had a briefcase before and I proudly carried my elegant status symbol in to work every morning. I even wore glasses. I had to or I'd have cut my thumbs off trimming timber and cutting shelf lengths up for customers who wouldn't buy their own saw, the tight-fisted buggers. In my briefcase I had paperwork, and on a good day a couple of cheques to put in the bank, and my sandwiches.

I was proud to announce I had 1,000 boards always in stock and I could talk metric long before we all went European and you could no longer buy spuds in 5lb bags on Burnley market. The design board I had in the office was where I planned out people's kitchens and cupboards. Sometimes they used to fit, which was always a relief.

In a business magazine I once read the fairy story of how some bloke set up a stationery business and promised to deliver anything, anywhere no matter how big or small. So one day someone phones up from miles away to ask for a packet of drawing pins. The bloke curses and swears but delivers the pins, true to his word. Unknown to him it's a giant multinational company that's testing him out. He passes the test and they give him a massive contract that sets him up for life. I pinned that story up behind my desk and sat and waited for some giant firm from 30 miles away to ring me to deliver an order for one packet of screws. I'm still waiting.

But we must have been doing something right; the customers turned up, and even came back. Many a night my briefcase was weighed down with over £1,000 in cash I took into the bank to count up. Customers would ask my advice about this and that, which in the first few months was certainly a case of the blind leading the blind. When a rather attractive lady came in once and asked, with a straight face, did I do nine-inch screws, for once I was lost for words. Of course people came in to chat about football and, with a bit of luck, buy a doorknob from the man who had once scored 37 goals in a season. There was one bloke in particular who used to love to come and chat away about football, to such an extent he used to come back into the office with me and we'd jaw away for hours. Sometimes when I was called out to serve a customer I'd let him wait in there. Silly Willie. One day I noticed £400 cash missing from a drawer in the desk after he'd visited. Of course I couldn't prove he'd taken it but that was the last visit he ever made. Trust people too easily, that was my trouble.

I did the bread and butter lines – there were 8,000 of them, would you believe – and customers came from Bolton, Blackburn, Preston and Clitheroe as well as Burnley. It thrived to the extent that we opened a second store in Keighley. We looked at bigger houses or extending the one we were in. I had my obligatory snooker and table tennis room and all the trimmings; spoiled the boys rotten. I appointed extra staff to look after the Burnley store. And there the happy story ends.

Maybe I was OK with self-tapping screws, but debit sheets, balances, statements, invoices and cash flows were things I left more and more to others.

Meanwhile I beavered away, and my bank manager prudently looked after my account, or at least that's what I thought was happening. I became fully conversant with all manner of screws, be they brass, traditional brass, traditional brass raised, traditional solid brass, buffed brass or burnished brass. Then there were dowel screws, square head screws, round head screws, twisted thread screws, self-drilling, concealed screws (buggers; I could never find them), adjustable, countersunk, runner or drywall.

I became an expert in advising people how to unblock sinks.

"Well, ahem… you could pour bleach down… or vinegar… or baking soda… or all three. You could use a plunger, or failing that a drain auger." At this point I would always feel so knowledgeable, nay superior.

"Pardon, Willie… an auger…?"

"Well, it's sometimes called a plumber's snake." (Guaranteed to make the ladies giggle).

"Pardon."

"Well, it's just a bit of bendy wire really. Shove it in, wiggle it around, in and out, up and down… as the actress said to the bishop… and Bob's your uncle, sink unblocked… or a bishop with a glazed look in his eyes."

I was so helpful; nothing was too much trouble. A fella came in one day, and this is a true story, and asked for a clothes line prop for his wife; well not actually to prop up his wife, it was to prop up the washing. "Well, we don't do them," I said, "but I can make you one. All you need is an eight feet length of two by one and I'll cut you a V in the middle at the end."

"Brilliant," he said when I had done this little job and away he went. Couple of days later he came back with it and don't forget this is a true story. "Willie," he said, "you've put the V at the wrong end." I looked at him and thought for a minute. "Bugger," I said. "I've made you an Irish one." So I cut him a V at the other end and away he went very pleased.

You'd be surprised at the questions I was asked. What do you say to the chap who comes in and says plaintively, "Willie, my Rawlplugs don't work?" What you do, dear reader, is move into DIY speak mode.

"Well now, let me see, there's nothing worse than a wobbly Rawlplug. Wobbly Rawlplug equals shelf that might fall down. I'll bet you didn't know that the Rawlplug was a Victorian invention by a man called Rawlings. What people those Victorians were. Did you know a man called Thomas Crapper designed one of the first flush loos… you didn't?… well there you go then. Anyway, Rawlplugs... To work correctly I would recommend that the hole, the plug and screw must all fit correctly... you're with me so far... stop me if I get too technical... for the majority of DIY work (in the trade we sometimes call it Destroy It Yourself, ha, ha), use a Number 8 masonry drill, 6mm, Number 8 plugs (red if from Rawlplug) and one half inch Number 8 screw. I further recommend supascrews; you'll recognise them because the heads are all posidrive; they do not taper, the thread runs all the way to the head (now here's where I really know what I'm talking about), and there are usually two threads running parallel."

At this point I would pause, one for effect and two for breath. The follow-up was equally impressive.

"And when you're drilling, do drill deep enough for the screw not to bottom out: use a hammer drill with the hammer action on – and above all... you need a clean hole; any excess dust and you're in big trouble." Here I'd halt again for maximum effect before finally adding the *coup de grâce* with as much gravitas as I could muster...

"And don't forget to tighten yer chuck, luv."

With performances like this, no wonder people travelled in from all four corners of east Lancashire. I doubt it was to hear my jokes. Like this one. A woman goes into a DIY shop one day to buy a fitted wardrobe. She soon goes back to say it's all fixed up and fitted but it keeps wobbling and shaking all the time. Just tighten up all the screws, the shopkeeper tells her, it will be right as rain. A few days later she goes back. "Now what," the bloke asks her. "Er, it's still shaking but we live near the railway line and it seems to be every time a train goes by." "OK," he says. "I'll come and take a look."

So a couple of days later he goes to the house and she shows him the wardrobe and he gets inside it to have a look. Meanwhile her husband comes home, hears his wife upstairs, goes up to the bedroom and finds her by the wardrobe door talking to someone inside it. So he yanks open the door and is furious to find another bloke in his bedroom. "What the hell are you doing in there?" he thunders. "Whoops, you won't believe this," the bloke says, "but I'm just waiting for the train."

And so my DIY empire thrived and prospered, or at least I thought it did, until, after several years of working my fingers to the bone, what became blindingly obvious even to me was that it didn't seem to be making much money. For reasons I won't bother going into I'd had to move premises. I had six months to move out and as soon as the old premises were vacated another DIY firm moved in and set up business in direct competition. The trouble was, though, people continued to go to the old premises thinking it was still mine, so trade in the new premises was terrible. We'd worked our socks off moving out of one and into the other and all for nothing. It was a disaster. The penny dropped that there'd be far less hassle, and more money to be made, and far more peace of mind to be found, if I had just a nice little corner newspaper shop, in my home village of Worsthorne. It seemed so sensible, so simple, so much less stressful, even if you did have to get up at the ungodly hour of five in the morning to sort the papers, even if Rita did fall and break her foot on the ice one winter morning delivering them. And anyway, didn't the great Ronnie Clayton, ex-Blackburn and England, once have a paper shop? So, when the local corner shop went up for sale, we made our decision. I had someone lined up to buy the DIY business – or so I thought.

We took out a bridging loan to pay for the shop and my purchaser agreed to buy the business. We sorted everything out with the bank and the manager. We left the paperwork to our solicitor. What was there to worry about; everything fine, no problems. Smooth as a baby's bottom. We moved into the paper shop, but continued to live in the big house with the games room. My purchaser informed me he was having difficulties raising the money to buy the business, but everything would be OK, it was just a temporary thing; in a few weeks he'd have the money. The alarm bells should have rung there and then but they didn't. Am I not Willie Irvine? Do I not trust people?

No problem, I told him. We had the shop, a house in the village and a cottage that we rented out, a nice big car and the briefcase could from now on stay in the bottom of the cupboard. How sweet life was, how simple was my day, how nice it was to stand in the tiny shop, serve customers with the simple things of life, while away the day in chat and gossip, no more stress, no pressure, until one day we had a visit from the solicitor and the bank manager.

It struck me in no way odd that they turned up together. I seem to recall they played tennis together; maybe they were just calling in for a paper.

They looked uncomfortable, if not embarrassed; they looked at the floor before they looked at me, they waited until the shop was empty, and then one of them, I can't remember which, asked, could we talk. We went into the privacy of the back room and they hit me with the news that the bank overdraft now stood at some enormous figure that I just didn't possess. The events of that day remain a blur even now and so do the following weeks and even months. The figure of £44,000 rings a bell, a huge amount for the mid '80s. I recall just standing there bemused, disbelieving, then total shock set in and numbness and a sickness in the pit of my stomach. Where in God's name did anyone find that amount of money? I blurted out that someone had agreed to buy the business. I asked the pathetic predictable questions: how had this happened, why had I not been told long before, and just what did we do? I felt lost, helpless; the enormity of it caused my mind to go blank. Then my head started operating again. Denial temporarily took over. I challenged them: there must be some mistake, this couldn't possibly be correct, I had had someone running the warehouse who intended to purchase it, and the bank and my solicitor couldn't possibly have let this happen... surely?

I can't remember if they made soothing, calming noises, or how long they stayed, but what was certainly said was that there would have to be more meetings to discuss how to resolve things, and that there could certainly be no further continuation of the overdraft.

And my purchaser? For legal reasons I'll say allegedly, but it would seem he had never been in any position to buy the business: he'd provided no security, had signed nothing, was not legally responsible for the debts racked up by the business which was still in my name but which I had left in his hands, and he had disappeared to France. According to the bank manager a few cheques had been paid into the bank account but precious little cash. The building wasn't mine and the value of the stock in the warehouse was a pitiful £2,000. It's a cliché I know, but there's no other way to describe it. The bottom had fallen out of my world.

The blurred days continued. I'd rack my brain to find a way out of this mess. Mess isn't strong enough a word; nightmare isn't adequate either. I sat in the chair that night and didn't have a clue what to do. It was Rita who took things in hand. The shop would have to be sold, the house and the cottage; there was some insurance money due after my Volvo had been damaged. An accountant called Dave Edmundson became involved and reached a settlement figure with the bank. It was less than what we really owed, but crippling nevertheless. At the end of this harrowing process we moved into a smaller house, and somehow managed to retain the princely sum of £700. We committed ourselves to making monthly payments to the bank, on top of the proceeds of all that we had sold. Bearing in mind that the job I eventually managed to find paid me just £360 a month you can judge how difficult finding the bank repayment was. We depended on Rita working as well. During one of the meetings we'd had with the solicitor and bank manager, they had offered to help Rita find a job. She looked at them in disgust, turned, walked out of the room and slammed the door in their faces.

The boys were knocked for six. From having it all; nice big house, own bedrooms, snooker and games room, spoiled rotten especially at Christmas; from all that to having next to nothing. The middle one, Stephen, took it especially hard and began to run us ragged.

If we had a saviour in this sorry saga it was Dave Edmundson, who I should say is no relation to the current Chief Executive at Burnley Football Club. We asked Lloyds Bank to undertake an investigation into the way in which the bank had handled our account and allowed this overdraft to build up. Of course they would, but then pointed out that if the investigation cleared their branch of mishandling or incompetence, then we would face further costs. Of course we declined. The frightened minnows versus the big boys; how could we possibly risk further debt?

What use are green international jerseys and memories of glory days when something like this happens? How will 37 goals scored in one magic season put food on the table and feed three hungry boys? Those boys who I love so much now received only neglect, and precious little attention from me in the weeks that followed.

In fact my moods were such that Rita kept them out of my way. How old was I? Not much more than 40 – in my prime, or should have been. But the collapse of everything I thought was sound and secure left me emptied of all pride and sense of achievement. I aged almost overnight, began to lose my hair, and what was left turned grey. There were days when I looked in the mirror and didn't recognise the face staring back. I felt useless, helpless and hopeless; a wreck, a shell, devoid of any interest in anything. Without Rita I wouldn't be here today. She became the rock, the indestructible one, and the one who kept things going and stayed on her feet. She worked full-time, but for a while we lived on benefits, and she still brought up the three boys. I, meanwhile, could barely look them in the eye when in my own mind I had let them all down so badly. I remember actually fighting with one of my own sons who was so angry with me. They were dark days.

CHAPTER SIXTEEN

TO THE BOTTOM AND BACK

For a number of weeks – I can't remember how many – after what I call "the crash" I mooched about, avoided people and rarely left the house. If I wandered occasionally in a sort of haze up to the Bay Horse for a drink I stood alone, glass in hand, staring at the walls or floor, and kept my troubles to myself. You stand "small", shoulders down, head looking at the floor, hunched, almost apologetic for being there. You don't want to be noticed because you don't want people coming up to you. The last thing you want to be asked is "How are you Willie?" You've only gone there in the first place because somebody has said to you, "Go on, it will do you good to get out." Classic. I didn't even tell Andy Lochhead, my great friend, who was the landlord. Maybe I should have, but the sense of shame and inadequacy ran so deep. I didn't want people to know; I wanted to hide it, keep it to myself and pretend I was strong. I was anything but.

Have you ever been depressed? And by depressed I don't mean just fed up for an hour when something trivial has gone wrong, or your football team has lost, or you have put weight on when you'd kidded yourself you'd slimmed down a bit.

I didn't sleep, lost interest in everything, lost any energy I had and just felt totally washed out and continually tired. The question went continually through my head – how could this have happened? Then there'd be feelings of guilt and self-reproach. Losing hair and weight seemed a minor side-effect. I couldn't concentrate on anything, couldn't make a decision to save my life, wandered around the house, and it took an

232

effort to do even the simplest little job. The business crash made me feel a total failure.

The last thing I wanted was the people who told me to buck up: things can only get better; stop feeling sorry for yourself, we all have problems; do something about it; the answer is in your own hands; just stop thinking about it; everything will be fine, you'll see... There are 101 platitudes people come out with: I couldn't begin to list them all but they have one thing in common; they have the opposite effect to what is intended. What I needed was not someone talking at me but just someone who would listen, if you could find such a person. What I wanted to hear was that it wasn't my fault; I'm here if you need me, I can't imagine what it's like but I admire you for hanging on in there...

I had, in fact, made a mess of things big time, and it may well have been my own fault either through neglect or carelessness but the last thing I wanted was constant reminders of that from people who hadn't a clue about the state I was in. What I needed was sympathy, affection, friendship and compassion; someone to help and be on my side but who lets me think that I was helping myself.

Before recovery came, depression took me right to the edge; to a suicide attempt. This was a time when there were no magic pills on tap, no Prozac, no antidepressants available on demand simply by telling your doctor you were depressed. This was a time, even though it was only 20 years ago, before counselling had become an industry and medical knowledge and research was not quite ready to say that people like me were genuinely ill.

It was another night I'd stayed downstairs when everyone else had gone to bed. I sat in the kitchen. There was a wooden bench in there and I have a mental picture of myself sitting on that bench with my head feeling like it was swimming. We had a huge bottle of pills, paracetamol if I remember rightly. God knows how many I swallowed; I just emptied the bottle into the palm of my hand, shoved them into my mouth, half chewing, half swallowing and emptying a full glass of beer down me at the same time. Somehow I got them down, and afterwards we guessed I must have taken four or five dozen. I'd had enough, saw no solution, mind totally gone, right down in the depths of despair. Looking back it was interesting that I waited till it was dark and quiet. The darkness seemed important.

Today depression is seen as a clear illness: a chemical imbalance in the brain is the doctorspeak. Then, it was seen as taboo, a stigma and maybe some people still see it that way. They say it's the coward's way out. Others say it takes bravery to take these pills, whether it's one by one, or in great handfuls, knowing what the consequences will be. I say now it's neither, nor is it being irresponsible. It's none of these because the mind isn't functioning as it should any more and doesn't know the difference between responsibility and irresponsibility. Words like these are meaningless and irrelevant because there are no words you can use as labels. God knows what the decision-making process is except that it comes from a total lack of any ability to think clearly and logically. How can the mind be logical and clear to think that death is more attractive than life? But that is the state you have got to. Death becomes comforting and welcoming. Maybe that's why darkness is an attraction. It's like a cloak that gives protection and comfort from what you think is shame, and that is what you want to escape from; what in your own mind you perceive as the humiliation, what you see as the loss of control over the events of your life, and the embarrassment, and the lack of any answers.

Rita is a light sleeper, or maybe she's been a light sleeper ever since. She was upstairs but heard the sound of the bench hitting the floor when I passed out and fell off it. If I'd been sitting in the armchair in the living room there would have been no sound, she would never have heard and I'd have been lying there in the armchair in the morning when she and the boys came down. It's a horrific thought. The fact that I made the attempt in the kitchen, sitting on a wooden bench, saved my life. Hearing the crash, Rita came down and saw the bottle and the remaining scattered pills on the floor. She called a great friend of ours in the village, David Denson, who came round immediately. Somehow they lifted me and carried me into his car. They got me onto the back seat where I lay sprawled, unconscious, out to the world. Within minutes I was in hospital in Burnley with my stomach being pumped out.

Was I grateful my life had been saved? Was there a sense of relief? The truth is no, there was not. The following morning all I wanted to do was get out of that hospital bed and flee from any further humiliation. The shame at what I had done felt even greater. I signed myself out and got myself back home. I just wanted to hide and didn't want anyone to know what I had done.

Few people know until reading this of the attempt I made, but anyone I have ever told has responded with a sense of surprise. There's that brief minimal moment of silence before they say something and sometimes its just an "oh", with a barely repressed sense of shock.

If someone tells you they are feeling suicidal, then listen. You can't solve their problems, you can't personally "rescue" them, you can't take on all their ills as your own, but you can listen without making them feel unclean. These people need concern not disapproval.

But slowly, bit by bit, inch by inch I recovered. I can't explain the process by which I managed it. There were good days and bad days, days I felt in control but others when the old aimlessness came back. But I saw people rallying round, I saw the concern of family and friends, and when I saw them there I no longer felt the deep sense of isolation. Yes, it was a cry for help and when that came, and I learned I was still valued, life became worth living again. I learned that bottling things up, keeping all those emotions hidden beneath a "stiff upper lip" was a mistake. I learned that burying the anguish just perpetuates and feeds the illness. In my case, when I came round, I learned to look outwards not inwards and in looking outwards I saw my boys again properly. I saw that things weren't right.

I began to ask myself why I had made the attempt, and began to see the consequences of my actions had I succeeded in what I had tried to do. The good days were when I was able to put it to the back of my mind and start to get on with things and just not think about it. The bad days were when I remembered it all over again and the feelings of anguish flooded back and all I wanted to do was stay in the house, put a blanket over my head, hide from it. Three steps forward and then two steps back. I didn't work for quite a while; how could I? Rita stayed at home with me, and besides there were the three boys for her to look after and try to retain some semblance of normality. She watched me constantly and for a while we had no income other than benefits.

From international footballer, then successful businessman who brought a briefcase home every night, sometimes stuffed with more than £1,000, luxury home, top-of-the-range Volvo, to this – living on benefits – no wonder the boys didn't know what had hit them. I might have lost everything, but I didn't want to lose them. And through all of this Rita was the rock and pulled us all through.

Then, bit by bit, realisation grew that our situation was not the end of the world and that yes, with work and graft, we could cope and pay our bills. There was no magic medication, no special key, just a slow realisation. And for the first time in an age I noticed the boys and their needs. Maybe that was the key, recognising the needs of others, not just mine. I saw little things in the house that needed doing, gradually began to speak to neighbours; the healing process was under way. Rita saw a job advertised that might be suitable; part-time, work your way back into things slowly was the advice. "Willie, you have been ill in just the same way that someone has had a broken arm or any other injury; you have had a broken mind. These things are not your fault; they happen, to more people than you think. Take your time, step by step. When you broke your leg at Goodison it took months to recover and get back to full fitness; this is the same." Life began to feel better for the first time in an age.

The council job was evenings for just five hours a night. I met a chap called Gordon Waddington to talk about it. I smiled for the first time in weeks. That had been one of the first things to vanish, my sense of humour. It had been weeks since I had last told one of my pathetic jokes.

The job was helping and working with young people in community centre youth clubs. There were all kinds of kids and all ages, many from good homes with nice parents; but many were kids who got themselves into scrapes and came from difficult, troubled homes. There were disturbed kids, glue sniffers, shoplifters, disturbers of the peace, kids in conflict with parents; the whole range of teenage flotsam and jetsam. Some of them I felt sorry for and thought, "Poor sod, this just isn't your fault, what chance have you ever had?" They were the products of failing schools and poverty that was man-made and parents swamped by their inability to cope. Others deserved no sympathy whatsoever.

Many parts of Burnley in the '80s were not pretty: rows and rows of substandard housing, closed-down corner shops, derelict streets, boarded-up properties, once the homes of mill workers in the days when the cotton mills churned out their products. Some of the council estates, once the bright dream of an improved future, were no better and all of them were filled with the jobless and the unemployed. A lucky few did have work but it was rare in this job if I ever met them.

The estates were centres of poverty, deprivation, boredom, vandalism, litter, abandoned cars, and unrest. I had my eyes well and truly opened. I went into homes that were carpetless and almost without furniture. I went into homes where people slept on mattresses on the bare floorboards, where the rooms stank of stale urine and cigarette smoke, and empty beer bottles rolled about the floor; rooms lit by just one naked bulb. I went into homes where small children cowered in a corner while their parents argued and screamed abuse at each other. Some of these kids looked as if they hadn't eaten for a week and clothes hung off them like rags. In some homes electricity had been cut off for non-payment of bills. And into these homes, with these kids without a future, I was supposed to bring hope and then help them with their troubles. These were the places that politicians had failed, the politicians with their words and promises, their committees, action plans, visions and policies. Damn them, I thought, we live in a world where there are the haves and the have-nots and if you're unlucky enough to belong to the latter you're part of a group where hardship, squalor and debt is just the normal way of life. And it's not just a small group; there were times when I felt it was a huge part of the town. Is it any wonder,

I thought, that these kids, with their apathetic parents who have lost all interest, are discontented and kick back? I met all manner of parents but in too many cases there was an attitude that said they'd given in; what else could they do?

I don't think I came back home any night without ever thinking, "There but for the grace of God go I. My problems are nothing compared to these." And something else I thought as well; the poverty I saw in Burnley at that time was different to the poverty the Irvine family survived in Eden or Carrickfergus so many years before. There were times in the very early days when the Irvines never had two pennies to rub together, but we never resorted to the levels of behaviour or developed the attitudes that I saw in those derelict terraced rows, or on those badly planned shoddy council estates. There was a community spirit back in Carrick; laughter and optimism was never far away. I don't think it ever occurred to us just how poor we were in the very early days in Eden. We were too busy being happy and making the best of what we'd got. If there is such a thing as cheerful poverty then it's a description that would have suited us. There was a sort of cheeky defiance, I suppose, that we flung back at our lack of money, and a satisfaction from devouring a stew made of meat we'd conned from the butcher and filled with vegetables we'd liberated from the farmer's fields. Sweets from the shop tasted better when you had bought them with pennies earned from doing odd jobs or chopping firewood.

We did all kinds of things in those community youth clubs: played games, organised trips and visits, played music, sometimes just talked. Of course I did some football coaching and ran a team. There were a lot of happy moments but the memory of some of the kids you met stayed for a long time. Lisa, not her real name, of course, was just 13 going on 14 and already on the game. There came a night when she lingered and hung around the youth club even though it was closing time. I learned to recognise the signs. When kids were reluctant to go home it was because they were frightened of abuse or beatings. But Lisa was from a good home and had loving parents so this was unusual. We talked to her and the truth emerged. She was frightened that her parents would eventually find out the trouble she was in and what she was doing. She had discovered that performing simple sex acts for men made easy money, but then one man had encouraged her to dabble with drugs. She was hooked and simple sex became full sex to earn more money. She was trapped. In a case like that the senior youth club officials took over and then social services. What happened to her I never found out but often still wonder.

Then there were the glue sniffers and lighter-fuel sniffers. One disco night I went outside just to give my ears a rest for a few minutes and there round the corner was one lad having a cigarette and next to him a lad sniffing lighter fuel. There were occasions when I did home visits to see the parents of some of the kids.

I went to the house with the lad to let his parents know what he was getting up to. Knock, knock. We waited for the door to open and eventually a bloke who looked like King Kong opened the door and glowered at the pair of us. "Now what?" he grunted. "My God," I thought, "this bloke's a monster, what do I say?" I explained his lad had been lighter-fuel sniffing and maybe he needed some help.

"NO HE DOESN'T and who the fuck are you," the bloke roared towering over me, leaving me thinking, "Whoops be careful." With a bit of blather we all went into the house and I made damned sure there was nothing in between the door and me in case I had to make a quick exit. "Tell the truth," I said to the lad. "You tell your dad what you've been getting up to." Mercifully for me the lad did so. His giant father was silent and I made a polite exit, relieved that I had not been flattened. I can't say I ever saw that lad sniffing again, at least not at the youth club.

Of course there were good times and I met some lovely kids and families. Some of them have grown up now with families of their own and just occasionally I bump into them. That's when I feel good about what I did, when they ask, did I remember them, and proudly show off their children in the supermarket. There were indeed some good times such as a day trip to Rhyl I remember well and some remarkably giving colleagues.

But one afternoon it occurred to me I was ready and able to do more work than just five hours a night. I really did sit there racking my brains to think of ways of earning more money doing something that would allow me to work in the evenings as well. Life is strange in the way it works. And as I thought, fate, luck, happenstance; call it what you will; intervened.

As I sat there thinking, what should happen but the window cleaner noisily propped up his ladder against the wall in the yard outside and put his bucket on the ground with a great bang and a clatter that would have woken the dead. A thought grew. "Bloody hell, I could do that," I thought. "Cleaning windows, easy work, do it in the mornings, all you need is a bucket, a ladder, a leather..."

He was a local chap, Roy Holdsworth, and out I went to talk to him. He made it sound easy and a nice little earner. I felt like that Liverpool bloke, what was he called? Yes, Yosser, out of *Boys From The Blackstuff*. "Gizza job? I could do that." I found out about another round that was for sale in another part of Burnley, and rang the bloke who was selling it. He wanted £1,000 and for a £200 deposit it was mine there and then. Just one problem reared its ugly head: it was Saturday, and the banks were all shut; where to get £200 there and then? He didn't want a cheque; he wanted cash and somebody else wanted to buy his patch. No way did I have £200 in the house so it was quick thinking time; this was too good a chance to miss. Surely the corner shop would cash me a cheque. I knew the bloke in there, he'd have cash in the till, and round I went. To my disappointment he wasn't too keen, even though I explained everything. Perhaps he thought my cheque would bounce. No joy, so over I went to the Bay Horse and Andy Lochhead who was landlord there. No problem, he cashed me the cheque, I had a quick pint in celebration, and back I ran to the house to grab the car and beetle off to pay the £200. No problems. I was now the proud owner of my own business again. I sat in the car pleased as punch, like a cat that's found the cream. I was a transparent wall engineer, a glass hygiene consultant, more commonly known to you, dear reader, as a window cleaner. Bloody hell.

For the next few days Roy showed me how to wash a window without leaving smears. I never knew it was so easy to leave smudges and marks on a piece of glass. I'd thought it was simple. He made it look easy, but every window I practised on had more smudges than Liz Taylor's make-up. And this was before I went up a ladder; these were the easy windows on the ground floor with my feet firmly on terra firma. Stage two was climbing up a ladder with a wash-leather in one hand, another over the shoulder, and a bucket of water. A third hand would have been useful. You should try washing a window up the top of a ladder when you have to reach and stretch over to get into the corners. Then there were those leaded windows and little Georgian windows that were all the rage. Why couldn't they just have one big window? I sometimes came home after a day of this and my arms and shoulders ached.

This was the age when it was just a sponge and wash-leather; there were none of these gizmos on handles the modern lads use, with rubber blades and fancy attachments. All the times I'd driven or walked past a bloke up a ladder cleaning windows, some cheerfully whistling, others with a fag casually dangling from the corner of their mouth, a quick swish and a wipe, and, hey presto, window clean as a whistle. Now it was me up there, sometimes hanging on for grim life; don't look down, hold tight; and when it was an attic window or a very tall building, "Christ, Willie," I'd think, "one slip and you're a gonner. A while back you tried to end things deliberately; now you could do it by accident." My hands used to freeze on a winter's morning and as my fingers turned blue, so more than once did my language. I'd look at my hands all red, sore and numb, but no way was I going to be the first window cleaner in Burnley to wear rubber gloves or have a hot water bottle down my trousers.

But gradually I got the hang of it. Climbing a ladder became easier; casually working at the top, leaning over, one foot on the ladder and one foot casually on the window ledge became a piece of cake. Washing a window without leaving any marks became straightforward. My teacher taught me well. "The technique of cleaning windows is a bit like good sex, Willie. It's no good just going round and round; you've got to start in the right place, go up and down, then across and really get into all the corners." Willie Irvine, Window Cleaner: who'd have thought it? I'd sometimes be up the top of the ladder with the wind whistling round my ears and thinking, "Bloody hell, Willie, this is a long way from Wembley," but I was happy as Larry. My own boss again, money in my pocket, paying my bills, pride come back, sense of satisfaction, looking people in the eye again.

Of course there were some funny moments. Imagine being a Burnley fan and you'd seen games in the '60s when I'd played and been the bee's knees and after Willie Morgan I'd been pin-up boy number two, then 20 years later you're on the other side of the window and suddenly you see Willie Irvine's cheeky face looking in through the bedroom window with a wash-leather. The looks I got from people were a treat. In the early days, quite a few times somebody would come running out of the house and shout up, "Bloody hell, Willie, is that you, what you doin' 'ere?" Sometimes I'd hear a dad say to his son, "Gawd, I don't believe it, that's Willie Irvine cleanin' our windows."

Just occasionally, yes, there was a woman worth looking at through the window, but most times though if you saw someone in a state of undress it would have been a kindness had they drawn the curtains. One day I happened (never deliberately) to have seen a little old lady in her bedroom absolutely starkers with more wrinkles and creases than Nora Batty's stockings. Her grinning husband came out into the yard when I came down the ladder and said, "Sorry you had to see that, Willie; she's not been ironed today."

My son Darren used to go round every Friday night for me to collect the money I was owed from people who had been out at work. For God knows how long he collected money from one house which wasn't one I'd ever cleaned but he didn't collect the money from the house next door which was the one I did clean. This went on until the person in the house with the uncleaned windows came out one day when I was next door to ask me why he never saw any difference in his windows. "I've had these bloody bird droppings on my bathroom window for the last six months and they're still bloody there." "But I don't do your windows," I told him, baffled. "Then who's been collecting effing money off me for the last six months?" he asked, none too pleased. All I could do was offer to wash them free for a few weeks. The house which I had done, but where I hadn't collected the money, I just had to say, "Ah well, sod's law, you've had 'em done for nothing."

At one house I'd finished the job, packed up the ladders, loaded the roof rack and got ready to go and damn me if the car wouldn't start. "Don't worry," says the woman, "my husband can fix it." And he did, he worked on it for an hour or more. "Willie, don't mention it," he said when I thanked him profusely, and he wouldn't take a penny for his labours. Of course, Darren goes round on the next Friday night, not knowing, and calls to collect the money. "Cheeky bugger," the woman shouts at him, "my husband fixed his bloody car for him for nowt and you're here asking for money. Tell your dad to bugger off and I'll get a new window cleaner," Her husband is the bloke who today does all the photographs at Turf Moor and we still laugh about it.

The window round lasted for 12 months and, with working in the youth centre at night as well, words like knackered, buggered, exhausted were heard quite a few times around the house. No way could I carry on working most of the day on the window job and then all evening at the youth centre. I'm pleased to say I eventually sold the window round for a nice little profit, said my goodbyes to Burnley Council and youth work, and found a normal day job at an engineering works where I stayed for 14 years. One of the nice spinoffs of being a footballer was that I knew the boss, John Turkington. "Come and work for me," he said. After 14 years there and footballer's hips playing me up, I moved to an electrical firm, LED, and Derek Davies, a friend for years, for less hours and more money. Thanks, Derek. Today, I'm at Aeropia, an aircraft company, where I'm a stores manager and work with some really good lads. Trouble is some of them are from Blackburn.

Amazing how the wheel turns full circle, though. Whoever

would have thought I'd finish up working back at Burnley Football Club? If you'd told me that, while I lay on a trolley in the hospital with a stomach full of pills, or while I stood up the top of a ladder hanging on for grim death in a force nine gale, wondering if George Best had ever had to clean windows for a living, or while King Kong was deciding whether or not to batter me for taking home his fuel-sniffing son, I'd have just shook my head.

But when a few years ago the commercial manager at Turf Moor asked me to become a Saturday afternoon host at the club, what could I do but jump at the chance? I'd been down there often enough to watch a game, had often gone into the guest lounge to chat and mingle, and had shed tears in '87 when it looked like the club would fall out of the League and probably fold completely. By coincidence the three clubs I played for (I'm afraid I don't count Halifax) are all in the Championship, the old Division One. I've done my bit for them all, played my part, and am part of their history books. I'm proud of that.

So that's it then, I suppose. Story over. Yes, there are some big regrets, but I've survived, come through and can count up how lucky I am now: I have a wife who has stuck by me through thick and thin. She could write her own book about me, I'm sure, the good and the bad. I've got three fine sons whose love I once almost lost but have now regained: lovely grandchildren, a job, a warm home, food on the table, and my health. Maybe I don't have all my own teeth and not much hair, but what I do have is above all my self-respect. I can look at myself in a mirror and if I ask, "Have I done all right?" I can say it took some doing, but yes I have.

POSTSCRIPT

His home today is still in the village of Worsthorne, on the edges of Burnley. It's a small terraced house, cosy and warm, and on one wall of the living room is a trophy cabinet filled with mementoes of his short career. A green Northern Ireland shirt takes centre place; others that might have been there have been given away. But for his business misfortunes his home might today have been something grand and detached, but it would still have been in Burnley and more likely than not in just the same village where he feels at ease and comfortable.

His home faces west, with views of green fields and distant hills and in the saucer-shaped vale below you can just see the town. Some summer evenings when the sun is setting he can light the tiny barbecue and sip a beer, or just sit and bask in the sun's soft fading rays. It's at such times that he sits and thinks about what might have been; or on other days in a different mood, he feels a pride and contentment that he owes no man money, that he paid his debts, that he emerged from the dark tunnel of depression, and that even now in Burnley today he is known and recognised and loved.

A Preston fan once described how he showed his character through his play: he was determined but irreverent, focused but seemingly relaxed, exuberant but ice-cold in execution. The fan spoke of a sense of wistfulness about what he would have achieved had he not been injured, and the residual outrage that his career was ended by the clogging of some of the filthier players who were around in those days. A Brighton fan described him as charismatic, and a Burnley fan that he was simply his favourite player.

After the football finished he went through a time that would have laid low lesser men. His openness, trusting nature, and vulnerability, made him prey to less scrupulous men, but in the great scheme of things it is the meek, as someone once said, who shall inherit the earth. When Willie asks his sons and family, "Have I done all right?" the answer is a resounding "yes"; although the day has not yet come when he will have no need to ask.

Months ago, when he first began to jot down his thoughts in his battered notebook, it was just something for his grandchildren to read and to remember him by. But as he wrote more and more, and discovered more and more, and as together it was enlarged, his reminiscences grew into something bigger and more significant. They became a testament to a man's ability to lift himself again after being laid low by the callous manipulation of some, and the unfeeling deviousness of others. It enabled him to find out a few things more about his past and his roots, things that he had never known before. There are still things to learn and maybe one day he will find out more.

He belonged to an age when footballers made no great fortunes from the game. The chosen few may have struck lucky after their football years were over but the Willie Irvines of this world set out with their business ventures and tried to thrive in a cut-throat world. Some survived, some prospered, others did not. For some it was all too much and was nearly so for Willie, but somehow he hung on, fought his way back, surmounted his problems and today can proudly say, "I went through hell but here I am, still in one piece and not one penny do I owe."

He may have been 62 in 2005 but he still needs to work. On cold, damp, dark February mornings that might just be when he still feels the faint trace of lingering discontent and the regret that his career ended before it should. "I should have been up there with the best," he sometimes says to himself. Sometimes when he gets out of bed at 6.30am and the rain is hammering down outside or the mist is swirling around he'll ask himself why he is still having to do this and he'll curse that day his leg was broken and the day his knee was shattered. The tackle that broke his leg will be imprinted in his mind forever, for he was never to be the same again.

But one thing he does have now again is his pride, and his sense of humour remains intact. For one terrible period they were both gone, lost in an abyss of despair and gloom when all he could say to himself was that he had failed so terribly and let his family down. He could only watch as Rita brought up his three boys, held things together, stayed strong and bit by bit pulled him through.

To anyone who today suffers from the torments of deep depression, and whose misery is such that they too would contemplate ending their own life, Willie would say this: "Find one good friend if you can and just ask them to be there and to listen. Good friends do listen: that is what makes them good. They won't have answers and solutions but they do have strength for you to draw on. Don't live and exist in isolation avoiding others, shrinking into a shell, making yourself 'small'. Don't hide away, retreating into the house for days on end, get out if only to walk for half an hour so that you can look outwards again. And if late at night, when all is still and dark and quiet, the thought grows that death would so easily end all this, break that mood. Switch on the television or radio, a tape, a CD, anything to bring another human voice into that lonely room. Break the spell; end the silence. Don't forget it is not shameful to be this way: there is no stigma, it is not something that needs to be unmentionable and that you have to live with as a secret. Remember that more people than you think suffer in a similar way and this illness is something you have not chosen yourself to experience; it has chosen you. And today there is help if you need it."

His three sons today are his pride and joy. All of them look up to him with pride and affection. Maybe the burden of their upbringing did fall on Rita, but that's the football life; it's the wife so often who holds things together, sorts out the problems, worries about the schools, the new homes, the constant upheaval as players move from club to club, puts up with the moods and whims of a footballer husband which can change so much from day to day.

Darren is the eldest son. Big, strong, 6ft 2ins tall. His wife Sarah and he have two sons, William and George. Mention Willie's name to Darren and he bursts with pride and love. Like his father he is a Claret through and through. He remembers his father once taking him to Halifax to join in the training. He never saw his father play except once in a testimonial game. A glorious cross came over and Willie leapt like a salmon... but missed. But Darren goes misty-eyed when he watches the faded videos of Willie's games of yesteryear and the goals he scored. His three goals at Tottenham in the FA Cup game that Burnley lost 4-3 are there forever. He remembers the old Irish charm on show in the newspaper shop. It sold all manner of items including those old fashioned flypapers that unwitting flies landed on and then stuck forever – Willie was a great salesman – one for 50p or two for £1.

"Dad, I don't think that's quite right."

"Son, I don't think the flies are going to worry too much."

It was Darren who got his father interested in going back to a declining Turf Moor again after the times when Willie had little or no interest in anything.

"Why don't you come on down, Dad?"

"Because they never came to see me when I was bad, did they?" he says now.

But when Willie was bad, Darren too was hit hard and will readily say today that he wasn't the nicest teenage kid to have around. He's tried to make up for it ever since because whatever he has tried to do in his life, "my dad has always been there right behind me."

Stephen is the middle son who joined the army, and maintained the family tradition of military service, serving in Northern Ireland during the troubles. He knows what it is like to be shot at and spat on. There was the time a washing machine was thrown out of a bedroom window and just missed him as he patrolled the street below. He's thought ever since; there must be easier things to carry upstairs than a washing machine. But there were endless sleepless nights of worry and fear for Willie and Rita while he was there. It was Stephen who suffered most from the bad years his father went through. To say he became a tearaway would be an understatement. In the good days he'd helped his dad mow the lawns, counted the takings from the business, enjoyed the luxury life and then when it all went wrong, so did he. He was going to work for Dad in the DIY business and suddenly there was no business to work in. And suddenly there was no Dad either when Willie upped sticks and left home for a while, everything on top of him, unable to manage. Love

Postscript

turned to hate; just another problem for Willie to shoulder and handle. He fought with Willie, caused Willie and Rita no end of grief and today will say he is not proud of any of the disruption he caused at that time and that much of it was very bad. But whatever he did, whatever aggravation he caused, he remembers that his parents were there for him. Cars are his thing: rallying, navigating; a 21st birthday present driving at Oulton Park saw him putting in lap times faster than the pros. Both he and Willie cried when he left home to join the army and Willie took him to the station. In spite of all the problems Stephen caused, Willie stuck by him, supported him, raised £3,500 in sponsorship so he could take part in the Monte Carlo Rally. And then when Stephen's first marriage broke down and he was in Germany, it was Willie who went there to help him and was almost as distraught as Stephen himself. "But he was the rod in my back," says Stephen today and will readily add that "without his help and love" he wouldn't have coped and got himself back together. Today Stephen has married again, to Gaynor, and has given Willie a granddaughter, Natalya. Stephen takes Willie with him on MG rallies. His life is back on track and he will be the first to say he owes it to Willie.

Jonathan is the son who so nearly continued the football tradition. He's 30 now, married to Sharon, with two sons of his own, Connor and Ben. One of them is a goalkeeper, and who knows how far he can go with football genes in his blood? Maybe one day he too will live the dream. Jonathan can remember the good times clearly but the bad times are only a haze, though one of them was when his father collapsed with chest pains and Jonathan can still feel the panic he felt. Then there was the time that there was some kind of major row in the house, Dad wasn't at home for a while and Jonathan cried his eyes out as his Mum read a story to him on the settee. But then wasn't there a Cliff Richard record came out called *Daddy's Home* and, sure enough, Willie came home. He too remembers the fights between his father and Stephen. But the bad memories are now few and far between and maybe that's how things should be. Sure his dad liked a drink, and many an evening when the village church bells struck seven, that was the signal to nip round to The Bay Horse "for just an hour".

Willie Irvine

But a dad is a dad, and what do you do when he is asleep on the settee before he goes out for a drink and Mum's make-up bag is nearby? You paint his face so that when he wakes up he pretends he doesn't know and goes out for a drink all the same, leaving you chortling and laughing as he closes the door.

Yes, there were times when family life was stressed and difficult, when there were problems and differences, but as much as possible the boys were shielded from all of that and today instead of the bad they remember only the good. Jonathan came so close to following in his father's footsteps; he played for Northern Ireland Under-18's regularly, he signed as an apprentice for Blackpool, then, briefly, as a professional, scored goals easily, but was then released and moved to Wrexham, but there the lack of finances ended what chance he had. He remembers playing against, and rubbing shoulders with the Beckham, Scholes, Butt and Neville boys in an A team game years ago at The Cliff, Manchester United's old training ground; beating them 3-2 and scoring twice. What he remembers so clearly is being taught the difference between right and wrong, the interest his father showed in him, the encouragement he gave, the miles he travelled to watch him play. He remembers a game he played for his school when he was only nine years old. The rain bucketed down, the wind blew a gale and just one solitary parent stood watching the game, getting drenched. It was Willie, for if Willie had no father to watch the games he played in, he made damned sure that Jonathan had someone to watch over him. And when Jonathan brought home his first Irish shirt it was to Willie he gave it.

One thing none of those sons will ever forget is the weekend they took him back to Carrick for his 60th birthday. They watched him dance a jig on the top of Carrickfergus Castle to the sound of the music and the big bass drum as the band marched by and they saw the smile of joy on his face that would have lit a thousand rooms. The weekend in Carrick was a pilgrimage. They took him to the place where his father Alex was buried all those years ago. It was the first time he had seen his grave. They spread out and searched

250

through the graveyard until they found it and then they stood beside it and not just Willie wept. As they visited old haunts and places in Carrick and Eden, old memories flooded back and he could tell his sons of this and that and the things he got up to and the things he did in his boyhood days. They met old friends; they returned to Barn United and presented one of Willie's treasured shirts to his old club. And then in Carrick Town Hall the Mayor presented Willie with a commemorative coat of arms in recognition of his services and achievements. The sons would love to take him back again. Maybe one day they will.

For nearly a year he has put down his story in a dog-eared notebook, sometimes with it on his knee as he sits outside and catches the sun's last enveloping warmth. Sometimes his grandchildren have seen him write and have asked what it is that he is doing. "Something for you," he told them, "something for you to read one day so that you will remember me and know more about me than I ever knew about my family."

Of that family he wonders if he will one day find out more. After ten years without contact with his brother Bobby, the ice was broken with a phone call on St Patrick's Day and there are plans to see each other again; together again after all these years. He has a sister, Sandra; again whom he has not spoken to for years and who looked after his mother in the final years of her life. Maybe she knows more. Somewhere he thinks there was a huge old family bible with all manner of things recorded and written down. He remembers seeing it in his home before he left for England, but who has it now? Does it still exist or is it lost? Answers to so many questions may be locked inside it, the names of all his stepbrothers and stepsisters whom he never saw and what happened to them all. Maybe it would contain the answer to exactly who was killed in World War One, or what happened to William Black and then Herbert Hamilton.

He has had some journey through life. From dragging wood from the sea onto the beach at Carrickfergus and chopping firewood to earn pennies, walking barefoot through the snow to school, seeing his mother taken away from home to prison

251

for many months; he then became a professional footballer, one of the best, a record goalscorer and Northern Ireland international. Yet not much more than ten years on from that marvellous Brighton promotion season and the Wembley night when the Irish minnows beat the mighty English, he lay at the brink of death on a trolley in a dimly-lit Burnley hospital corridor while doctors fought to save his life and Rita stood there wondering if he would live or die.

Today he is still asking: what might he have been without that broken leg; how many more goals might he have scored; how far could he have gone? And of his family he is still asking: what happened to all those stepbrothers and sisters he never knew; how many uncles died in World War One; how different might life have been had his father not died so tragically? And that huge, ancient Bible: does it have the answers, where is it and who has it now? Of the problems that befell him in his life after football he's still asking: just how did it happen? But then he'll smile with pride for every home matchday he and Burnley Football Club are together again.

He'll tell you now he treasures every day and, though he still asks his sons, Darren, Stephen and Jonathan, that simple recurring question, "Have I done all right?" he knows what the answer will always be.

"Yes Dad, you've done all right, you've been through hell but come out on top. You've done us proud."

INDEX